Resolving Employment Disputes Without Litigation

Resolving Employment Disputes Without Litigation

Alan F. Westin
Alfred G. Feliu

The Bureau of National Affairs, Inc., Washington, D.C.

Library of Congress Cataloging-in-Publication Data

Westin, Alan F.
  Resolving employment disputes without litigation.

  Bibliography: p.
  Includes index.
  1. Grievance procedures—United States.
2. Conflict management—United States.   3. Dispute
resolution (Law)—United States.   I. Feliu, Alfred G.
II. Title.
HF5549.5.G7W47   1988   658.3'155   87-31989
ISBN 0-87179-558-2

Printed in the United States of America
International Standard Book Number 0-87179-558-2

Preface

The Center for Public Resources (CPR) is a national coalition of 170 major corporations, generally represented by their chief legal officer; 90 law firms, represented by a senior partner; and legal and social-scientist academics.

The CPR Legal Program is devoted to the field of alternative dispute resolution, or ADR, as it has come to be called. The mission of the CPR Legal Program is to develop, promote, and implement private alternatives to litigation. CPR is interested in techniques designed to prevent disputes and in collaborative approaches to the settlement of disputes that permit parties to resolve their differences without wasteful expenditure of resources and energies devoted to litigation.

CPR committees of leading experts are developing ADR approaches to disputes in a number of fields, including employment, government, hazardous waste, product liability, technology, toxic tort, and transnational business.

A common thread running through virtually all the activities of CPR is a strong emphasis on encouraging the prevention and settlement of disputes, including disputes between employers and their employees. CPR believes that adversarial approaches are often unnecessary, and that parties to disputes should be encouraged to resolve their differences, at least in the first instance, through nonadjudicative processes.

The CPR Employment Disputes Committee, chaired since 1984 by Joseph Barbash of Debevoise & Plimpton, is a diverse group—all leaders in the field—consisting of corporate in-house counsel and industrial relations directors, outside defense counsel, members of the plaintiffs' bar, and academics. Peter H. Kaskell, Senior Vice President of CPR, serves as staff director.

Professor Alan F. Westin has served most capably as an academic advisor to the Committee. With Professor Westin's advice and encouragement, the Committee studied approaches adopted by major corporations to deal with complaints by nonunion employees, who lack the protection of collective bargaining agreements. The Committee focused, in particular, on the various types of more or less formal internal dispute resolution systems adopted by a growing number of companies during recent years.

Professor Westin and Alfred G. Feliu proposed developing a book, consisting of case histories of innovative corporate internal dispute resolution systems, written by the organizational managers responsible for developing and administering such systems, together with commentaries on the case histories and on the evolution of relations between employers and nonunion employees. CPR and its Employment Disputes Committee concluded that such a book would make important contributions to the fields of alternative dispute resolution and industrial relations, and CPR provided a grant for the realization of this project.

A subcommittee consisting of Chairman Joseph Barbash, Professor Samuel Estreicher of New York University School of Law, Jerome B. Kauff of Pretzin & Kauff, and Bruce McLanahan of ITT Corporation reviewed a draft of the manuscript and made valuable comments.

In 1984 the Employment Disputes Committee developed a survey questionnaire on employee dispute resolution practices. The questionnaire was completed by 48 CPR member companies. The results were analyzed by Professor Westin and are reported in Chapter 4 of the book.

The Westin-Feliu manuscript represents a unique collection and analysis of the best practices developed by enlightened corporate managements for handling nonunion employee complaints. We congratulate the authors on an important task well done. We also thank Chairman Barbash and the members of his Committee for their support of this project. (Committee members are listed in the Appendix.)

James F. Henry
President
Center for Public Resources
New York City

Introduction

This book is jointly sponsored by two organizations, the Center for Public Resources and the Educational Fund for Individual Rights, both in New York City. The Center was established to support alternative methods for resolving business and social disputes without litigation; it has made alternative dispute resolution (ADR) for employee-employer conflicts one of its key areas of activity. The Educational Fund was created to study and support new ways to protect individual employee rights in the workplace, especially in a period of rapid change in technology, workplace relations, and employee expectations. One major area of the Fund's program has been new fair procedure systems which, by resolving equitably the grievances of nonunion employees internally, can make it unnecessary for employees to resort to courts or government agencies for redress.

This volume has been developed with four main audiences in mind:

1. The personnel and human resources managers who have primary responsibility for administration of employment policies. These specialists oversee the promulgation of employment rules, performance evaluation systems, promotion and assignment policies, application of discipline, handling of employee complaints, and arrangements for termination when this becomes necessary.

2. The legal counsel inside organizations who advise management on employment-policy matters, and the outside counsel who provide similar legal advice to their organizational clients. Increasingly, these counsel are being asked to help organizations develop ADR mechanisms that can reduce the volume and severity of employee-initiated litigation.

3. Senior managers and executives who not only run their organizations but establish an atmosphere and set the terms for dispute resolution within the company. These officials want to know

not only what new employee expectations and legal rules they must respond to but also what new programs and techniques of ADR for employee disputes have been created—and are working well—at other companies and private-sector organizations.

4. The growing body of scholars and journalists who are interested in ADR in private employment, and who also want as much detailed data as possible about what is going on within innovative organizations, and how new ADR systems are really working.

To serve these varied readerships, the book begins in Chapter 1 by summarizing the factors that have led to a major increase in employee complaints to Equal Employment Opportunity agencies and the courts over the past decade, and then describes the various responses that private employers have adopted. The most important reaction, we conclude, has been for a leading edge of private employers to develop new mechanisms for preventing or resolving employee complaints through internal programs. After sketching the main types of employee complaint processes that private employers had in the early 1970s, we use several surveys we conducted between 1979 and the present to trace the main types of new mechanisms in development (primarily among medium- to large-sized corporations). We then present a typology that classifies these mechanisms according to whether the company is addressing non-adversarial employee concerns, potentially adversarial concerns, or adversarial concerns in its programs. Using Security Pacific National Bank as an example, we illustrate how some large employers have installed programs to address all three of these types of employee concerns.

Having provided this historical backdrop and noted the efforts of some innovative private firms, we present in Chapter 2 a series of profiles in which employees themselves describe their problems with fair treatment at work. Most of these real employees, interviewed between 1981 and 1987 by the Educational Fund for Individual Right's staff, present stories of frustration over the absence of fair, meaningful, and available mechanisms within their companies to hear and resolve employee complaints. While we make no claim of statistical representativeness for these interviews, our judgment—and that of several hundred lawyers, personnel managers, and employee-protection-group leaders who have used these profiles at the Educational Fund's national seminars—is that these stories ring true. They do describe both the conditions and the resulting feelings of unfair treatment that employees encounter in most of America's well know and often otherwise well managed business or nonprofit organizations.

Having seen what does *not* work, we turn in Chapter 3 to the heart of our volume. This is the presentation, after a brief overview, of 12 organizations whose innovative programs for internal resolution of employee disputes were written expressly for this volume by the managers who run these systems.

The 12 organizations are:

Bank of America
Cleveland Clinic
Aetna Life and Casualty
Citibank
Michael Reese Hospital and Medical Center
Northrop Corporation
Life Savers Division, Squibb
Chicago and North Western Transportation Company
Chemical Bank
National Broadcasting Company
Massachusetts Institute of Technology
American Telephone and Telegraph-Information Systems

We asked these organizational officials to relate the kinds of systems the organizations had before they installed their current programs; why they decided to create the new systems; how their programs actually work, with types of issues, processes, and outcomes described in detail; and what effects they see their programs having on employee attitudes and actions, managerial effectiveness, overall employee relations, and levels of employee recourse to outside legal forums.

We believe these organizational profiles are a unique and important contribution to the literature on ADR in private employment. Some of these descriptions were first made at conferences organized by the Center for Public Resources and the Educational Fund for Individual Rights. Others have been written especially for this volume. All of them have been shaped by the editors of this volume to provide readers with a level of detail and of self-examination that has not been available until now in published form. As a resource for organizational managers, scholars, and public policy makers, we believe this collection should be of great value.

Following the organizational profiles, we present, in Chapter 4, a discussion of 15 factors that we have derived from our study of not only the 12 organizations profiled here but almost 150 organizations over the past 8 years. In our judgment, these are the critical factors without which no internal dispute prevention or dispute resolution system can operate effectively.

Finally, in Chapter 5, we present an analysis of the current legal environment for private employment that is making it so important for private employers to develop fair and effective internal systems. After this overview of major changes in American law, we show the costs—internal as well as external—that employers face today if they are unable to resolve the great majority of employee complaints internally, and have to resort to legal proceedings over charges of unfair, discriminatory, or abusive employer conduct. The final section of Chapter 5 shows how courts have begun to take notice of internal company systems, and the considerable advantage that employers may obtain if they design and operate good, fair procedure systems.

Like the society of which they are a part, most employees and employers in the America of the 1980s believe that among the golden rules of the workplace are that hiring and advancement must be based on merit; fair treatment is required in the daily administration of the employment relationship; and fair procedures for resolving disputes are essential to peace on the job. The new social and legal ethos of the 1980s suggests that such internal policies and procedures are both needed by employers and in their enlightened self-interest. A further incentive for the development and institution of such systems is the growing possibility of increased legislative oversight of management's personnel actions if employers do not demonstrate that voluntary mechanisms are developing well and widely.

In short, the topic this book explores is not an esoteric matter of interest only to specialists in a new form of unarmed combat called alternative dispute resolution. These are issues that involve 80 million employees, 50,000 employer organizations with substantial work forces, and many basic institutional and social balances in our democratic society. This volume's collection of historical and legal analysis, individual organizational experiences, trend data, and discussions of future policy alternatives should, we hope, help our society to preserve important private-sector autonomy while also providing equity and justice to the employees who make America work.

The Educational Fund gratefully acknowledges the support of two foundations whose grants underwrote much of the field work during 1979–1984 from which our trend analysis and identification of innovative programs for this edited collection were developed. First was Russell Sage Foundation, whose interest was in the fact that private employers in the late 1970s were becoming concerned with ways to create private dispute resolution systems without adopting paralyzing legalistic procedures, and how students of law and organizational behavior might study and possibly enhance this important development. The second sponsor was the Ford Foundation, whose interest was specifically in the presentation and internal handling of equal employment opportunity complaints by corporate employees.

This volume presents the first of two publications on this topic produced by the Educational Fund for Individual Rights. The second, to appear later, is an in-depth case study of one of the best and most fully developed internal systems—the Guaranteed Fair Treatment procedure of Federal Express Corporation.

In terms of primary responsibility for sections of this volume, Chapters 1 through 4 were mainly written or edited by Alan Westin, and Chapter 5 by Alfred Feliu. However, we share responsibility for the whole volume; its virtues and its defects are our joint product.

A word of special thanks is due to Luceil Sullivan, Executive Director of the Educational Fund for Individual Rights, for her constant support of this project in its administrative, financial, and personal odyssey. Hope Campbell, Margaret Marino, and Debra Westin were vital to the final typing and editing process. Al Feliu would like especially to thank Susan Haire for her patience in enduring the countless revisions of this text (and for the friendship that survived them) and his wife, Susan, for sharing a courtship with a "green-eyed" manuscript. And we reserve the last appreciation to James Henry and the Center for Public Resources, whose financial support and concern for improving the processes of employment dispute resolution gave this book its necessary final push.

Alan F. Westin

Alfred G. Feliu

August, 1987

Contents

Chapter 1

The Movement to Create Alternative Dispute Resolution Systems in Nonunion Employment

For corporations, litigation by employees and ex-employees represents one of the "growth industries" of the 1980s. It is obviously not an expansion that cheers the hearts of executives, and there are no signs that the situation is going to be easily or quickly reversed. Consider some of the hard trends.

The Rise of an Employee Litigation Explosion

- In 1986–1987, 66,305 charges of employment discrimination against private-sector employers were received by the Equal Employment Opportunity Commission (EEOC). (The EEOC predicted that during 1988 such charges would increase to over 67,000.) In 1986–1987, state and local human rights agencies received 52,139 charges of employment discrimination. This produced a 1986–1987 total of 119,289 charges of unlawful employment discrimination.

- During 1986–1987, over 10,000 cases alleging employment discrimination were filed in the federal or state courts, either directly by private individuals, or on their behalf by government antidiscrimination agencies.

- The list of companies that entered into consent or settlement decrees with EEOC during 1986–1987 as a result of discrimination charges filed against them included many well known firms. The list featured Great Atlantic and Pacific Tea Co. (A&P); Westinghouse Electric; Goodyear Tire and Rubber; Trans World Airlines (TWA); Lucky Stores; Macmillan Publishing Co.; United Airlines; and Gulf States United Telephone Co.

- From an estimated total of less than 200 unjust discharge cases filed annually in the state courts by private-sector employees in the late 1970s, when the Educational Fund for Individual Rights started tracking these developments, we estimate that more than 20,000 cases are now pending in state courts. The immediate cause of the explosion in wrongful discharge litigation is the broadening judicial recognition and application of the various exceptions to the traditional "employment-at-will" doctrine previously relied on by management. As a result, courts and juries are increasingly called upon to review the merits of management personnel decisions and, when necessary, to determine damage awards.

- Decisions against private employers in unjust discharge cases are becoming frequent and substantial. A recent study of unjust discharge cases in California found employees winning 78 percent of the jury verdicts, with punitive damages being awarded in 40 percent of these cases. The average damages award in these cases was $424,527. Many well known companies have been the defendants in such cases, including IBM, Bank of America, McGraw-Hill, Blue Cross and Blue Shield of Michigan, International Harvester, and Arco.

- Though minorities and women remain primary litigants in the EEO areas, an increasing number of age discrimination and unjust discharge cases are being brought by white male employees over 40 years old from professional, sales, and management ranks, who have had long-term service with their employers. These employees are highly knowledgeable about the inner workings of their companies, have excellent lawyers, and are often able to make the employer's public and legal defense very difficult.

- In 1987, Montana became the first state to enact a law giving private-sector employees a right to have dismissals reviewed by the courts; similar legislation providing a right to arbitration for private employees is pending in several other states. Advocates argue that some right of outside appeal is necessary in the United States to see that employers have a proper business or performance basis for discharging non-union employees.

- In terms of what may lie ahead, in the non-EEO areas, it has been estimated that about 1.4 million nonprobationary, nonunion employees are discharged annually in the private sector. This estimate may be either too high or too low, but a substantial annual discharge rate is clearly part of the nonunion scene.

If the state courts continue to expand employee litigation opportunities, if the plaintiff's bar continues to find this an attractive area of new legal business, and if only 1 in 20 such discharged employees decided to file a lawsuit, this would mean 70,000 new unjust discharge cases per year. If we look at either the employee-prevails rate in unjust discharge labor arbitration cases (50 percent), or the jury-verdict rate for employees in California courts (78 percent), the potential implication in judgments against private employers appears clear.

The primary causes for a greatly expanded employee activism in regulatory agencies and the courts are not hard to understand. They include: a more educated, assertive, and minority-proportioned work force; the addition of "antireprisal" protections and review procedures for employees in almost all EEO, Occupational Safety and Health, Employee Retirement Income Security, environmental protection, and consumer protection legislation; a value-system of the "baby-boom generation" that expects fair treatment at work and will resist "arbitrary" actions; the central importance of employment for access to health and pension benefits in a non-socialist society; and the current weakness of the alternative job market, which makes efforts to be reinstated in a job or to protect an employment reference a far greater concern to employees than in the 1970s. Add to this the widespread efforts by companies to become more competitive by paring back their work forces—often choosing older employees in professional and management ranks as the preferred pushouts—and the main sources of the current litigative explosion are defined.

How Companies Are Responding

What responses have these trends evoked from American corporations? Some managements have rewritten their employment contracts, employee handbooks, performance evaluations, and other documents to eliminate any implication that job security is promised, that termination requires a "just" cause, or that any internal hearing or appeal system is guaranteed before termination. Other companies are training managers and supervisors to operate more effectively in the new legal climate, through better documentation of employee performance, violation of rules, and disciplinary steps.

The most important response, however, and the one that this book focuses upon, is the decision by a growing number of companies to either create new dispute resolution systems inside their organizations, or to improve existing systems they have had for some time.

To understand the significance of this trend, it is useful to sketch a profile of how American companies traditionally handled nonunion employee complaints, and then describe the new techniques that are being adopted.

Corporate Complaint Systems in 1979

In 1979, under a grant from Russell Sage Foundation, the Educational Fund for Individual Rights conducted a field study of complaint and appeal mechanisms in nonunion corporate employment. Focusing on the practices of large employers—the 10,000 or so companies with 100 employees or more—we discerned the following patterns:

1. Approximately 50–65 percent of large employers were using a "chain of command" system, in which employees were told to "see their supervisors" and then progress up the management ladder.

2. Another 20–25 percent of companies had this basic system but added to it a declaration that "management's door is always open" if an employee wanted to complain, by making an appointment to see the general manager or executive in charge of their division, or someone even higher in the firm.

3. About 10–15 percent of large employers were using formalized systems of employee complaint resolution, usually step-

by-step hearings modeled after the union grievance system; often, as at Trans World Airlines, these were installed after a union decertification election or in anticipation of a union challenge.

4. Finally, perhaps 50–100 companies, about 10–12 percent, had developed complaint systems providing what we would call a "fair procedure" oriented mechanism for nonunion production and clerical employees. Sometimes this was extended to professional and technical employees as well. Such systems were in operation in 1979 at IBM, Bank of America, Control Data, Xerox, Citibank, General Electric Aircraft Frame Division, and other innovators in this area.

When we looked at how these various systems performed in 1979–1982, we found that the chain-of-command, open door, and union-style formal systems had developed grave weaknesses in the new environment of employee rights expectations and access to legal review of our current era. Employees we interviewed reported that they were afraid to use such systems for fear of reprisal from supervisors and managers; that the personnel managing these systems were almost always defensive about management interests and protective of their fellow managers; that the procedures to follow were difficult for the average employee to comprehend and use effectively; and that employees, especially with serious EEO complaints, felt they would fare much better by going to public agencies than by "wasting time" inside. Our interviews were confirmed by the rising tide of EEO charges and unjust discharge lawsuits that we cited at the beginning of this section.

Survey Results on New Trends in Corporate Complaint Systems

How management actions have begun to change is well documented by the results of a January 1984 survey of company complaint systems, which was part of a national conference on resolving EEO disputes without litigation that we conducted in Washington, D.C. Executives and staffs from 175 business, government, and nonprofit employers attended, and 85 filled out a detailed survey of their internal programs. Sixty-four of these were corporations, and it is their responses that will be used here.

The 64 companies surveyed obviously were interested enough in EEO complaints and alternative dispute resolution approaches to attend a two-day conference on these issues. About 60 percent were manufacturing firms and the remaining 40 percent were in the financial, insurance, and service industries. The size of their employee forces was as follows:

SIZE OF WORKFORCE

Over 50,000 employees	11%
10,000–50,000	44
5,000–10,000	10
1,000–5,000	23
Under 1,000	12

When asked what changes they expected in the level of employee complaints on EEO issues filed *within their organizations* in the "next few years," a majority said they expected "substantial increases" in age discrimination and sexual harassment issues; "moderate increases" in race and sex complaints; and "about the same levels" of religion and handicap complaints. Virtually all reported an expected rise in unjust discharge litigation.

The following table indicates the kind of internal complaint system these companies reported they had in early 1984:

TYPE OF COMPLAINT AND APPEAL SYSTEM FOR
NONUNION EMPLOYEES

Mechanism	Production workers	Clerical workers	Professional/ technical	Supervisors/ managers
Chain-of-command	39%	53%	46%	5%
Informal open door	46	62	64	64
Formal complaint and appeal	32	39	35	32

Among these companies, about one-third had formal complaint and appeal systems, twice as many as we estimated for large companies in 1979. What was even more important was that two-thirds of these companies (42), reported that they were currently "taking concrete actions to reduce the volume of employee complaints to regulatory agencies or the courts." The two main types of actions reported were:

- Companies without a formal complaint system said they were presently developing such a mechanism.
- Companies *with* formal systems said they were installing new features to make their systems more effective. These included: adding employee representation on appeals committees; designating an Ombudsman type official; giving staffs who handled complaints special training in mediation and dispute resolution techniques; and considering outside, voluntary mediation or arbitration as a final step to their programs.

When asked why they were taking such actions, two out of three companies said that these approaches were what an "expanded, human-resources approach" to personnel management required in the mid-1980s. When asked about reasons relating to outside litigation, they checked the following, which are presented in the order most frequently cited:

- Desire to try new dispute resolution techniques,
- Concern about reducing legal costs,
- Number of outside complaints too high,
- Concern about class actions,
- Size of awards growing too high,
- Settlement amounts growing too high,
- Costs of several recent "big cases," and
- Outside complaints hurt credibility.

Another view of trends developing in the corporate community is supplied by a survey in late 1984 conducted by the Center for Public Resources (CPR). CPR mailed to its 130 corporate members a survey questionnaire asking about company experiences with employment disputes in nonunion employment and recent company practices designed to reduce such disputes. The survey was an activity of CPR's Employee Disputes Task Force, chaired by Joseph Barbash of the New York law firm of Debevoise & Plimpton, with Professor Alan F. Westin of Columbia University serving as the Task Force's Academic Advisor.

Forty-eight of 130 CPR companies replied to the survey, representing a 37 percent return rate. Of the 48 respondents:

- 31 (64.5 percent) are in manufacturing;
- 7 (8.7 percent) are in financial services or insurance; and
- 10 (20.8 percent) are engaged in "other" activity (of which the largest categories were mining and public utilities).

Slightly over half of the respondent firms (54 percent) are large employers, reporting that they have work forces in the 25,000–100,000 range. An additional 37 percent report having 5,000–25,000 employees. No respondent reported having more than 100,000 employees, and only 1 respondent had fewer than 5,000 employees.

In sum, the CPR respondent group consists primarily of manufacturing firms in the medium-large to large-sized work force category.

Forty-two companies supplied figures on pending external employment disputes. Cumulatively, they reported a total of 1,801 cases pending before *EEO agencies*, and 665 employee *lawsuits pending in state and federal courts*. (This comes to an average of 42.8 EEO complaints per company, and 15.8 employee lawsuits.)

Forty-two companies also supplied figures, at another point in the survey, on the number of *unjust dismissal cases* they had currently pending in the courts. The total was 245 cases, for an average of 5.8 per company.

Companies were asked to check *all* of the following "internal mechanisms" they currently provide for their nonunion employees:

- No formal complaint system; follow chain of command;
- Open Line, Speak-Up, or other employee communication system;
- Informal open door policy;
- Formal complaint and appeal system;
- Private outside arbitration; and
- Quality Circle or other employee participation program.

These mechanisms were organized by occupational level of employee, and produced the following results. (The total number

Type of employee	No formal complaint system; "follow chain of command"	Open Line, Speak-Up, or other employee communication system	Informal open-door policy	Formal complaint and appeal system	Private outside arbitration	Quality Circle or other forms of employee participation program
Production workers	16	18	27	18	5	20
Clerical/secretarial	25	23	36	17	2	18
Professional/technical	27	24	36	16	1	19
Supervisors	27	23	36	15	0	16
Managers	27	21	37	14	0	13
Senior executives	25	17	36	12	0	10

of respondents here is 47. One company that reported results on 32 subunits could not be used in the analysis.)

Looking more closely at the companies indicating they had a formal complaint and appeal system for one or more categories of their nonunion employees, 21 out of the 47 respondents (44 percent) indicated they were using such a system.

Occupational level	Have formal complaint and appeal system	Number of employees Over 25,000	Under 25,000	Industry Manufact-uring	Financial	Other
Production	17 (36%)	10	7	14	3	0
Clerical/secretary	17 (36%)	9	8	11	4	2
Professional/technical	15 (32%)	9	7	10	4	2
Supervisors	15 (32%)	9	6	9	4	2
Managers	14 (29%)	9	5	8	4	2
Senior executives	11 (23%)	7	4	7	3	1

We provided firms having a formal complaint system with a series of statements about the possible effects of having such a system on various personnel, legal, and management interests. The following chart shows the responses of 21 companies.

Statement given in survey	Agree	Disagree	Can't say
Helps screen out meritorious claims for resolution by management	20	0	1
Helps identify weak or poor management practices or supervisory administration	20	1	0
Has helped identify company policies that needed revision or clarification	19	1	1
Probably reduces the number of EEO complaints filed with EEO agencies	19	1	1
Is considered cost-effective by our management in terms of reducing negative employee behavior (poor work, absenteeism, excessive quits, etc.)	19	1	1
Probably reduces the number of employee lawsuits filed for unjust dismissal (other than EEO suits)	14	3	4
Has had a positive effect on employee morale	12	0	8

Statement given in survey	*Agree*	*Disagree*	*Can't say*
Has helped in the way some EEO agencies treat employee EEO complaints, because the agency staff believe our internal procedures are fair and sound EEO policies are applied	11	2	8

When given a set of reasons why the firm had created a formal complaint system, or was expanding it, and asked to check all that applied, the most frequently checked reason was "an expanded 'human-resources' approach to supervision." Next in order was the desire to "reduce the number of employee complaints to outside agencies and the courts" and a "concern over the size of awards." Low-ranked factors were work force changes, costs of several big cases, and concern to reduce legal costs.

The 1984 CPR study indicates, and studies by the Educational Fund for Individual Rights confirm, that in the EEO category age discrimination complaints are expected to rise dramatically in the next three years. Age suits by *professionals* and *managers* are expected to be higher than those brought by clerical/production workers. (For example, 75 percent of the firms expect managerial and professional age suits to increase, while 55 percent expect increased age suits by clerical/production employees.)

Sex discrimination and sexual harassment complaints are about equal in expected increases (about 35–38 percent, across the three occupational categories).

Race and handicap external complaints are seen as least likely to increase.

Eight CPR firms reported that they were considering changes in the handling of employee complaints in the EEO area. The changes described were as follows:

- Formal complaint procedure.
- We have considered, within the Office of the General Counsel, the possibility of adopting arbitration for all grievances, but no formal proposal has been drafted or considered.
- Mandatory supervision, training, and published complaint system.
- Formalizing the current system into a full-blown alternative to employee relations litigation.
- We are considering a formal complaint system.

- Ombudsman-type approach involving corporate, division, or staff offices outside of employee's normal chain of command is being considered for all complaints.
- Possibility of implementing a formal employee complaint procedure in divisions other than ____Division.
- Formal complaint system is being developed and is under consideration. It would deal with complaints in EEO area, as well as other areas.

The survey asked companies whether they had made changes during the past three years in various company documents "to make clearer that employment is at will and terminable at the option of the employer." The responses were as follows:

Company document	Percent of all companies making changes	Percent with formal compliance system	Percent with informal systems
Personnel handbook	43%	47%	40%
Employment application	36	38	36
Policy statement to employees	25	38	11
Offer letter	20	23	15

These responses show that almost half the CPR firms have revised their personnel handbooks in the past three years to strengthen at-will prerogatives. The difference here between companies having formal systems (47 percent) and those having informal systems (40 percent) is minimal.

As already noted, 42 reporting CPR firms have a total of 665 employee lawsuits pending in the courts, of which 245 are unjust dismissal cases. In the detailed responses as to outcomes of unjust dismissal cases, the clear trend is that most lawsuits are either being won by companies, abandoned by plaintiffs, or settled by "nominal payments." Very few cases are reported to be won in court by the employee or resulting in reinstatement.

The data show that only a minority of employees first raise their complaints *within* the company before filing with outside agencies (in either formal or informal systems). Presumably, those who start inside are able to resolve most of them there, and those employees who are distrustful of employer fairness or are uninformed about the availability of internal systems are the ones who file outside. Specifically, of 23 firms reporting on use of inside forums in *EEO cases* before the claim was filed outside, 15 said less than 29 percent of these employees used the inside system. Twelve firms said less than 29 percent of employees used the inside mechanisms in *court cases*.

Among the other activities or trends relating to dispute avoidance or management were the following:

- 35 of 47 firms (74 percent) have changed their performance evaluation procedures recently "to provide more objective actions" by management.
- 41 of 47 firms (87 percent) have put more emphasis on "training supervisors to conduct terminations properly."
- 16 of 27 firms (60 percent) say they are giving managers and staff formal training in mediation or conflict resolution; 11 of these do this in-house.
- 5 of 46 firms report they have used arbitration, mediation, or a "minitrial" in a nonunion employment dispute.
- 3 of 43 firms say they are *considering* providing an outside arbitration or mediation option for their complaint system.
- 25 of 47 firms (53 percent) report that their legal costs for defending unjust dismissal suits have increased *substantially* over the past 3 years.

The primary trends indicated by this survey can be summed up as follows:

- Most of these CPR companies are experiencing larger numbers of employee lawsuits, are spending "significantly" more in legal costs to defend such cases, and anticipate significant increases in the age discrimination area in the next 3 years.
- These firms have in general moved in recent years toward establishing formal complaint and appeal systems, or toward expanding the scope of existing programs (both to cover more types of employees and more issues).
- This trend is continuing, with eight firms reporting that they are either considering adopting a formal system or expanding an existing one.
- Three firms are considering adding mediation or arbitration to their systems.
- The 21 firms that have formal systems report a high level of satisfaction with them, stating they they see positive effects in the personnel administration and the legal areas.

While this may reflect a desire to justify what their firms have done, the level of candor in an anonymous survey of this kind allows some confidence to be placed in the intended objectivity of these evaluations.

Having documented the move by leading companies to create new "fair procedure" systems, what are the key elements of such systems, and how effective are they in keeping employee complaints out of litigation?

Patterns of Emerging Internal Systems

During the period of 1982–1987, the authors examined over 150 internal complaint systems in large- and medium sized companies. As might be expected, the systems vary according to the nature of the work forces, organizational patterns, and company cultures of different firms, including their previous EEO/affirmative action experiences. They also vary as to which employees can use the systems: some are available only to production and clerical employees; some are open also to sales, professional, and technical employees; and a few allow lower and middle management to use the system.

However, in about a third of the firms we have studied, a number of multifaceted mechanisms for avoiding and/or resolving employment disputes are emerging. These generally consist of five elements. The assumption of this mixed-mechanism approach is that employees inevitably have "concerns" and "problems," and that *most* of these should be responded to by nonadjudicative approaches (e.g., information-giving, counseling, and mediating) to forestall concerns becoming adversarial. However, the governing assumption is that *some* concerns are or will become adversarial, because of what the employer's agents have done or what the employee perceives as an unfair action. Therefore, an adjudicative system is a necessary mechanism to include in a full-fledged dispute prevention and dispute resolution program. (The chart on the following page illustrates this mixed-mechanisms approach.) Briefly described, here are the five elements used:

1. An *employee-communication* mechanism involves receiving written queries or telephone questions from individual employees about anything that "concerns them" and produces a direct written or oral answer to the employee, in confidence. Such programs (e.g.,

INTERNAL CHANNELS FOR RESPONDING
TO EMPLOYEE CONCERNS

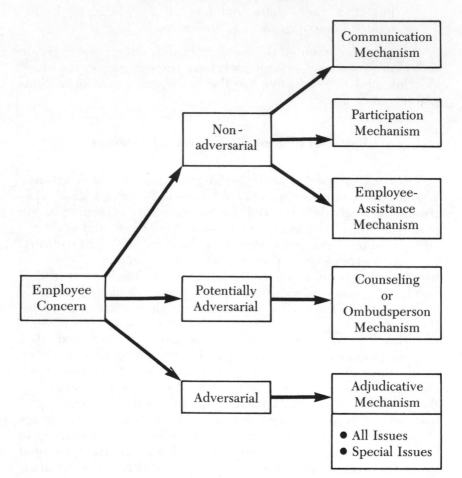

Speak Up at IBM, *Question Line* at Security Pacific National Bank, and *Action Line* at Prudential) allow managements to receive and reply to employee concerns before they turn into grievances, and from there into complaints.

  2. An *employee-participation mechanism*, such as Quality Circles, Quality Teams, Involvement Programs, and Participative Management, in which potential employee complaints can be resolved as part of a small-group "work problem-solving" procedure. Our studies and others show that many issues which otherwise

would produce grievances in unionized firms or internal or external complaints in nonunion firms are effectively resolved in the course of a strong employee participation program.

3. An *employee-assistance mechanism*, by which employees whose problems at work stem from personal troubles, such as alcohol or drugs, family difficulties, and financial crises, can be connected by the company to outside, confidential counseling services. Companies such as Control Data have found after a decade of having an Employee Assistance Resource that failure to provide such assistance is very costly in terms of bad work, employee complaints, and outside litigation.

4. An *employee-counseling mechanism* provides staff experts trained in mediation skills whose assignment it is to listen, investigate, counsel, mediate, and, whenever possible, negotiate solutions acceptable to the employee and the management.

5. A *formal adjudicative mechanism*, in which the company provides a complaint forum at which the facts of a dispute are heard and determined, with strong assistance to the employee from counselors who support the hearing process, plus one or more higher appeal committees that review the judgment and basis of the hearing body. These systems provide explicit guarantees to employees against any overt or covert reprisals for using these systems, and usually guarantee that using the system does not generate a record in the employee's personnel file.

Of the 90 companies we surveyed in 1984 that had such an adjudicative system:

- Most provide facilitators to help the employee who files a complaint to sharpen and clarify his or her concerns.
- About one in five uses some kind of independent investigator (from management) who interviews parties and witnesses and makes a judgment that management will almost always accept.
- One in five companies provides that a fellow employee can be selected to assist the complaining employee or represent him/her at hearings, or have employees as members of hearing and appeal committees.
- Only 5 percent of these companies provide voluntary, outside mediation or arbitration of the final internal appeal, though several other companies said they were currently considering such a measure.

How Well Do the New Dispute Resolution Systems Work?

In 1984, in cooperation with the Center for Public Resources, we conducted confidential interviews at eight diverse companies that have the internal mechanisms we have just described. We asked them how well their systems were working in light of growing employee litigation and especially unjust discharge cases in the state courts.

All the firms reported a rise in the percentage of *internal* employee complaints involving involuntary terminations. At one company, these complaints made up 14 percent of the total annual case load inside the company in 1983 and 16 percent in 1984. At another company, terminations were 23 percent of the total number of complaints. Termination cases are also the single issue most likely to be carried by employees up to the highest "appellate" stage of the internal company systems. This is true in both the systems that culminate in an "inside the firm" review board (with or without employee members) and those that offer outside arbitration. The reason given was the bad job market which makes employees fight harder to retain their present employment.

All eight firms report their internal systems are providing major payoffs for the companies using them, even though their presence does not deter *all* employee lawsuits or complaints to regulatory agencies. The reasons given were:

- The internal systems allow management to learn about and have the opportunity to deal equitably with almost all the employee complaints that are truly meritorious—for example, where line management (1) did not follow the company policies or violated legal-regulatory duties, (2) did not document their actions as called for, and (3) put the company into an embarrassing though legally defensible position.
- The small number of cases that do go into court after being heard inside are, in these employers' judgment, cases that the company expects to win and not to have to settle. This gives the corporate legal departments a much greater sense of confidence and much better advance preparation than would otherwise be true.
- Seven of the eight companies estimated that their case load of wrongful discharge suits was significantly lower than that of companies of similar size and type, in each geographic

zone relating to judicial doctrines and plaintiff's lawyer activity.

Example: Security Pacific National Bank

A good example of a multiple-channel set of mechanisms in action is at Security Pacific National Bank, headquartered in California.

Security Pacific is the tenth largest commercial bank in the United States and the second largest in California, with more than 600 branch banking offices within the state and corporate and international banking offices in 12 states and 24 foreign countries.

Over 12,000 members of Security Pacific's work force are located in the branch banking office system, with an additional 10,000 employees in staff support and central administration positions. Of these 22,000 employees, approximately 5,000 are classified as officers and 17,000 as nonofficers. None of the bank's operations is unionized.

Grievance Procedure. Security Pacific instituted a formal grievance procedure in 1970; it is unusual among large banks in calling this a grievance system, rather than using the softer language of complaint system or problem resolution procedure that most other banks favor. In a 1977 article in *American Banker*, Irving Margol, now Executive Vice President, Management Services Group, explained the origins of the bank's formalized grievance system as follows:

> The first [of the bank's mechanisms for two-way communication on employee problems], implemented in June 1970, was a formal Grievance Procedure. Management realized the increased trend of union activity among white collar workers in the banking community and met head-on the need to take affirmative steps to provide effective management practices and systems to maintain a total work environment in which employees do not feel a need for a union to represent them.

Margol also mentioned concern over loss of productivity from "employees who are not working to their full capacities because of dissatisfaction with some aspect of their job and/or working conditions. . . ." Such behavior can arise from the "unrest" of employees who feel that the only way to get management to pay attention to a problem is to "tell them you're going to the Fair Employment Practices Commission—FEPC—or the Equal Employment Opportunity Commission—EEOC," or those employees who believe "management doesn't want to hear your complaint. If you don't like it here, quit or just do enough to get by."

Security Pacific's Grievance Procedure meets these problems, said Margol, by "providing a very necessary two-way communication" that allows the employee "to appeal to higher levels when a problem which has been reviewed with the supervisor appears beyond resolution."

> The procedure has three decision steps allowing employees to present the problems to three levels of management, the third step being the appropriate member of the management committee. The grievance is prepared in written form and the employee is assisted by a Personnel Officer. The Personnel Officer's role is to help the employee clarify the grievance and outline it into three segments: the Situation, the Problem, the Expected Outcome.
>
> The procedure has been advantageous as a monitoring device of employee dissatisfaction, application of personnel policies and effectiveness of supervision. It has additionally provided an input to management regarding "HOT SPOTS" such as union or concerted activities, eliminated outside agency complaints, and provided management with a channel to demonstrate interest and willingness to solve problems for employees.

From its inception in 1970 until 1977, Margol reported, about 500 grievances had been filed by bank employees, with the majority involving dissatisfaction with supervisory actions, denials of salary increases, or failure to be transferred or promoted. Discrimination complaints appeared in the program from the start, generally at a 5 percent level of the total.

An excellent portrait of the Grievance Procedure at work was presented to bank employees through a 1982 article published in *Security News*, the employee newspaper. The article quoted Peter Kiefer, vice president of employee relations, as stating that 113 grievances were filed in 1981, and "by people from all levels of the bank." Officers filed 20 of the 113 grievances and nonofficers 93; females filed 84 grievances and males 29; and 63 of the total came from banking offices compared with 50 from staff units. "The majority," Kiefer said, "had to do with performance, advancement, and concern for fair treatment." Six of the 113 (about 5 percent) grievances were classified as "affirmative-action related." The three largest categories were classified as "situation counseling" (33 percent), "training/advancement" (25 percent), and "supervision" (dealing with "personality conflict, communication, performance appraisal ratings") (16 percent).

In discussing what happened to the 113 grievances that employees filed, Kiefer reported that 70 employees withdrew their grievances after discussing them with personnel. This was, he felt, because their situations had changed since the grievance was filed, or because the grievance was resolved without having to go through higher steps, or because the employee was satisfied "once bank policy was explained and verified." Of the 43 grievances that did go further, 35 were resolved at Step 1 (meeting with a regional vice president or department/division manager); 4 at Step 2 (meeting with a division administrator or department head); and 4 at Step 3 (meeting with the appropriate bank executive vice president). Seventy-five percent of the 43 grievances carried beyond the personnel department, Kiefer reported, "were either granted in the employee's favor or at a compromise." In the other 25 percent, the employee's grievance was denied.

Kiefer believes the grievance procedure is a good one and is working well. "The entire grievance procedure," he notes, "is completely confidential—neither the grievance forms nor the fact that an employee wishes to file a grievance will ever become part of a personnel file." In addition, the employee handbook assures employees that "You can be absolutely certain that your standing with the bank will not be adversely affected in any way," as a result of filing a grievance.

Question Line. The *Question Line* program was instituted by the bank in June 1974. Irving Margol explained that while the formal grievance procedure "was and is successful, we also realized that it did not meet all of the varying needs of our employees."

> It became apparent [that] many employees had situations or questions that needed management's attention, but employees did not want to openly file a grievance and identify themselves for a solution unless it was actually necessary to do so.

The *Question Line* program created to meet this need is described to employees as "a confidential, two-way channel of communication," available to raise questions about "bank policy, personnel practices, benefits, compensation and operating procedures." Printed, postage-paid forms located throughout the bank's offices are used by employees to send in their questions, which go to a *Question Line* coordinator. The coordinator detaches the name of the employee and then sends the inquiry to the bank official best qualified to respond to it. A written answer is then sent by the coordinator to the employee's home address.

No communication is made by the coordinator to the employee's supervisor; however, if the *Question Line* inquiry indicates an individual personnel problem, the Coordinator will ask the employee whether he or she wishes to talk it over with a personnel specialist, or may even suggest that the employee file a grievance and have the matter officially resolved.

Those questions and answers that are considered to be of general interest to the bank's staff are published monthly in the employee publication, *Security News.* This practice, observes Margol, "allows us to communicate to our total staff the management's position or reasons for specific decisions, issues, policies or practices." A regular stream of published Question Lines have dealt with EEO issues at the bank during the seven years the program has been in operation.

Overall, Margol stresses, "The confidential nature of this program cannot be overemphasized to the employees, as anonymity is guaranteed. If assistance cannot be given to the employee through this program without identifying the employee, the employee makes the decision to pursue the matter through alternative channels." Margol remarks that "Many problems have surfaced and have been prevented prior to outside intervention. Management's feedback in this program is possible while protecting the employee."

About 1,000 *Question Line* inquiries are filed and answered each year, and responses are usually made to the employee in a few days, or within a week or two for any questions that require more time for response. Discrimination issues appear in the Question Line at about the same percentage as in the Grievance Procedure.

The Q-Line. The third and final element of Security Pacific's program is called *Q-Line.* It is described to employees as "a special telephone line reserved as the place to call for an immediate response to any job-related inquiries. This program confidentially provides information, direction, and assistance to you." The employee need not identify himself or herself when dialing the special *Q-Line* number, which is open for 2½ hours in the morning of each weekday. Calls are received, collect, from bank employees anywhere in the world. About 1,500–2,000 *Q-Line* calls are received a year, also including questions relating to EEO issues. Margol explains that:

> The caller does not have to identify his or herself but merely ask or state the question that concerns them. The Personnel Department

will attempt to channel the caller through the proper chain of command but if this is not satisfactory, will investigate the situation. . . .
Employees can use this program to seek, on a confidential basis,
guidance or counseling about a particular situation, to get a quick
answer to a policy question, or to request direction to the appropriate
person who can assist them.

The reasons the bank added this hot line in 1977 to the existing
complaint machinery was explained in an interesting observation
by Margol:

> We were experiencing a trend of employees contacting outside
> agencies without first using internal problem solving sources pres-
> ently available to them. It was apparent employees needed a for-
> malized method of talking to someone immediately about a problem
> or concern. Realizing some employees do not wish to directly con-
> front management with their situation or wish to remain completely
> anonymous, the Hot Line Program utilizes the telephone system.

Security Pacific officers with whom we discussed the handling
of discrimination complaints within the bank had several observations to offer. Overall, they believe, Security Pacific has an excellent record in terms of resolving discrimination complaints
internally, and has a good record with external EEO agencies. It
has not had any class action suits filed against it, nor has any
employee complaint filed with EEOC gone to official fact-finding
in the past five or six years. Generally, employee complaints filed
with local EEO agencies are resolved through settlements worked
out with the employees. Only a small number of employees—well
below industry averages or experiences of other California companies of Security Pacific's size—have produced lawsuits on EEO
issues. One personnel official at the Bank remarked to us that, "in
keeping with the litigiousness of the times, more of our employees,
as a whole, are going to outside agencies and attorneys these days
and do not start by using our internal process at first. However,
when they do, the local EEO staffs know that we have a strong
and fair internal program, and they will generally recommend to
such employees that they try our program first, before proceeding
further with the complaint. Most of them then do that."

The internal complaint system is well regarded by such agencies not because of any unique procedures per se but because the
bank has achieved a solid "bottom line" performance in the hiring
and advancement of minorities and women, and EEO agencies
therefore view the bank as ready to apply that policy fairly through
its internal grievance procedures.

Overall, Kiefer believes that the bank has done the right thing by handling employee complaints about EEO issues through its three general complaint mechanisms, rather than creating a special EEO adjudicative system. "Discrimination issues are wrapped up with pay, promotion, appraisal, and all the other basic employee relations issues. We felt during the 1970s that our general employee communication and feedback programs were the correct place to deal with them. We still do today."

With the aid of its multipronged internal system, Security Pacific has maintained an unusually strong record in EEO cases (e.g., no class action suits and most EEO complaints settled with EEO agencies) and a much lower employment-lawsuit case load in litigious California than most other banks. In fact, the bank has not lost a single termination case in a jury trial, a record that few other California banks can match.

"The reason our system works," Kiefer observed, "is that it is committed to fairness and equity in the application of management policies, legal rules, and good employee relations. And we will correct or overturn any manager actions that do not meet those standards."

The Growing Trend Toward Internal Systems

The survey taken at our 1984 national conference showed that two out of three of these 64 corporations were engaged in installing the kind of internal dispute prevention or dispute resolution systems we will be examining in this book. This is probably higher than the proportion of activity in the 10,000 largest firms for which such issues are relevant today, though the CPR survey shows the steady movement of large companies in this direction. The start of a basic trend in the corporate world seems clear. Any nonunion firm that: (1) seeks to draw the greatest creativity and commitment from its work force, (2) seeks to resolve employee complaints before they generate appeals to outside agencies and the courts, and (3) wants to meet both employee expectations of fairness and organizational interests in sound administration is—or ought to be—actively considering the creation of a multifaceted fair procedure system.

Chapter 2

Employee Perceptions of Unfair Treatment on the Job

Between 1978 and 1987, researchers at the Educational Fund for Individual Rights conducted formal and informal interviews with over 250 employees of nonunion companies. About 100 of these employees were people who were actual or potential whistleblowers—employees who believed their organizations were engaging in illegal, dangerous, or unethical conduct, had tried to raise and remedy their concerns internally, had been rebuffed by management, and were thinking of "going public" or had chosen to go public with their complaints.

In 1981, the Fund published first-person accounts by 10 such corporate employees, in a book titled: *Whistle-Blowing: Loyalty and Dissent in the Corporation.** The situations selected for that collection spanned a wide range of whistleblower settings. Whistleblower cases raise the most dramatic and extreme cases of employee complaints. And, since they directly challenge what management is doing, they pose special problems for any dispute resolution system administered by management itself. While some companies have developed special procedures for receiving and responding to issues of ethical dissent or whistleblower concerns (see the Citibank profile in Chapter 3), whistleblower cases are increasingly being adjudicated by state courts examining wrongful discharge claims, or under state or federal laws that provide a judicial hearing for persons who allege that they were fired or disciplined by private or public employers because the employee reported illegal conduct to public authorities.

---

*Alan F. Westin, ed. New York, McGraw-Hill.

What we focus on in this section are employee complaints and experiences that involve more of the everyday, nonexceptional aspects of employee-employer relations. Many of the profiles presented involve discrimination claims, or at least personnel decisions such as assignments, performance evaluations, promotions, discipline, or discharge in which employees felt some element of discrimination was present.

It should be emphasized that we did not conduct independent investigations of these reports. We screened out any in which our fairly practiced eye led us to believe that the employees we interviewed were displaying obvious bias, poor judgment, or distorted notions of employment realities. What we draw on, therefore, is a pool of over 100 interviews in which a genuine dispute had arisen between employees and employers, and there was no meaningful and trusted dispute resolution mechanism to be used. Our sense is that these personal accounts paint in vivid terms the "employee's-eye view" of dispute problems in the nonunion firm. They show what can go wrong with systems that are formalistic, poorly administered, lacking in top-management attention to retaliation problems, and lacking in meaningful employee-level participation in their operations. As such, they serve as an ideal backdrop for presentations of systems in Chapter 3 that *do* address the central problems these employees raise.

Overall Impressions

Most of the employees we interviewed said they knew about some kind of procedure for handling workplace complaints, and some were able to describe their company's procedures in detail. Those employees usually mentioned that written materials explaining the procedures were distributed to employees, and briefings were provided for new employees in initial orientation sessions. Some employees—presumably correctly—said that their companies had no specific procedures for handling complaints—"you just talk to your supervisor" or "I suppose you can go to personnel."

Whether the issue involved discrimination or not, many employees said that they and their colleagues had genuine fears of reprisal from supervisors and management if they invoked the complaint machinery, despite official promises that this would not happen. "The problem with reprisals here is real," one employee commented, "especially for lower level employees and blacks and minorities."

To appreciate the feelings generated by unfair treatment by inadequate internal complaint mechanisms to address employee problems, we have selected a representative group of reports from corporate employees and present them here. As readers will see, these employees span the full range of corporate employment, from secretaries to technical and professional specialists, salespeople, and management.

Realities of the "Open Door": Karen's Story

Karen currently works as an executive secretary at a large communications firm. It was during her job several years ago with a division promoting rock and roll albums, however, that she began to experience two sets of problems—a work-assignment and pay-level issue and a steadily recurring sexual harassment condition.

"The sexual harassment began right from the start, from the first three hours I was there. I work in rock and roll, which is very sexually oriented—life in the fast lane and all that. Lifestyles are very high. And, women aren't respected much in the rock and roll world." She then related a series of blatant and humiliating sexual demands made upon her by superiors in her division. Given the culture of the division, and its huge money-making position in the company, she did not feel she could make any formal complaint or expect anything to be done. "I went into therapy. I felt working there was like learning to play a delicate chess game. I was furious at the way I was being treated but you get to be very ambitious in the big corporate world, and you try to find ways to play the game."

At the same time that the sexual harassment was taking place, and continuing, Karen experienced a growing problem with her work assignments: "From the first day I worked there," Karen recalled, "there was confusion over which of two bosses I should actually report to. Both bosses would assign me work to do, and I often had twice as much as anyone else. Each man would also ask for personal items to be typed, during my normal work time. It became a power play between the two men. I complained to my bosses that this wasn't fair. I thought it had been worked out and I wouldn't be required to do that any more, but from time to time, personal items were still given to me. Then, one day, one boss saw me doing personal work for the other, and he told me I had no right to do that without his permission. I told him that I did personal work for him, and that it wasn't fair for him to yell at me. He got mad and threatened that he would never ask me to do anything personal for him again.

"About the same time, I had absorbed someone else's work and was doing her job. I felt I should be paid her salary, which was higher, and I wanted to raise that issue as well as the problem of my being asked to do personal work and getting caught between the two bosses.

"Under our 'Open Door' policy, you are supposed to take a problem to the personnel department, and if personnel can't help, you can then appeal to management. There isn't supposed to be any reprisal if you do. But using the Open Door poses a threat to your boss,' and they can view it as your going 'over their heads.' After I complained to personnel, and they must have asked my boss about what I had related, I suddenly received a 30-day notice of dismissal for (inattentiveness to work).

"When I had told the personnel people that I was going to raise my work-assignment and pay problems through the Open Door, they had warned me that it would be dangerous and asked me to reconsider. I didn't believe them. Then the 30-days notice arrived. When I told the people at Personnel about it, they said that since this had been issued without any previous warning, as expressly required by the company's personnel policies, it was against the firing policy. If I appealed this through the Open Door, they said, I would win. But they added that, if I did, and was upheld by management, my life would be unbearable in that department. They suggested I take a job elsewhere in the company, and they would fix it up for me to do that. So, when an opening came up in another department a few days later, I took it. I wanted to stay and fight the improper discharge, but everyone—including a Woman's Employee Committee we have—told me it would be better to get a fresh start somewhere else. I was treated for depression for eight months. So, I learned what reprisal can take place when you try to use the Open Door. Now, I advise anyone who asks me against using that program. It is dangerous."

Diminished Black Prospects at a Manufacturing Firm: Charles' Story

Charles is a black executive in his late forties. He works for a large manufacturing firm in the textile and chemical industry with over 20,000 employees in installations throughout the country. Charles is a vice president in the personnel division at the Corporate Headquarters in a large northeastern city. He is an Ivy League graduate, well educated and well spoken, living in an integrated suburb. He has worked for this partially unionized firm for about 15 years.

Charles' firm has a typical grievance/arbitration system for its unionized employees. It had also created a 3-step, formalized procedure for its 5,000 nonunionized hourly production employees. Step 1 of the nonunion process is to file a written complaint with the immediate supervisor, Step 2 is to carry the issue to the unit superintendent, and Step 3 is to go to a Review Board, which includes the plant or division manager. About 50 to 75 cases go to Step 3 annually.

Salaried employees do not have this 3-step system. They are expected to go to their supervisor with a complaint, and if this is not resolved to their satisfaction, they can go to Personnel, "if they trust them," said Charles. Beyond Personnel, "there is not much to do." Charles notes that this is *not* a company with an Open Door philosophy or policy; such language is not used with salaried employees. However, in one division, Charles noted, the open personality of the head makes it easy for professional employees to talk over problems; the man who held that post previously was not so inclined, and no one complained to him. In short, there is no *system* of open resort to top management in this company.

Charles reports that the company instituted a good performance appraisal system in the early 1970s, as a result of serious EEO problems and several plant closings that required the firm to find ways to select the best performers for relocation to other plant opportunities. In the 1970s, the firm also worked up a good outplacement program to help terminated employees, and is now instituting a job-posting program in some of its units. Charles feels "the job-posting program does a lot to demystify how people get promoted, and to eliminate unfounded skepticism." However, "it makes big demands on staff at a time of lean resources. We're not like IBM or Control Data with rich staffs to use."

When this man joined the firm, in the mid-1960s, there was no EEO consciousness, and federal law and regulation were only beginning to get under way. He was added to the corporate staff as a black Ivy League graduate, clearly an illustration of the "talented tenth" phenomenon of black high achievers rather than a result of any minority-outreach program. The firm experienced major audits, class actions, and litigation in racial and female discrimination suits in the early 1970s, with external pressures reaching a serious point about 1972–1973.

Management responded with several steps:

- a serious performance appraisal system, in quarterly evaluations;
- the job-posting system already described; and
- an EEO committee in each division, mixing management, staff, and representatives of minorities and females.

The EEO committees, Charles stressed, do *not* operate as a grievance processing body; they raise and identify "problems to be solved." The firm will then bring in outside experts and consultants, do attitude surveys, develop pilot programs, and so forth. The committees are really used, Charles reports, to "discuss the health of the division or plant in its EEO program. They can take up pending class actions [there are several] or discuss individual cases, but only to assess the 'problem,' not to render a judgment on the merits. For example, when the issue was raised of opportunity for females, a nationally known women's civil rights expert was brought in to conduct awareness sessions with managers. Top women's rights leaders were also brought in to meet with the CEO and top management." This led to a special progress plan for women, and it is operating well. "In fact," Charles observed, "women are moving faster here than minority males."

Overall Charles sees his firm as a "me-too" responder in the EEO area, not a leader. He drew a distinction between the "consumer" companies that have marketing incentives to be perceived as good in minority hiring and opportunity—such as Pepsi Cola, Bristol Myers, Miller Brewing, and Philip Morris—and those like his firm—along with Dow Chemical, Olin, Norton Simon, and Union Carbide—that he feels respond to minority issues only when government regulatory pressures are on them.

Among salaried black employees at his firm, both female and male, Charles believes, the belief is strong that "management will now drag its feet. It won't do as much as in the past. It will seek people with impeccable credentials at corporate, and management in the divisions will cease active recruitment of minorities. Neglect will start to be the rule."

Speaking from his many contacts with black executives in corporate employment, Charles commented that "blacks are not at all optimistic about our opportunities to keep climbing the management ladder, given the Reagan administration's policies in Washington, to which top management in this firm are very sympathetic."

In terms of EEO complaints, he said they have not had sexual harassment complaints at his firm, but they have several dozen race and sex discrimination cases currently pending with EEO agencies. These have been declining from earlier levels. "We are doing better with inside counseling and settlement," he felt. They have had very few age discrimination suits. He feels this is because the firm's performance appraisal system operates well to flag and document poor performance, and this serves to support their personnel decisions. Also, they do a good job of relocating employees when plants close, rather than firing them or using these opportunities to eliminate older workers.

In response to a question about how blacks in salaried ranks— professional people like financial analysts, lawyers, management science people, and technical people—would be likely to handle an EEO issue under the new, Reagan-era atmosphere, Charles was quite firm in his judgments. "If a minority male or female decided to raise an EEO complaint now, it would be as part of a plan to leave the company and then file it. You wouldn't expect—as was true in the 70s—to be able to file it and stay working here." He explained that filing such a complaint would be considered "disloyal," a "break with the team." You "would not be openly harassed, but you'd only be 'tolerated' thereafter, and you wouldn't have much of a future."

In addition, he noted that there had been no "huge settlements at this company in EEO cases, as there have been in some other companies," so that a minority employee filing an EEO complaint today would know to expect "a long arduous process and probably little financial return." He also said that "under the Reagan administration, you'd have the burden of showing the company was wrong, rather than them having to show that they hadn't based their judgment on discrimination. It's going to be a lot harder for minorities in the future."

He could not say whether white females at his firm are less reluctant now to file EEO claims, but he is sure black men and women are. "There's deep skepticism at this firm now among black professionals and managers that opportunities will really be equal in the mid-80s."

Limits on the Jurisdiction of a Complaint System: Two Women at an Educational Corporation

Martha is an executive secretary and Betsy is a senior executive at a large company that provides services and issues publications in education. The firm has several thousand employees at its headquarters in a northeastern state, primarily professionals and their clerical support staffs, with sales and administrative staffs located in half a dozen other states. Almost 50 percent of the employees hold a bachelor's degree or higher. The company is nonunion, with low employee turnover compared with other companies in its field. The management sees its personnel style as very "open," "communicative," and "participative," with job postings for new openings, solicitation of staff inputs on drafts of new personnel policies, and an "open" policy toward salary levels and ranges.

The company's present system of complaint handling was instituted, according to company officials, because the management decided that its formal, Open Door mechanism, supported by employee relations professionals, had become less satisfactory as the size of the staff grew and individual rights and group rights consciousness increased in the nation. A proposal for a formalized, multistep complaint system was rejected as too rigid and inappropriate to the professional character of the work force. After trying to improve its informal system for several years, the company moved in 1976 to try a "peer review" system for resolving personnel "disagreements."

Under the system, an employee who wishes to go above the supervisor with a complaint may invoke the "disagreements procedure" by contacting the Vice President for Personnel. A panel of 20 employees (below the officer level) are selected at random from the total headquarters roster and asked whether they would be willing to serve on a peer-review panel. The employee with a complaint chooses one employee from the volunteer panel, the vice president from the area where the complaint arose chooses another employee volunteer, and these two panelists choose a third panel member, who serves as the chair.

Panel members are told they they are not to serve as representatives or advocates of the "side" that chose them but as an independent and impartial committee. Materials are provided by the parties, statements are obtained, and hearings are held where necessary. The panel submits its conclusion and recommendations to the Vice President for Personnel. Any staff member who is not satisfied with the action of the Vice President can then appeal to the company's Executive Vice President for a review, and, finally, to the President. A guarantee of nonreprisal for using the procedure is made and publicized frequently. Over four years of operation, the personnel director has indicated that about two dozen employees have used the disagreements procedure and he sees the system as working well.

What Martha and Betsy believe is that the disagreements policy has rarely if ever been used by women or black employees to challenge the "gross inequities" they see in this company's pay and promotion policies. "Inside the organization, with one exception, no one other than a white male has ever been proposed by management for a vice president's spot," Betsy observed. Furthermore, in "job-slotting, performance appraisals, and promotions, the company systematically and continually discriminates against women and racial minorities all up and down the line, at clerical levels, technical, professional, and senior staff." Given the continued discriminatory practices by top management, the two women said, making a challenge through the disagreements policy "would be a waste of time. You'd probably be considered to be 'disloyal' for bucking the system. Even if no reprisal were taken, the complaint would fall on deaf ears." Both Martha and Betsy have been quite angry at the discriminatory treatment they believe they have received from management, but neither has ever used the disagreements policy.

For reasons that neither woman could fully explain, very few employees at this company had filed complaints with EEOC or other human rights agencies. As a result, there had been little outside investigation and no agency adjudication of the equity of this company's practices. Instead of using the adjudicative machinery, women employees had organized a Women's Equity Commiteee and black employees had formed a similar action group, and, recently, both took what could be called "political action." The women's group saw to it that documents showing inequitable treatment of women were leaked to the company's Board of Directors. The black group drew up a protest memo signed by over

100 black employees at all levels complaining about similar ine-quitable treatment of blacks; this was not only sent to the Board but also leaked to the national press.

"Under the old management," Betsy observed, "all of this probably wouldn't have accomplished anything." But a new chair-man was recently brought in by the Board, primarily to improve the firm's business performance and its public image. On reviewing the treatment of women and miniorites, he concluded that the company's past practices were a "disgrace." He has promised to not only correct these practices but to see that "reparations" are made for previous discriminatory practices.

Reflecting on this possible new approach, Betsy observed that no complaint system can hope to win equal opportunity when the top management does not even recognize that it is carrying out highly discriminatory policies. "Now," she said, "with what the new chairman has promised to do, and with new top personnel people to carry that out, we could have a disagreements policy that would mean something in handling discrimination issues that in-dividual employees have. But, we'll have to wait and see how the new chairman's intentions are carried out."

Panel Interviews With Employees and Managers at "Transatlantic Company"

Transatlantic is the name we will give to a service company with more than 15,000 employees. This nonunion firm has a pro-gressive approach to human resources policies, with, for example, strong EEO programs, employee privacy policies, and encourage-ment of employee involvement. The firm has a formal multistep complaint procedure, as well as a write- and call-in communications program that allows employees to get problems answered by higher management on a confidential basis, without having to go through the supervisor and up the steps of the complaint system.

We conducted one-hour panel discussions with a dozen ran-domly selected clerical employees. In the course of asking about their experiences and opinions relating to personnel policies, a question was asked about the company's formal complaint system. The clerical employees volunteered the view that many employees "are afraid to use the complaint system." They fear that reprisals would be taken against them for challenging actions of their su-pervisors or of higher management. Despite the company's explicit assurance that employees could use the complaint procedure freely and without fear, some employees (including those who had been at the firm for a substantial period of time) were convinced that ways would be found to limit their opportunities or "make it hard for them" if they asked higher management to overturn lower management decisions.

When the clerical employees were asked whether they felt confident in using, and were actually making use of, the write- or call-in communication mechanisms, they said that they had no hesitation in using that system. One employee volunteered after the formal discussion session had broken up that, if she had an EEO complaint, her real choice would be between using the write-in mechanism or filing a complaint with the local EEO agency.

When the gist of these panel reactions were communicated to the executive in charge of personnel relations, she was both surprised and somewhat dismayed. "We would take serious action against any manager who punished an employee for using our complaint system," she said, "and we say clearly that no reprisals will be permitted. It's comforting to know that our write- and call-in systems are providing a vehicle for employees who don't feel comfortable using the formal machinery, but we may have to find ways to convince more of our employees that they will be completely protected if they use the formal system."

Political Constraints on a Bank's Complaint System

Elvira, vice president for a service function at a major bank we will call First American Financial, is a 34-year-old black woman. She came to First Financial seven years ago, after working for five years at another bank. She has an MBA from a leading private university.

Cooperation and loyalty are highly valued in the corporate world, Elvira points out, and First Financial is no exception to that rule. "No one wants a whistleblower on his or her team," she says frankly. Employees who complain about the company or their situation within it are also not sought after. "Malcontents and whiners," as the bank sees complainers, are soon identified and are not promoted. "You either learn that the hard way, by complaining," she says, "or, if you're smart, by observing what happened to others." Out of more than 20,000 employees in her sector of the company, only 34 have used the grievance system since 1978. She calls such people "crazy."

When grievance procedures at the bank are begun, there are two different tracks, one for managers and the other for line workers. She believes the complaint system works pretty well for most simple line-worker disputes—salary, promotion, and discipline problems. The line worker who complains formally needs to have a solid foundation of fact, because he or she will be scrutinized closely by management. Anything other than "perfect employee behavior" will be remembered, and could contribute to greater problems with management further down the line. "After all, anyone making a complaint becomes highly visible. They upset the normal company operations, an action unlikely to win managerial friends," she points out.

Managers rarely use the formal complaint system. And the likelihood of a potential manager resolving a complaint informally largely depends on his or her political talents, Elvira says. A successful effort is likely to depend on having the support of a number of superiors, and tends to be in direct proportion to the person's reputation, according to Elvira. "A good manager needs to be a good politician, so top managers look favorably on someone who uses political talents to obtain satisfaction, just as they look unfavorably on someone who is reduced to using the formal grievance system," Elvira says.

If a manager who is well thought of uses the system to raise a major complaint, and that complaint is rejected, a "termination deal" will usually be worked out. The manager will be allowed to resign under favorable terms, continuing with the company in a position of little responsibility for three months to a year while he or she locates appropriate employment elsewhere. The "outplacement" services of the company's Personnel Department may even be put at the "lame duck" manager's disposal. Such a proceeding is contingent upon the manager's willingness not to "create scenes" or "air the complaint in public," Elvira says.

Elvira is unaware of any instance during her seven years with the bank when a management position was reversed because of an employee's complaints, although the statement that this does happen is made in the company's brochure for employees. She also says that, to her knowledge, management informs employees only verbally of its decisions in a grievance proceeding. "The cardinal rule," she says, is "Put nothing in writing."

Because Elvira is part of management, she raised her own salary and promotion complaints outside the grievance system. She feels she had to "threaten, cajole, and intimidate" her superiors at every one of her meetings with them on such matters, and to present "absolutely irrefutable evidence" of how sexism and racism were involved. Elvira claims that in her complaint meetings, "I submitted my attorney's business card and said that I would take my case to civil court. And I always won."

Elvira says blacks, Hispanics, some white women, and Jews ("if their names are readily discernible") do not "fare well" at the bank, and the grievance system is not able to help them. Recent black and Hispanic MBA graduates tend to fall out of favor with management by failing to develop political savvy and to make use of "mentors" to correct problems.

Elvira's recommendation for fairer treatment of employee and manager grievances at the bank is to detach the Personnel Department from the rest of the organization. If personnel managers were independent and neutral, the grievance process might be effective, she feels. But in its present location, she believes, "Personnel is too supportive of top management everywhere in the company to act impartially."

Pushing Out Older Salespeople

Shawn, a university graduate, went to work in the late 1940s for a famous, family-owned company that manufactured a consumer product. He became a star salesman, working territories in the Northeastern states. In the early 1970s, he became metropolitan manager in a large city, which involved training other sales personnel and managing the office along with handling his own major accounts.

In the early 1970s, a large conglomerate bought the family firm. While production workers did not lose their pension rights in this takeover, because they had union protection, the salespeople were not so treated. Shawn lost 19 years of accumulated benefits.

As the new management took over, Shawn continued to be a top performer, always in the top 10 percent and sometimes in the top 2 or 3 percent of the sales force. However, when the new management acquired another company in a related consumer-product field, and merged that into a division with Shawn's product, major changes in sales force policies were introduced. In the place of the experienced, "20–30 year men" who were the rule in selling the product that Shawn and his colleagues represented, the management began filling all retirements and vacancies with very young salespeople, just out of business school or with only a few years' experience. Simultaneously, senior salespeople were taken off the straight commission basis that they had been on for years, and were told they would now be on a salary-plus-commission basis with quotas and rates that reduced salesperson returns significantly. In addition, changes were made in the assignment of large customers within sales territories, without any advance notice to the salesperson who had that territory, and in ways that further reduced the ability of senior salespeople to continue earning at the levels they had maintained for many years.

Shawn experienced both these new policies. He was forced to accept the new, reduced salary-plus-commission system. He also found that a major new customer in his multistate territory had been assigned to another salesperson without notice or consultation with him; this salesperson was also allowed to sell to customers at a lower discount rate than Shawn was allowed to offer.

By this time—the late 1970s—Shawn had three grievances: the loss of his pension accumulations, the reduction in reimbursement, and the "violation" of "his" sales territory. Since all these changes had been made without management discussions with employees, in a "top-down" directive fashion, Shawn began in the early 1980s a series of attempts to raise these questions formally through the company channels. He put his concerns into writing to the regional manager, phrasing them moderately, carefully, and seeking to create a dialogue with the new management. (Shawn had gone to law school during the 1950s and had received his law degree, though he loved sales work and had never practiced law.)

Shawn received no reply from the regional manager. In 1981, he spoke to the division sales manager when he ran into that executive at a trade show. The sales manager went to lunch with Shawn, but told him that the company had a new view of sales: years of sales experience did not count; one year could be as good as 30 (which Shawn had); and senior salespeople were now going to have to compete on an equal basis with new and younger salespeople. Since Shawn had always been a top sales performer, he was not bothered about competition. But he felt the new management was really trying to push out as many of the older salespeople as possible, or forcing them to retire, as a way to cut the company's operating costs. And, they were doing this, Shawn felt, in a way that tried to avoid lawsuits for age discrimination.

To see whether he could at least protect his ability to earn the substantial commissions he had always produced from his territory, Shawn wrote the regional sales manager again for an answer about the assignment of accounts in this territory to another salesperson. Shawn documented how much in commissions he had lost by this action, noted that this was against many years of previous practice, and indicated how all of the older salespersons were being hurt. He asked for restitution of what he would have earned and exclusive coverage of his territory.

When he received no reply, he went to the headquarters of the conglomerate parent and tried to talk to people in the personnel office. He could not get a formal appointment with anyone there, but he did talk informally, in the halls, with several senior executives. They told him that "all the doors are open here." But they declined formal meetings or official action about his complaints.

However, shortly thereafter, Shawn was called in by his regional managers and told that he "had some nerve" saying such things to upper management. He should have known about the special discount marketing that the company was pursuing, and he should now accept the changes "or else."

At this point, Shawn contacted a lawyer. He felt that he was getting nowhere in his complaints, that the company was deliberately trying to harass and get rid of the older, better paid salespersons, and that he was going to be fired if he did not shut up. Shawn's lawyer advised him that if he filed an age discrimination complaint, he would probably prevail in the state EEO agency. But although the company would be told to cease discriminatory sales policy practices, the company would still be free to fight him in the courts and find other ways to punish him. It was a "no win" route, his lawyer advised.

Instead, the lawyer asked Shawn if he had ever thought of trying to organize older salespeople into a union, and to notify the company that he was doing that. This would bring into play strong protections under state and federal law against interference with union organizing activities, and would also allow a damage claim for wrongful discharge if he was fired.

Shawn decided to try the union route. He had contacted most of the sales force—about 100—and 20 percent of them quickly signed union authorization cards. He was working to secure 33 percent—the number needed to have the National Labor Relations

Board hold a supervised union election—before going to management. Suddenly, he received several direct responses from the management to his own case. He was told it was the prerogative of the company to change the accounts and the remuneration as they wished, and there would be further changes. He would be expected to follow all of them. "I felt they were telling me, if you don't play ball with us, we'll change the accounts and make your life impossible."

Shawn's lawyer advised him that meetings with management were no longer of any use. Shawn's lawyer officially notified the company that Shawn was engaged in union activities, and that any detrimental change in his financial relationship or other status would be deemed unlawful reprisal. The letter offered to meet with the management and work out a fair arrangement on territories and lost revenues. If the company refused, and continued its harmful policies, the letter stated, Shawn would sue for damages suffered.

The company replied that Shawn's claims were "groundless" and that the law provides remedies for employers who are subjected to "frivolous legal actions." At the same time, the company mounted a campaign with the sales force against the union organizing effort, saying that a few disgruntled employees were behind it, that the company was a fine place to work, and that no "outsiders" were needed for employees to be fairly treated.

Shawn says, the "harassment really got heavy." He was told, for the first time in 33 years of outstanding sales performance, that he would have to make line-by-line explanations for each item in his expense accounts, a process that took many extra hours for every report submitted. He heard from customers in his territory that management people had told them Shawn would not be with the company much longer. Some of his accounts were called on by other company salespeople and were offered better discounts than Shawn could give, if the customer would shift its orders away from Shawn. His sales volumes and commissions fell. Then, one state was removed from his territory and reassigned to someone else; no other area was given to Shawn to replace it. Shawn's lawyer wrote the company to complain about its harassment tactics, and said Shawn "would not accept" the withdrawal of the state territory. The company replied that disciplinary action would be taken if Shawn in any way disobeyed the assignment.

Shawn filed a state-court lawsuit against the company, saying that the removal of accounts from him and the lowering of his commissions had been reprisals for his union activity. However, he was careful not to violate the reassignment decision, to avoid creating grounds for charging him with insubordination.

Shawn has about 42 percent of the sales force signed up with union cards, and is waiting for 50 percent to make the best impression when the election is held. Women are signing up also, especially young women. "This company starts men off at $25,000 but starts women at about $14,000," Shawn explains. "'Equal pay for equal work' is the cause that's getting women into our group."

Some other older salespeople, however, succumbed to the pressure and have taken early retirement. One such man was at a company retirement dinner in honor of someone else during the Christmas season. When he was asked to say a few words, he rose and remarked "I have worked a long time for this company, over 30 years. And this is what I have to say." He pinned a sprig of mistletoe to the back of his suit coat, stood for a moment to let the message sink in, then walked out of the room . "I loved the 'Mistletoe Speech'," Shawn says, "but I'm staying to fight. This company has made me a union organizer."

Watching Them Come and Go

Mrs. A. is a black woman of Hispanic descent in her early fifties. She is a nurse at a large primary care hospital in an eastern metropolitan area. She is an articulate and observant person who has become increasingly active in labor issues at her hospital, particularly issues that affect nurses.

Unlike others in this study, she has not pressed an EEO complaint. But she considers her employment setting one where the number of serious complaints is high and turnover rates remarkable because few credible mechanisms exist for resolving disputes or venting grievances. "Nurses have always been afraid to say or do anything because they are afraid of what will happen on the job. You really can't win if it's anything important because of the way it is set up. So nurses don't complain. They leave, instead." Mrs. A. often commented that she felt frustrated and depressed at watching good nurses leave rather than endure the limiting conditions of employment.

"If you try to do anything, they think that you are a radical, even if what you are doing is something simple, or right," she says, "such as reporting incompetent workers," seeking redress for abuses of supervisorial power, or pressing for more adequate security during night shifts. "Management provides lots of ways to handle your grievances," says Mrs. A., "but none of them work, so people don't bother with them. Besides, you usually have to go first to the senior nurse, then the supervisor, and it's their job to make sure that everything is going right. Like if you asked them to do something different, make a change, and they did it, it's like admitting that they were doing it wrong in the first place, so they aren't going to do that."

Mrs. A. reported the widespread perception of hospital employees that reporting to immediate supervisors is likely to antagonize those superiors without having the grievance addressed satisfactorily. Even if a particular issue is addressed and resolved, the employees feel they are inviting long-term, low-grade harassment, eventually making continued employment at the institution undesirable. "You pay the price, and it's usually too high. Things start to happen. You suddenly can't get the days off you used to get, like say, Friday nights. And there are lots of little errors that you can make, like not initialing a medication order, that everybody does sometimes. But you get written up, and it goes in your record, or it goes to the supervisor nurse and you get a warning and something in your file. Usually, people just ask you if you gave the medicine and then tell you to put your initials in, so what happens is according to the strict rules, but it's different. They're just trying to pressure you to transfer or to leave the hospital."

The first step of the standard grievance procedure is to document the complaint. Mrs. A. observes, "so if you think a nurse is making mistakes, or a senior nurse is harassing somebody, you have to write down all the information—date, time, what happened. A lot of nurses won't want to document other nurses because they are afraid of what might happen if you write things down, so it just ends right there. Besides, if you are going to do it, you could spend more time writing than nursing, so it's usually easier to transfer or just leave and get another job at another hospital."

The documentation should then be submitted to the senior nurse. Mrs. A. described a senior nurse who had been remiss in her duties and abusive of staff, and noted the irony of beginning the complaint procedure with the person most directly involved. "Usually, though, the senior nurse says, 'I'll look into it,' but weeks go by and you don't hear about it again. Or she'll tell you to get more documentation."

If the nurse wishes to press her complaint, she then takes the issue and the documentation to the Supervising Nurse (if on the day shift) or the Assistant Director II (if on the night shift). "They usually say they are going to do something about it, but they'll delay and hope you forget about it because they don't want it passed on up. Most of the time it just ends here. See, the Senior Nurse is responsible for things going OK, and the Supervising Nurse and the Assistant Director II are responsible for the Senior Nurse. They don't want to admit that things aren't being done right. They are all on the same side."

If the complaint is serious enough for the nurse to press it further, the nurse must go to the Assistant Director I with all documentation and comments from all supervisory levels. Mrs. A. commented that "although they are in nursing, the supervisors are also mixed up with administration, so they don't want to go against management decisions even when they are sympathetic with you. When it comes to doing something about it, they just get cold feet, and it's easier to ignore you."

Mrs. A. was more positive about the ultimate level of the grievance procedure, the Nurses' Council. "They are nurses from the floor, and they know what's going on." But to reach this point, a nurse would have to be willing to alienate all of her supervisors. The general feeling, according to Mrs. A., is that this would be an unwise move unless the issue is felt to be critical. "The Nurses' Council works, and I think they're okay, but the trouble is back down the chain. It's easier to just leave, and even if you stay, they look you over for every little thing and you don't get such good evaluations after that."

Mrs. A. knew of no one who had pressed a complaint with the Director of Nursing, or who had made use of the hospital ombudsman service. She felt that, in any event, pursuit of those avenues would not solve the problems down the chain of command. She was concerned about the rigidity of the system and the fears it produced. Mrs. A. recalled an incident involving a nurse who was flagrantly incompetent and a threat to the welfare of the patients, yet who remained on the service for several months after her incompetence was first recognized. When the senior nurse finally acted, "suggesting a council where we would all meet and talk with her," the nurse in question simply quit and within days had found employment at another hospital.

Mrs. A. shrugged her shoulders when asked why she stayed in nursing, and spoke of her sense of responsibility to her patients. "If you took a poll today about the situation, you'd find that nurses are, well, disenchanted. It's hard to nurse. It's so easy to leave that if you stay, you just see new faces all the time. You can see it in one thing that happened this year. We usually have a Nurses' Recognition Day, where we meet and have lunch and get a chance to talk with each other. But not this year. It was cancelled. Oh, they gave us something so we could buy like a coffee maker for each floor, but that was it, and that's not what it's about."

What These Employee Stories Suggest

Most employment disputes have two sides. If the management perception of what happened in these conflict situations were to be obtained and analyzed, the employees' perception might be seen as distorted or unbalanced. What seems clear is that these employees did *not* believe there was an accessible, meaningful, and trustworthy system they could invoke to obtain a *fair hearing* and a *reasonably objective decision* for their complaint.

With these employee perceptions in mind, we will examine the kinds of responsive systems that have been developing in the nonunion organization over the past decade.

Chapter 3

New Organizational Programs in Action

The Scope and Variety of Internal Mechanisms

The 12 organizations whose dispute prevention or dispute resolution programs we have selected for presentation illustrate the diversity of industries and nonprofit organizations, work force characteristics, and organizational cultures that mark private employment in the United States. As the following chart shows, the 12 examples have been divided into two groups.

The first eight profiles illustrate adjudicative mechanisms. In seven of them, an employee can raise any issue of concern, while the eighth, Chicago and North Western Transportation Company, illustrates a special program for hearing and resolving equal employment opportunity (EEO) complaints. The seven "omnibus" or all-issues programs have been chosen to illustrate the variety of mechanisms which private employers have established.

- Bank of America uses an "independent investigator" system modeled after IBM's long-established *Open Door* program, which is administered from the Office of the IBM Chairman by a staff of Administrative Assistants.
- Cleveland Clinic and Aetna Life and Casualty illustrate 4-step complaint, investigation, and appeal systems in which Senior Management is the final authority.
- Citibank illustrates two important additional elements in adjudicative systems: peer participation by fellow employees in a *Problem Review Board* and a special mechanism

for reviewing "whistleblowing" type complaints by Citibank employees.

- Michael Reese Hospital, Northrop, and Life Savers are examples of organizations that provide the option of outside, professional arbitration. In the case of Michael Reese, this is "advisory" to the Chief Executive, while with Northrop and Life Savers, the companies accept binding outside arbitration. The Life Savers example also illustrates a system designed for a small-sized firm—a 500-employee production facility.

The second group of profiles, beginning with Chemical Bank's *Intercom* system on page 159, illustrates organizational mechanisms designed to help resolve as large a number of employee concerns as possible *before* they become grievances and settle into an adversarial mode requiring formal adjudication:

- Chemical Bank and NBC exemplify counselor systems, in which trained staff members listen, advise, investigate, negotiate with all parties, and, where justified, attempt to "sell solutions" that are acceptable to employee and management.
- Massachusetts Institute of Technology illustrates an *Upward Feedback, Mediation Process* system administered by two Special Assistants to the President.
- The *Ombudsperson* system at American Telephone and Telegraph's Information System's Division applies the orientation and techniques of the ombudsperson approach, which is nonadjudicative and aims to negotiate actions or settlements according to the merits and equities of each situation.

A word should be said at the outset about our asking organizational managers or staff members to describe their own systems and then publishing these presentations. Clearly, there is a trade-off involved in employing such a method. The positive side is that these managers and staffs have agreed to supply detailed accounts that most of these companies had never revealed before. They represent, therefore, an important addition to the empirical literature. Also, having motivations, choices, operations, experiences, modifications, and program assessments made by organizational spokespersons provides readers with a statement of organizational purpose and self-evaluation as those are officially voiced by program managers themselves.

ADJUDICATIVE MECHANISMS IN PROFILES

Organization	Industry	No. of U.S. Employees	Union status	Type of System in Profile	Final review	Employees covered	Issue covered
Bank of America	Financial	62,000	Nonunion	Independent investigation	Chairman's office	All	Any work-related
Cleveland Clinic	Hospital	7,400	Nonunion	4-step process	Senior management	All	Any work-related
Aetna Life and Casualty	Insurance	40,000	Nonunion	4-step process	Senior management	All	Any work-related
Citibank	Financial	20,000	Nonunion	Problem review with peer participation	Senior management	All	Any work-related
Michael Reese Hospital	Hospital	4,400	1/3rd union	4-step process	Advisory outside arbitration	Nonunion employees	Any work-related
Northrop Corporation	Manufacturing	42,000	8% union	4-step process	Binding outside arbitration	All non-supervisors	Any work-related
Life Savers	Manufacturing	500	Nonunion	4-step process	Binding outside arbitration	All production workers	Any work-related
Chicago and Northwestern Transportation Company	Transportation	12,000	90% union	4-step; special EEO mechanism	Vice President of personnel	All	EEO issues

NONADJUDICATIVE MECHANISMS IN PROFILES

Organization	Industry	No. of U.S. employees	Union status	Type of System in Profile	Final review	Employees covered	Issue covered
Chemical Bank	Financial	15,000	Nonunion	Communication counselor	Senior management	Clerical	Any work-related
NBC	Communications	8,000	40% Union	Grievance counselor	Senior management	All	Any work-related
Massachusetts Institute of Technology	Education	20,000	⅓rd Union	Mediation	Senior management	All nonunion	Any work-related
AT&T Information Systems	Manufacturing and communications	1,800	Nonunion	Ombudsperson	Senior management	All	Any non-EEO work-related

At the same time, this technique has an obvious limitation. These are approved accounts from organizational spokespersons, not independent studies or outside evaluations. These descriptions do not include the views of employees who have used these systems, whether satisfactorily or unsatisfactorily, of nonuser employees, or of supervisors and managers whose actions have been reviewed in such systems. (The Educational Fund for Individual Rights will publish in 1988 such an in-depth case study of one company, Federal Express, based on several hundred interviews with employees, supervisors, and managers.)

However, the value to readers of this collection is that contributors agreed to write their profiles according to a common format provided by the authors; to supply previously unpublished and detailed descriptions and statistics on the workings of their systems; to give case examples of dispositions; and to respond to the editors' basic questions about positive and negative effects of their programs. Our sense is that these 12 accounts present fairly open and candid narratives, in a manner that stems from the confidence of these managers that their systems have proved their worth over time, and can be openly discussed for peers and serious readers to examine.

Finally, we suggest to readers that they could profitably have the following themes and factors in mind when they read these 12 profiles:

- How work force characteristics and company culture shaped the choice of a particular dispute prevention or dispute resolution mechanism.
- What the actual source of legitimacy and protection for controversial decisions is for each of these programs, and how such protection is communicated.
- How the organizations go about the key task of fact-finding, and the spectrum from independent-investigator to employee-management fact-finding board that is represented in the profiles of adjudicative systems.
- Why the four organizations with mediation-oriented mechanisms put most of their efforts into this approach, and not into new adjudicative programs.
- How the central issues of confidentiality and protection against reprisal have been addressed in each of these mechanisms.
- The deliberate exclusion of lawyers and legalized due-process mechanisms from virtually all the programs, reflect-

ing the judgment that legalism would inevitably corrupt the speed and low cost of procedures without producing fairer judgments.

- The key role of EEO issues and of increasing unjust dismissal suits in stimulating the creation or expansion of these systems.
- The critical and difficult role assigned to personnel officials or staff counselors and mediators in these systems, and how managements go about protecting these members of management from pressures or reprisals if they question or contest line or top management actions that employees have complained about.
- What levels of use by employees and outcomes of the systems say about the likely level of credibility these programs have with employees.
- How each program deals with the question of the final appeal, and the credibility to employees of the persons or institution that exercises such final authority.
- How mechanisms have been modified over time since their original formulation, and the factors to which such changes are responding.
- How the organizational officials presenting these programs assess their costs and benefits, and especially their estimate of how their programs affect the pivotal issues of employee morale and commitment, organizational effectiveness, and reduction of outside complaints and litigation.

The Independent Investigator System at Bank of America (*Let's Talk*)

*Frederick P. Martin**

BankAmerica is a bank holding company. In mid-1987, there were 62,900 employees within the entire BankAmerica Corporation. Of these, 45,090 worked in California, another 1,891 worked elsewhere in the United States, and 7,143 worked for nonbanking subsidiaries. The balance represented World Banking Division's offshore employees, nearly all of which are indigenous to the countries in which the offices and subsidiaries are located. The principal subsidiary, Bank of America has 888 domestic branches and 82 foreign branches. Total assets stood at $97 billion, total deposits in January 1987 amounted to $82 billion, and net loans outstanding totaled $66.4 billion.

Program Background

BankAmerica is committed to providing a positive work environment that fosters individual job satisfaction and responsiveness to employee concerns. The *Let's Talk* program has been designed to assist employees with work-related concerns. Through this process, employees may seek resolution of problems or concerns about a wide range of work-related issues. These may include, but are not limited to, problems relating to performance planning, coaching, evaluation, job assignment, and disciplinary action including termination, promotion, and equal opportunity.

These concerns are dealt with promptly and confidentially and no record of the *Let's Talk* review is placed in the employees' personnel file. Use of the *Let's Talk* program does not affect the employee's future career or present position with BankAmerica.

Our current *Let's Talk* program has evolved over the last 15 years. It has been revised twice in an effort to provide employees an effective means to have their work concerns reviewed in a prompt

*Vice President and Manager, Personnel Relations Programs, U.S., San Francisco.

49

and objective manner by bank management. This concept embodies the spirit and intent of BankAmerica's philosophy of promoting dignity and respect for our employees and openness and trust between employees and managers throughout the organization.

The original program called *Let's Talk It Over* was implemented in 1969. The procedure consisted of three informal steps. In the first step, employees had the right to discuss their concerns with all levels of management in their division. Employees were encouraged to first discuss their concern with their immediate manager. If the situation was not resolved to the employee's satisfaction after discussions with their immediate manager, they had the right to proceed to the second step. Step two involved discussing the situation with a higher level of management, usually a department head or regional administrative representative. If the second step did not produce the desired results, employees could avail themselves of the third, and final step, Personnel Relations. In step three, employees discussed their concerns with a Personnel Relations Specialist, who had no direct authority to resolve the situation to the employee's satisfaction unless a company policy had been violated. The Personnel Relations Specialist functioned primarily in an impartial advisory capacity. When contacted by an employee, the Personnel Relations Specialist made an objective analysis of the situation and informed the employee of his or her remaining options for solving the problem. Generally, these options were either to have the employee go back to discuss the situation with their management or have the Personnel Relations Specialist speak with the employee's management and attempt to resolve the situation on the individual's behalf.

An important feature of the program was that employees did not have to follow these steps in sequential order. If the employee felt uncomfortable discussing the situation with his or her immediate manager, the employee could proceed directly to a higher level of management or to Personnel Relations. Employees were also guaranteed that their discussions with a Personnel Relations Specialist would remain confidential unless they gave the Personnel Relations Specialist permission to get involved on their behalf with their management.

The program did not, however, provide any formal avenue that allowed employees to pursue unresolved concerns with the bank's top level management. Some executive officers had established an internal "open door" policy which facilitated their involvement in employee problems; however, there was no vehicle beyond Personnel Relations to have problems heard outside of the unit.

In 1980, the *Let's Talk It Over* program was revised to better meet the needs of both the corporation and its employees and to provide a more structured review process. Under the old program, some problems simply could not be resolved within the framework of the informal review process. These unresolved problems had to be dealt with on a case basis, but usually they were resolved by the intervention of the Director of Personnel Relations or, in some instances, by the Director of Human Resources. The need to make senior management a part of the review process was evident.

The revised program was renamed *Let's Talk* and consisted of six steps, the first three of which were identical to the original program. The last three steps involved written statements and responses to the employee's concern by successively higher levels of management until the sixth step was reached. However, an employee could only initiate a formal review after a discussion with a Personnel Relations Specialist. At least one attempt to resolve the situation through verbal discussion had to be made by the employee or a Personnel Relations Specialist before a written review could be initiated. Once this condition had been met, the employee could advance to the following steps:

Step 4. In most units of the bank the manager in Step 4 was the same person as in Step 2. This was built into the program to ensure that a manager who was relatively close, organizationally, to the employee's unit would have an opportunity to resolve a situation before it was reviewed by a senior manager. These officers responded to employees in writing.

It is important to note that when the six steps were first conceptualized by Personnel Relations it was thought that Step 4 review should be mandatory even if the employee had discussed the situation with this same person in Step 2. However, during a review of the program proposal by a senior officer representing the retail branch system, it was suggested that Step 4 be optional. That is to say, if an employee had already discussed the situation with the Step 2 manager it would be the employee's option to initiate the written review at Step 4 or 5. The senior officer who suggested this change thought that making Step 4 mandatory was an unnecessary complication and might discourage some employees from using the formal part of the program. Personnel Relations agreed with this recommendation and the change was adopted.

Step 5. For employees in the retail branch banking system this review was conducted by their Regional Senior Vice President. Employees from other divisions had this review conducted by the Senior Administrative Officer for their unit, generally a Senior Vice President, who responded to employees in writing.

Step 6. This review was made by three officers who were either Vice Chairmen or Executive Vice Presidents. One was the Executive Officer for the division where the employee worked. The other two officers were the Executive Officers of Human Resources and the Legal departments, respectively. Each member of the Senior Review Committee received a copy of all documents related to the problem and made an independent review of the situation. Each Committee members' decision was communicated back to Personnel Relations. The majority opinion on the matter was communicated to the employee in writing and was signed by the Director of Human Resources, who was the Committee Secretary. The Committee's decision was the final step in the review process.

Personnel Relations coordinated the flow of written reviews and responses in Steps 4, 5, and 6. Initially, all written review requests were sent to a Personnel Relations Specialist by the employee. The Personnel Relations Specialist would review the write-up for content and completeness and forward it to the Step 4 or 5 manager for response. The written response of this manager was also reviewed by the Personnel Relations Specialist before it was sent to the employee. The Personnel Relations Specialist reviewed the write-up and response at each subsequent step until the situation was resolved.

Time frames were established for the program to ensure the prompt resolution to problems. The employee had to initiate a written review within 20 days of the time the problem/concern occurred. The individuals in Steps 4 and 5 had 7 working days to respond to reviews and the senior review committee had 10 working days to respond. The employee had 5 working days from the receipt of a written response to decide if it was necessary to proceed to the next step. These time frames were guidelines and a reasonable degree of flexibility to extend them was acceptable.

In 1984, *Let's Talk* was revised once again. The formal review process created in 1980 proved to be cumbersome, generating an excessive amount of correspondence and documentation. The fact that employees and managers had to put everything in writing was also time-consuming and discouraged many employees from using the formal process.

Personnel Relations again set about to develop a more effective approach to helping employees resolve work concerns. The goals of this project were to cut through the "red tape" by eliminating the excessive paperwork by bringing employees and senior managers together in an effort to resolve the problem quickly and equitably. To accomplish this mission, all the formal steps were eliminated and the process totally streamlined.

Current Program

Using Let's Talk

Under the new program, employees are again encouraged to talk with their immediate manager in an effort to resolve a work-related concern. The bank has found that most problems can be resolved by the first line manager. However, employees may discuss their concerns with their manager's manager, or any level of management within their division they believe will assist them in resolving their concern. Employees may also discuss their situation with a Personnel Relations Specialist, who will make an objective assessment of their concern and advise them accordingly of the various approaches they may take in seeking a resolution.

If an employee believes the situation has not been resolved, he/she may write to the Executive Officer responsible for the division, outlining the concern. This letter should identify the employee, provide a phone number where the employee can be contacted, state why he/she is requesting an investigation under the *Let's Talk* program, indicate what the concern is, explain the steps already taken to resolve the problem, and what he/she believes would be an appropriate solution to the problem.

The Executive Officer will either meet with the employee or appoint someone to act on his or her behalf as an independent investigator. The investigator will meet with the employee and conduct a brief investigation into his or her concern. After the investigation is completed, the employee will be told of the findings by the investigator, who will then review the results with the Executive Officer. The Executive Officer will then communicate his or her decision to the employee either verbally or in writing.

If the employee is not satisfied with the decision he/she may refer the concern directly to the Vice Chairman or equivalent officer responsible for the division. The process for doing this is the same as that described earlier.

The Vice Chairman will either meet with the employee, or appoint a different investigator who will meet with the employee and review the results of the first investigation as part of the final investigative process. The Vice Chairman will review the investigation and advise the employee of his/her conclusions.

Receipt, Acknowledgment, and Appointment of Investigator

Employee problems directed to the Vice Chairman or Executive Officer of the division the employee works for should be acknowledged within 72 hours. This response can be verbal or written, stating that the *Let's Talk* concern has been received and who the investigator will be. The communication should also state that the results of the investigation will be reviewed personally by the Executive, who will make the decision pertaining to the resolution of the concern.

If the recipient of a *Let's Talk* concern does not investigate the issue personally, it should be assigned to an individual who is in a recognized and responsible position, removed from the employee's immediate management, and who has not had previous involvement in the circumstances of the employee's appeal. Those positions eligible to be investigators include: Senior Line Manager, Regional Personnel Administrator, Corporate Human Resource Manager or Director, Division Human Resource Manager or Director.

Investigation Process

The employee originating the *Let's Talk* appeal should be interviewed as soon as possible after its acknowledgment. The facts of the complaint should be analyzed and a decision made as quickly as possible, normally within 15 working days after acknowledgment. If, for some reason, the response cannot be made within this time frame, the investigator should advise the employee of the delay and establish a new conclusion date.

The investigator must contact the employee and make arrangements to discuss the issues raised in the *Let's Talk* appeal *before* contacting line management. The investigator must be certain to clearly identify himself/herself and the fact that the Executive has asked him/her to investigate the concerns stated in the employee's letter.

At the initial meeting, the investigator should determine precisely the issues, concerns, or allegations raised by the employee, as well as what the employee believes to be an appropriate solution. The investigator should view the situation from the perspective of the employee making the complaint. In addition, the investigator should explain the investigation process, advising the employee that:

1. An impartial review of the relevant facts will be made.
2. Management views have not yet been obtained.
3. The employee may submit any written documentation that he/she believes is appropriate to the investigation.
4. The investigation cannot be anonymous; however, discussion will be restricted to those necessary to resolve the issues. Those interviewed will be advised to keep the matter confidential.
5. A recommendation will be made to the Executive for his/her decision after the employee has had an opportunity to hear the findings of the investigation and provide any additional input he/she desires.

The *Let's Talk* investigation should be completed with only as much visibility as is necessary to gather pertinent facts, and should be confined to factors relating to the complaint. The investigator should feel free to interview any appropriate member of management who has been involved with the employee's concern—including those in Personnel Relations. During the interviews, the investigator should take notes to ensure accuracy and to review when preparing the final report. He/she should remind those individuals involved not to discuss the investigation with others.

When the investigation has been completed, the investigator will verbally review the findings with the employee. This will enable the employee to correct any misunderstandings, suggest additional information, and react to the findings prior to the Executive Officer's reviewing the information. At the conclusion of this meeting, the investigator should advise the employee of the approximate date by which the employee can expect to hear from the Executive.

After reviewing the investigation's findings with the employee, the investigator will prepare a written report which must be submitted to the Division's Director of Human Resources for review before being sent to the Executive Officer.

After the Division's Director of Human Resources has reviewed the report with the investigator, it should be sent to the Executive Officer. The Executive Officer will review the information and make a decision that will be communicated in writing or verbally to the employee. Other managers who have been involved may be notified of the conclusions as appropriate.

All documentation, correspondence, and other information accumulated as a result of the investigation should be sent to the Director of Human Resources for the employee's division. Absolutely no record of the employee's complaint or investigation should be placed in the employee's personnel file.

Managers should not keep any files regarding this specific complaint. If a commitment is made for a particular personnel action to take place at a later date, that commitment may be documented and placed in the employee's personnel file, but no reference is to be made of the *Let's Talk* appeal.

All managers are expected to fully support the *Let's Talk* program, and are responsible for ensuring that their employees understand and have confidence in the process.

At this time the bank is reasonably satisfied with the activity and results of *Let's Talk*. Employee activity continues to be quite heavy during the informal process where the employees are encouraged to discuss their concerns with management or Personnel Relations. The following chart illustrates the number and types of work concerns or questions that were addressed by the Personnel Relations Specialists during the years 1983 and 1984.

INFORMAL ACTIVITY
MOST FREQUENTLY ADDRESSED EMPLOYEE
QUESTIONS/CONCERNS

	1983 Totals		*1984 Totals*	
Issue	*No.*	*%*	*No.*	*%*
Benefits	883	10.7	1,160	11.3
Chemical substance abuse	223	2.7	274	2.7
Job opportunity/career counseling/promotions	314	3.8	328	3.2
Leave of absence	254	3.1	284	2.8
Performance planning, coaching, and evaluation	366	4.4	594	5.8
Personal crisis intervention	564	6.8	646	6.3
Policy and procedures	1,113	13.5	1,240	12.0

Issue	1983 Totals		1984 Totals	
	No.	*%*	*No.*	*%*
Problems with manager	947	11.5	1,110	10.8
Salary	259	3.1	436	4.2
Surplus staff	140	1.7	318	3.1
Termination	350	4.3	372	3.6
Transfers	598	7.3	496	4.8
Others	2,222	27.0	3,018	29.4
TOTAL	8,233		10,276	

Less than one-tenth of one percent of the concerns addressed during the informal process of *Let's Talk* ever become requests for a formal review by the Executive Officer or Vice Chairman of the division in which the employee works. The vast majority of these deal with terminations, performance planning, coaching, evaluation, and promotions. The chart below indicates, for 1982 and 1983, the stage of resolution, subject matter, and resolution outcome for the formal cases processed by *Let's Talk*.

An excellent example of how the formal process of *Let's Talk* works occurred recently. A Vice President who had been employed

FORMAL
LET'S TALK ACTIVITY
1982/1983

	1982		1983	
Total number of cases	28		31	
Decisions:				
Employee	10	(36%)	6	(20%)
Management	11	(39%)	20	(64%)
Withdrawn by employee	7	(25%)	5	(16%)
Concluded at:				
Step 4	15	(53%)	11	(35%)
Step 5	9	(32%)	9	(29%)
Step 6	4	(14%)	9	(29%)
Subject:				
Termination	14	(50%)	23	(75%)
Performance	8	(28%)	5	(16%)
Promotions	3	(11%)	1	(3%)
Work assignment	2	(7%)	0	(0%)
Transfer	1	(3%)	0	(0%)
Benefits	0	(0%)	1	(3%)
Surplus staff	0	(0%)	1	(3%)

at the bank 23 years was terminated for poor job performance. The employee's job performance had declined for several consecutive years until finally management transferred the individual to a different position, hoping a new environment would generate better results. Unfortunately, the opposite occurred. The employee was placed into a position for which he did not have sufficient job skills to perform satisfactorily. Despite progressive counseling efforts by management, the situation continued to deteriorate until his manager recommended to the Division Executive Officer that he be terminated. After reviewing this situation with the Division's Director of Human Resources, the termination recommendation was approved.

The employee appealed the dismissal in the *Let's Talk* program to the Executive Officer of the Division who had approved the termination. Since the Division's Director of Human Resources had also been involved in the termination decision, the Executive Officer appointed a senior line manager within the division who had no previous involvement or knowledge pertaining to this situation to act as an independent investigator.

Following the guidelines of the *Let's Talk* program, the investigation was completed. After meeting with other impartial members of management and carefully reviewing the dismissed employee's performance objectives, the investigator came to the conclusion that the termination was not the proper solution to the problem. The investigator had concluded that the performance standards established for the dismissed employee had not been clearly defined, nor had the standards been consistently utilized to measure the performance of other employees in similar positions. Therefore the recommendation was made to the Executive Officer to reinstate the employee into a new position with less responsibility within a different part of the division. Despite the fact that the Executive Officer was the one who approved the termination, he agreed with the investigator's recommendation. The dismissed employee was reinstated into the new position and received the salary and benefits to which he was entitled.

The *Let's Talk* program has become a part of the Bank of America's culture and has evolved over the course of 18 years to be an effective Personnel Relations program. It places the emphasis for resolving work problems with line management by opening up the channels of communication between managers and employees. *Let's Talk* means exactly what the name implies.

The Dispute Resolution Process at Cleveland Clinic

Fred P. Buck*

Background

The Cleveland Clinic Foundation is an independent nonprofit health center dedicated to addressing the health needs of Americans with the best in medical care and technology. Established as a group practice by four physicians in 1921, the foundation has grown to become a National Health Resource, treating patients from throughout the United States and the world. Over 7,400 persons now work for the foundation.

Currently, foundation physicians provide care in 38 medical and surgical specialties and 67 subspecialties in the Clinic and Hospital, while participating in comprehensive programs of medical education and research.

Today the foundation is the largest postgraduate medical facility in the United States which is not connected with a medical school or university. In providing continuing education for medical students, practicing physicians, nurses, and allied health professionals, the Division of Education employs program coordinators, medical librarians, medical communicators, graphic artists, medical illustrators, photographers, scientific editors, registrars, and secretarial support personnel.

The clinic is also one of the largest ambulatory care centers in the world. Servicing approximately 500,000 outpatient visits yearly, the clinic is supported by appointment secretaries, medical receptionists, medical secretaries, allied health professionals, physical and occupational therapists, respiratory technicians, medical technologists, and social workers.

One-fourth of the hospital is set aside for heart patients, and the Department of Cardiology is the largest such department in

*Director, Division of Human Resources, Cleveland, Ohio.

the world. Assisting physicians in the care of patients in the hospital are perfusionists, electrocardiograph technicians, radiology technicians, dietitians, pharmacists, surgical nurses and technicians, patient transportation assistants, and unit secretaries.

Lending overall operations support to all functioning areas of the foundation are housekeepers, security guards, skilled craftsmen, and facilities and biomedical engineers. Men and women in the laundry and kitchens as well as business, insurance, and billing offices are important members of the foundation team. File clerks, medical record technicians, biostatisticians, admitting and registration interviewers, secretaries, and many others contribute to the quality care the Cleveland Clinic Foundation is dedicated to providing.

Health care organizations of all kinds have changed dramatically over the last 5–10 years, from organizations in which a sacred physician/patient relationship existed to big businesses where "caveat emptor" is the rule. The growth of health care as part of the Gross National Product is an illustration.

Year	% GNP
1950	4.5
1970	7.2
1983	10.0

Since health care organizations are now big business, they must be run more like a business while maintaining their reason for being, namely, patient care.

The Cleveland Clinic Foundation is unique within the arenas of business and health care. One example of this is the percentage of employment, for example:

Other Employers		Cleveland Clinic Foundation	
Managers, professional/ technical, clerical	50%	Managers, professional/ technical, clerical	80%
Craft, service/labor	50%	Craft, service/labor	20%

We are a diverse, people-intensive, professional culture, and as such, are dependent upon high quality interrelationships among many team members. The development of dispute resolution processes, which minimize dysfunctional behavior and maximize our ability to provide optimal patient care, is critically influenced by these characteristics of our organization.

Developmental Influences

During the early 1970s and continuing until early 1975, the Cleveland Clinic Foundation had an informal, unstructured, and little-used complaint resolution process. The process consisted of individual employees taking their complaints to whomever they had access to in the physician/managerial structure. Consequently, employees were totally dependent for response upon the whims of individual managers who possessed varying levels of interest and expertise. Unfortunately, many of the managers of that era were not enlightened, and employees received little, if any, response. Unless they had significant political backing, most complaints remained unresolved. As a matter of fact, our files are devoid of records regarding the types of complaints and how they were processed prior to 1975. As a result, many employees utilized external processes, and by 1975, some 43 discrimination charges, both state and federal, had been filed.

Dr. William S. Kiser, Chief Executive Officer, appointed Douglas Saarel, Director of Human Resources in 1974, and the organization provided him with the means to establish a highly viable and effective Human Resources program which contained a conflict resolution plan. Saarel, in turn, created an Employee Relations Department and appointed Fred P. Buck as its first director. Saarel and Buck began the development of formal and informal dispute modification/resolution processes which have continued to date. Buck assumed full responsibility for the processes in mid-1977.

Five factors greatly influenced the development of these processes and they are:

1. The Amendment of the Taft-Hartley Act in August 1974 to cover health care organizations for the first time. Prior to that date, no single, rational process existed for determining appropriate bargaining units in health care. Health care was fertile ground for union organizing, because while it was the fastest growing industry within our economy, it was also one of the lowest paid. Union organizing will remain a threat to health care because the industry is so labor intensive and embodies *such volatile social issues* concerning women and minorities. This legislation made it much easier

for unions to organize health care as evidenced by the following statistics:

Percent of hospitals unionized

1967	6
1970	15
1983	27
1990 (Projected)	65

2. The unsuccessful unionization attempts at the Cleveland Clinic Foundation during the 1970s taught management that current processes for listening and responding to employees' concerns did not work well and needed to be changed.

3. An Equal Employment Opportunity Commission Conciliation Agreement entered into in the mid-1970s by the foundation brought affirmative action to the Cleveland Clinic Foundation for the first time. The foundation was, as are many health care employers, outside the mainstream of social and business issues which affected U.S. employers. A large number of unresolved discrimination complaints, some of which related to this conciliation agreement, were analyzed by the Human Resources staff to determine cause and possible corrective action. The Cleveland Clinic Foundation was required to report its progress annually to the EEOC. This regular review by an external third party helped the Division of Human Resources convince management of the necessity and importance of being sensitive to group and individual discrimination issues.

4. The size of the Cleveland Clinic Foundation doubled in less than 15 years (1970–1984). During the early 1970s, the foundation employed fewer than 3,000 employees in an informal environment where most individuals knew everyone and felt that they were part of a familial group. New hospital construction between 1973 and 1975 resulted in the addition of 1,500 people in 2 years' time. Today, over 7,400 employees work at the Cleveland Clinic Foundation. This magnitude and rapidity of change greatly strained lines of communication between management and employees within our organization and complicated changes brought about by other influences.

5. The delivery of health care has become more sophisticated, more technology intensive, and has resulted in the development of a highly professional culture which demands participation and

input. Human Resources managers, educators, social scientists, and others recognize that employees in business organizations today are very different from what they were 5 or 10 years ago. They are much more interested in being involved in the decisions that affect their day-to-day work environment. This cultural change has given rise to the movement within the United States today. Since health care is so people-intensive, this issue presents us with a more complex and acute challenge than most other types of organizations are facing.

During the early 1980s, the Cleveland Clinic Foundation undertook efforts to ascertain the values that members of the organization deemed important and to evaluate how patient care and productivity were influenced by these values. These efforts resulted in the development and articulation of the primary cultural themes of our organization. They are:

1. The foundation is an experimental organization constantly in a state of "becoming." There is a high tolerance for uncertainty.
2. The foundation inspires the best in its members and minimizes its constraints on them.
3. Our work requires high collaboration. Plans and directions are based on free, informed choice and the consent of members.
4. The quest for ongoing dialogue is more important than the search for permanent solutions.
5. Our members are ambitious and devoted to ongoing learning, discovery, and excellence.

Formal Dispute Modification and Resolution Processes

Saarel and Buck and their staffs created both formal and informal dispute modification/resolution processes and persuaded the employees, managers, and various approval groups of the organization that these processes were needed.

Many of the early proposals, which were intended for the organizational good, were perceived as a form of employee advocacy. This misperception was based, in part, on the approval methodology used and consisted of a take-it-or-leave-it attitude with little room for modification. Management was unsophisticated and uneducated as to its responsibilities and the realities of legal and social requirements. Out of this situation evolved the development of complex change, communication, and approval models through which nearly everyone who is concerned with the proposed change has an opportunity to participate in its design and communication prior to its implementation. A copy of the model is shown in Figure 1. This approach is consonant with the third primary theme of the organization (collaboration and consent) and with the societal changes that have occurred in general during the last 5–10 years.

Dispute management in large organizations is a complex process. The optimal level of conflict resolution is a problem-solving mode wherein common interests dominate, conflicting interests are known, and friendliness and trust exist.

The foundation developed five primary formal dispute modification processes:

1. Retention of an outside expert counsel, which gives both the external and internal processes more validity and political clout. Counsel is utilized in those situations where internal discussions between management have reached an impasse. This allows for an impartial review and results in a low-scale conclusion.

2. Development of a job evaluation and salary administration process that creates a climate of equity, fairness, and trust throughout the organization and eliminates dispute questions regarding pay.

3. Development of a job-posting system that allowed Cleveland Clinic Foundation employees to move from a closed to an open system of promotion wherein self-nomination by the individual is the primary feature.

4. Development of Human Resources, primarily an Employee Relations Department, to proactively respond to employee and managerial questions and issues. The establishment of the em-

FIGURE 1
CUTTING EDGE CHANGE MODEL

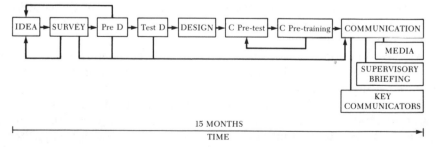

ployee relations function symbolized to employees and supervisors that the organization was serious about resolving complaints and issues. During 1984, seven employee relations professionals will make nearly 12,000 significant contacts with employees and supervisors in the organization.

5. Consensus participation by supervisors and employees in the development of all Human Resources related policies.

The formal dispute resolution processes that have been developed are:

1. The right-of-review procedure gave employees the opportunity to use a formal internal system where none previously existed. This procedure had four steps:

a. Supervisor,
b. Department Head,
c. Division Clearance, and
d. Chief Executive Officer.

Our past right-of-review system has allowed both employees and the organization to resolve many questions concerning health plan, pensions, job posting, time off, discipline, discrimination, and compensation.

Case Examples

- An employee raised a question concerning health plan coverage for an adoption which was in process and not yet consummated. The plan was amended to cover in-process situations.
- A concern was raised regarding job posting and medical leave of absence and return to work. The employee was returned to work and received five months back pay. Procedural changes in the posting process were also made.
- With relation to time off, a question arose concerning the accrual of paid time off during military leave and the policy was changed to allow for this accrual.
- Many of the rights of review were related to discipline and employees have been made whole, compensated for time lost from work, or reinstated.
- Discrimination rights of review have been filed and adjudicated as appropriate. The government agencies responsible for managing the charge/complaint process have

encouraged our employees to utilize the internal mechanism first.

- A compensation issue involved job classification and resulted in a group of employees receiving a payment in aggregate of $75,000.
- Many of the rights of review are individual in nature and require specific solutions. Others involve systemic issues and have resulted in substantive organizational changes as a result of the matter being brought forward. In this respect, the relief valve concept does work and makes a difference.

Changes have been made again in the right-of-review policy, effective July 1, 1984, consonant with the needs of the organization and its employees and our culture. Groups of supervisors and employees were asked for input regarding the changes they wished to see in the old policy; a process which took about 18 months. Before the right of review policy was approved, 146 employees and supervisors were interviewed and also responded to a questionnaire about the policy (Figure 2). The changes involve redefinition of what a grievance is, reduction of time limits for processing, and, most importantly, the establishment of a 10-member Right-of-Review Committee as a fourth and final step in the right-of-review process. This committee consists of a cross-section of managers and supervisors with several years of experience in a supervisory capacity. The new system has a 4-step process (Figure 3):

a. Formalized response from the supervisor,
b. Response from the next level of management,
c. Response from the administrative/division chairman, and
d. Response from the Right-of-Review Committee.

The Right-of-Review Committee members attend a training program to learn about due process, arbitration/labor law policy procedures, and grievance procedures so that they would be able to function effectively in grievance resolution cases.

The new policy covers all nonstaff physicians and nonprobationary employees who initiate their Right-of-Review within 30 days of a causal incident or knowledge of an incident. The Right-of-Review will be processed within time limits even if management does not respond in a timely manner. The Employee Relations Counselor has the responsibility of facilitating the process and assisting the grievant's response when necessary. The Legal Department will be advised and involved in the process as significant litigation issues are identified.

FIGURE 2
REVISED RIGHT OF REVIEW POLICY

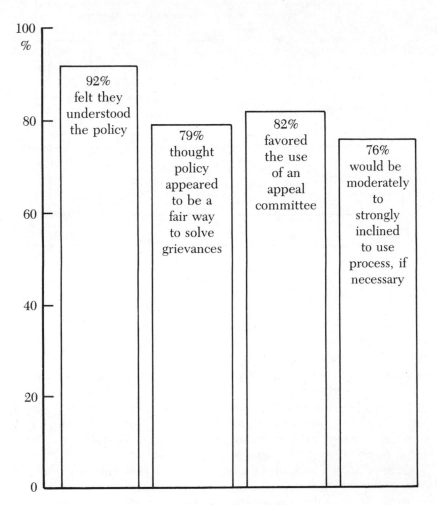

Employee Reaction

2. The Cleveland Clinic Foundation has always had an "open-door" policy which allows an employee to talk to any member of management or staff about his/her concerns and receive a prompt and courteous response.

3. Communication/sensing meetings in which individual employees or groups can voice their concerns to management and receive responses are frequently covered.

FIGURE 3
RIGHT OF REVIEW PROCESS

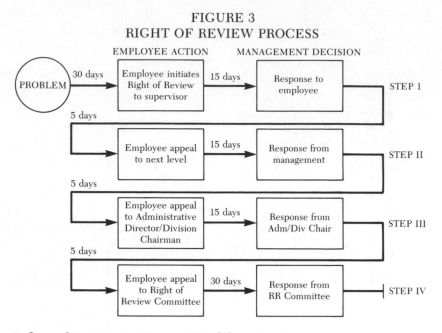

Informal Systemic Dispute Modification Processes

There are six major, informal systemic processes:

1. Human Resources has been assisting medical and operational departments in the development of organizational effectiveness programs which identify issues and opportunities and provide for response strategies.

2. We have created problem-solving groups across departmental and organizational lines to deal with group issues. Individuals and groups explore differences, generate flexible alternatives, and reach consensus decisions. As a result, an atmosphere is established which provides mutual benefit, creates alternatives, and encourages future problem-solving endeavors.

3. Human Resources has changed significantly from serving a traditional maintenance function to having a client-centered orientation as a result of organizational effectiveness programs.

4. Employee benefits surveys have been conducted since 1980. The initial one was the first time we had ever asked employees how they felt about benefit issues. The results were conveyed to employees in small discussion groups with a series of smaller surveys being utilized. Both were intended to involve employees in decision making and to provide valuable input to management. As

a consequence, we created and implemented "BeneFlex," a flexible benefits program wherein employees can select, within certain limits, the benefits they need most. In the past, many of the professional and social interest groups within the foundation wanted separate programs. With BeneFlex, we have offered one program with multiple options. It offers a variety to employees and is less costly and easier for the organization to administer.

5. The foundation has conducted various physician and executive management development programs, with each of our approximately 300 managers receiving 16 hours of training per year.

6. The Division of Human Resources has utilized formal communication processes through the supervisory hierarchy and various publications and have also, through necessity, created parallel processes using other media to keep employees and supervisors informed.

Results

In the past nine years there has been significant overall improvement in our ratio of discrimination charges, computed per thousand employees with the variation occurring in 1983 (Figure 4). This recent variation from our past experience was a solemn reminder that dispute management and resolution are continuous and not periodic processes which must be approached with unremitting intensity year in and year out.

The frequency of rights of review exercised by employees has increased dramatically over the same time period, which suggests that this process has been a positive and useful one, particularly for employees (Figure 4).

By far the great majority of external discrimination charges over the past nine years have related to discharge and promotional issues (Figure 5). This trend is consistent with data in recent EEOC employment annual reports. We have attempted to make every effort to be fair in mediating discharge issues. The individual, however, feels that he or she has everything to gain and nothing to lose by filing a complaint. Our position has been sustained in 92 percent of all the external charges filed.

Rights of Review, on the other hand, have related predominantly to discipline in the face of termination, suspension, benefits, and job posting (Figure 6). On the average, over this nine-year period, 30–40 percent of our employees have received favorable

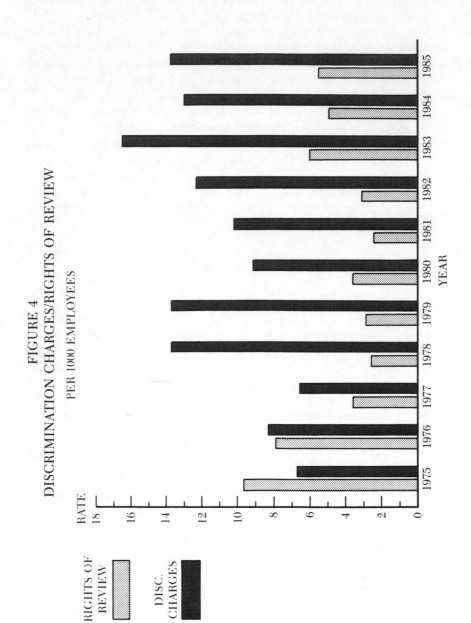

FIGURE 4
DISCRIMINATION CHARGES/RIGHTS OF REVIEW
PER 1000 EMPLOYEES

FIGURE 5
DISCRIMINATION CHARGES

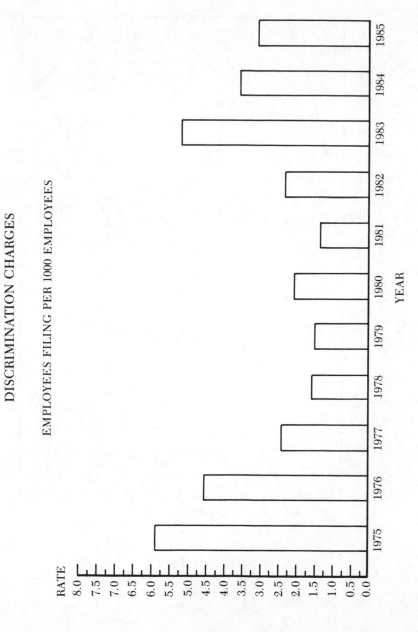

EMPLOYEES FILING PER 1000 EMPLOYEES

YEAR

RATE

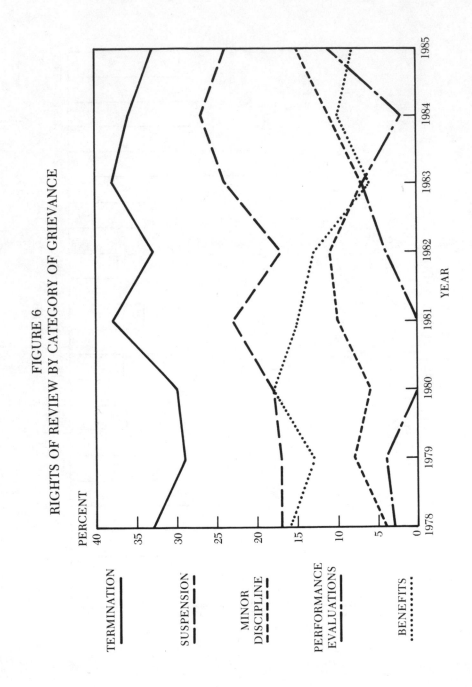

FIGURE 6
RIGHTS OF REVIEW BY CATEGORY OF GRIEVANCE

determinations concerning their rights of review. Certainly, it has proved to be more advantageous for individuals to process their complaints internally than externally.

The majority of the grievances come from the largest employee population areas. In 1983 the grievance process was used by Service, 30 percent; Professional, 20 percent; Technical, 18 percent; and Clerical, 16 percent. This has varied historically, but these are the four major groups who use the process. The tighter the job market is in the region, the more the grievance procedure is used due to employees desperate to keep their jobs.

Turnover is another area in which the foundation has a rate consistently one-half the general health care average, even with the changes occurring in the health-care environment involving reimbursement and competition.

	% National	% Foundation
1983	18	8
1982	18	10
1981	21	13

We have developed a more positive systemic approach to problem solving and have been able to gain our employees' participation in developing programs which better meet their needs while also saving time and money.

We have experienced significantly fewer cases of litigation with their corresponding costs than other organizations of comparable size. We are, of course, still a nonunion setting and believe that the organization and its members can best solve their differences together rather than through a third party.

Learnings

The first and perhaps most important lesson is that successful dispute modification/resolution processes can be developed and implemented in large organizations. However, no single model works in all settings. Organizations must develop a variety of complementary processes to meet different needs.

Other learnings about organizational policy, beliefs, and norms that must be created and in place for successful dispute modification and resolution processes to occur are:

● Policies must have a supportive culture. It takes time, usually 3–5 years.

- The organization must have an expert human relations unit, which is resourceful and flexible enough to handle all the changes which will be required.
- The goal must be excellence, and nothing less will be accepted.
- Experimentation on a small scale is a requirement.
- Two-way communication is essential.
- Individuals must collaborate across the organization.

Management of conflict is a never-ending task and an extremely challenging one. It can be rewarding to those who meet it if the measures of success are identified and opportunities for improvement are developed and implemented.

The foundation as an organization is not perfect; if it were, there would be nothing to change. We do, however, recognize our imperfections and are always striving to improve in order to assure that the Cleveland Clinic Foundation is a satisfying place to work for both current and future employees.

The *Resolution* Process at Aetna Life and Casualty

*Jack Massey**
and
*Roberto Rosario**

Organizational Profile

Aetna Life and Casualty is one of the 15 largest corporations in the United States and is the nation's largest investor-owned insurance and financial services organization. Aetna is headquartered in Hartford, Connecticut, and maintains offices in every state. Its work force numbers approximately 40,000 employees—two-thirds of them located in field offices.

Corporate operations are conducted through eight company divisions and several subsidiaries. The organizational cultures of each are quite different. To accommodate the different cultures and in some cases a different physical location, six of the divisions have their own human resource department, responsible for administering corporate personnel programs and practices. This decentralization of the personnel function emphasizes the importance of interaction and communication at a level closest to the employee/supervisor relationship. The focus of the corporate personnel department is development and monitoring of policies, programs, and practices. None of the operating divisions are unionized.

Aetna is an equal opportunity employer and government contractor. Currently, 68 percent of the work force is female while minorities make up 19 percent of the work force. Females account for 13 percent of the company's officials and managers category and 56 percent of Aetna's professional category. Minorities account for 9% of the officials and managers category and 15% of the professional category. Aetna will continue to initiate steps to reach a balanced, representative work force.

*Consulting Resources Group, Corporate Human Resources Department, Hartford, Connecticut.

Aetna has a strong tradition of responding to and resolving employee concerns. This tradition is based upon a long-standing expectation that supervisors and managers have a clear responsibility for maintaining a positive employee relations climate. The critical element to this approach is our management philosophy of letting the manager manage while holding him or her accountable for the decisions made.

Origins of Present Complaint System

Aetna's approach to employee dispute resolution has evolved over the years from "don't make waves" to "chain of command" to "corporate counselor" to a "structured problem resolution process." A growing and diversified labor force, a nationwide geographic span of operations, the philosophy of entitlement among employees, and management's desire to provide due process to employees were factors in developing the structured resolution approach currently in place.

Employee counseling developed as the initial focus of Aetna's dispute resolution program. Aetna began in the early 1970s with equal opportunity counseling, followed by career development counseling, and extending by the late 1970s to employee relations counseling. Employee relations and career guidance counseling was primarily informal; rarely were counselors in a position to contact management to discuss a counseled employee's concerns. In most cases the employees were urged to pursue their problems via the chain of command. Equal opportunity counseling, on the other hand, often necessitated the involvement of equal opportunity counselors with management. Management's interest in fair treatment and its desire to limit its equal employment opportunity liability explains the willingness of counselors to more actively pursue claims within the organization.

In 1981, in anticipation of the decentralization of personnel, all three counseling areas were merged into one counseling unit. Counselors were cross-trained in all three specialties and were expected to counsel employees regarding their equal opportunity, employee relations, and career guidance concerns.

Discussions about instituting an employee grievance procedure at Aetna were first held in the late 1970s. Aetna's Employee Relations Department conducted research and held discussions with a number of companies (insurance and noninsurance) which had initiated internal grievance procedures to learn of their experiences. The company also explored the potential legal liability of instituting and employing an internal complaint process with counsel and labor relations consultants.

The proposal was presented and discussed with key executives and personnel professionals. Senior management was very receptive to the proposal and their support was critical in the decision to implement the process. Each level of review led to refinements of the proposed program. Aetna's top management decided to implement the program throughout the company, effective January 1, 1983.

Overall Description of the Current System

Aetna's internal process is known as *Resolution* and covers all employees—supervisors and nonsupervisors alike. *Resolution* allows employees to appeal their individual treatment resulting from a particular personnel policy.

Aetna's published personnel policies and programs had been available to all employees for years. These publications (*Personnel Policies and Programs Manual, Working with You, Second Paycheck, Compliance Manual*) reflect Aetna's philosophy of fair and equitable treatment for all employees, and contain specific policies and programs which serve to guide the company's everyday operations. Consequently, an individual with a policy-related concern referred to in a company publication may raise his or her concern through the *Resolution* process. *Resolution* is not an appropriate means, however, to challenge or appeal the policy itself.

Information about *Resolution* was published in several company publications, including Aetna's *Personnel Policies and Programs Manual* and the employee handbook. In addition, articles were featured in a monthly employee communications newsletter and bimonthly employee communications magazine. The Vice President of Corporate Human Resources contributed by distributing a memorandum to all officers of the company informing them about the process. The Senior Vice Presidents from the operating divisions were responsible for direct communications to their employees.

Aetna's 4-step *Resolution* process is designed to provide a review by distinctive levels of management within and then (if necessary) outside the employee's chain of command in order to ensure that employees are treated in compliance with company policy. The process also serves to affirm Aetna's responsive management style and encourage problem resolution at the lowest possible level. Employees can proceed with any individual policy-related concerns they have, although they cannot appeal the policy itself. This is not to say that a policy cannot be *modified* as a result of an employee utilizing the *Resolution* process. In this instance, the policy modification is a result of the process, not the reason for the process.

The 4-step process consists of:

Step I. Discussion between the employee and the supervisor. Employees are encouraged to use the chain of command as high as their comfort level allows.

Step II. Involvement of a divisional personnel consultant in fact-finding and problem solving.

Step III. Involvement of a Corporate Personnel consultant in fact-finding and problem solving.

Step IV. Senior Management Committee Review of decision. The Committee is composed of the Vice President, Corporate Personnel; Vice President of Corporate Public Involvement; and the Senior Vice President or Vice President designate from the employee's division. The Vice President of Corporate Personnel chairs the meeting.

A change of a personnel decision must be made by management. Consequently, a revision of a personnel decision can only be *mandated* at Steps I and IV, that is, an employee must use the chain of command or use *Resolution* to the final step. Steps II and III can *recommend* that management decisions be modified. Management, however, has the final decision on whether to accept or reject the recommendations. The divisional or corporate areas may proceed up the department's chain of command if their recommendation was not accepted in an attempt to reverse the decision or inform the employee of the decision with instructions on how to proceed with the next step. The end result for all steps is that any and all changes to management decisions are made by management.

Steps I and II are largely informal and are *initiated verbally* by the employee. The divisional consultant serves a dual role within the system: first, as an internal consultant for both management and employees interested in clarifying policy concerns; and two, as a fact-finder/arbiter in a Step II proceeding. A consulting role can evolve into a fact finding/arbiter role only at the request of the employee. Otherwise, all consultations are kept confidential.

Step II investigations begin when the employee contacts a divisional consultant to seek his or her involvement in resolving policy-related concerns. During this meeting, the consultant will attempt to identify the specific management decision or practice at issue. The divisional consultant will then meet with the employee's supervisor to acquaint him or her with *Resolution* and get management's perspective.

Investigations will typically require some form of review (personnel files, department policies) and comparison of the employee's treatment with others similarly situated.

The *Resolution* process becomes much more formal at Steps III and IV. An employee must initiate a Step III review within 30 days of a Step II decision and a Step IV review must be initiated within 15 days of a Step III decision. In both steps, the employee's correspondence must:

- Summarize the problem,
- Summarize steps the employee has taken to resolve the problem,
- Summarize the responses of management and divisional or corporate consulting areas, and
- State the desired outcome.

Requests for Step IVs are not automatically approved. Employees must provide *new* or *additional* information that was not covered during the Step III proceedings.

Many of the Step II investigation procedures are repeated at Step III. The corporate consultant will meet with the employee, management, and divisional consultant and conduct any additional meetings or interviews deemed necessary. The Step III investigations are undertaken with the role of the neutral fact finder/arbiter in mind. The investigations tend to be more extensive and require more interviews and analysis than a Step II meeting. Both the specific issues raised by the employee and peripheral issues (legal liabilities, wrongful discharge, Title VII violation, breach of the covenant of fair dealing) are examined at this time. This typically requires the review of personnel files, demographic information, performance appraisals, merit ratings and increases, and department policies or practices. An internal investigation summary is prepared on each of the issues raised by the employee with an assessment as to whether the employee's position is supported. The summary is the basis of any Step III recommendations which are then shared with the divisional human resource area and management. The management members involved in this step are typically one to two levels below the senior vice-president. The Step III decision is provided to the employee in writing.

The Step IV process entails developing a position paper for members of the Senior Management Review Committee. The position paper is prepared by the corporate Employee Relations Department and outlines the issues raised by the employee, management's response, a summary of previous steps and recommendations, potential legal liabilities, and a recommendation for consideration by the committee. The committee members meet to discuss the case and question each other and representatives from the Law Department and/or Employee Relations Department. A consensus is reached and the decision again is provided to the employee in writing.

The *Resolution* process, as it is currently in place, is not a legal proceeding and therefore does not envision the participation of third parties such as lawyers, mediators, and arbitrators. Some employees have retained counsel while pursuing *Resolution*, but counsel has not been allowed at any interview or fact-finding steps. The results of the various steps are discussed with an employee's counsel if the employee so desires. Although the employee's counsel would not be allowed before the Senior Management Committee, the Senior Management Committee could request that an employee appear at the meeting. To date, no such request has been made.

Both the divisional human resource departments and corporate human resources department are responsible for ensuring that all relevant information has been uncovered in order to assess whether policy was followed. Neither party acts as an employee or management advocate. The consultant's primary role is one of neutral fact finder/arbiter. In essence, the allegiance of both the divisional and corporate human resource areas is to the proper interpretation and administration of company policy.

The involvement of the Law Department in the process is minimal. A member of the Law Department is always present at the Senior Management Review meeting to provide a legal perspective or response to questions from members of the committee. Any involvement of the Law Department during Steps I–III is predicated by the issues involved or the need of the divisional or corporate areas to assess legal liabilities in a particular case. In such instances, the legal perspective is shared with management when Step II or III recommendations are made.

To preserve the employee's right to privacy, any records and documentation involved in an employee's use of the *Resolution* process is handled confidentially. Documentation of Steps II through IV of the process are not kept in the employee's personnel file but are kept in confidential divisional and corporate consulting files.

The System in Action

During 1986, divisional and corporate consultants handled 4,549 consulting cases. Utilization of the consulting service bears a good resemblance to the demographic profile of the company.

Of the 4,549 consulting cases, 300 progressed to Step II, 10 to Step III, and two to Step IV. Typically, half of the Step II cases are generated by termination, progressive discipline, disparate treatment, or harassment issues.

From 1983 until the end of 1986, we had 45 Step III cases and 10 Step IVs. Termination issues accounted for 26 of the Step III cases and six of the Step IVs. There were five progressive discipline cases at the Step III level, with a host of other issues involved in the remaining cases (job posting, promotion, harassment, job elimination).

Management decisions were upheld in 33 of the Step IIIs. Modifications were recommended in the remaining 12 cases, of which seven were accepted by management. In the five cases where recommendations were not accepted, two went on to Step IV, where the decision was modified; two were settled; and one case was dropped entirely.

Resolution was developed to address all employee concerns, including allegations of discrimination. Divisional and corporate personnel consultants are trained so that their equal opportunity investigations simulate those of the EEOC and of state civil rights agencies. Any liabilities from an EO perspective are handled as part of the Step II and III recommendations. Since 1983, several Step III and IV cases alluded to discrimination, but none specifically raised discrimination as an issue to be pursued.

Case Study

A male technical level supervisor with 13 years of service was terminated for failing to meet the terms of probation. The employee had previously received a verbal and written warning in accordance with the requirements of the company's progressive discipline process. The employee believed that his termination was unfair and that his supervisor did not provide him with support and guidance. The employee admitted to performance deficiencies while holding that the deficiencies did not warrant termination. Furthermore, he believed his supervisor had made the decision to terminate him prior to initiating progressive discipline and, therefore, was just going through the motions of the disciplinary process. The employee also believed that females in his unit received preferential treatment.

The investigation consisted of meetings with the employee, the employee's first and second level supervisors, and the divisional consultant. A thorough review of the employee's personnel file, significant incident file, and divisional consulting file was conducted along with a review of appraisals for all first level supervisors. The progressive discipline memos were assessed for reasonableness and management stated that termination was the rule for employees found committing similar offenses.

The Step III investigation included a file review and interviews with all the employees in the grievant's former section. Although employee interviews are rare, they are conducted whenever employee perceptions are critical to the outcome of the case. In this instance, the interviews revealed that the employees were not aware that the first infraction of the regulation could lead to termination. Additionally, while management stated that termination was the rule for similar offenses, it had happened only once previously and the person had been allowed to resign. A review of the disciplinary action for department employees revealed that one other person had committed as serious an offense and was not terminated. Consequently, the Step III investigation concluded that the employee was not treated in a manner consistent with company policy or previous departmental practice. Step III recommended the employee's reinstatement but management refused to do so.

The Senior Management Review Committee discussed at great length the treatment of the terminated employee and management's treatment of other employee infractions. Though the consensus held that the employee should not have been terminated, his failure to perform a key job function could not be overlooked. After much discussion, the Committee agreed to offer the employee a job requiring a demotion or three months' severance pay. The employee chose the monetary award. Further, the department was advised to reorient employees to preclude any future similar actions and was required to revise its policy to state any infractions which would lead to immediate termination.

No employee attitude survey has been conducted since *Resolution* has been instituted. The support of senior management for the process, however, is clear. This support is evidenced whenever the Senior Management Review Committee meets. The members take their responsibilities seriously and are guided by Aetna's philosophy of treating all employees fairly and equitably.

Some general statements about management attitudes toward *Resolution* can be made based on Aetna's experience so far. The attitudes of both employees and management toward the process have been generally positive. Some management members, however, still view the process much like they view external laws and regulations which affect operations, that is, as an encroachment on their management rights. Others view the process as a form of vindication—final proof that their actions were appropriate and consequently they are not "guilty." Most supervisors, however, view the process in its proper context—as an appeal process for employees who believe management actions to be inappropriate. In essence, *Resolution* provides a form of checks and balances to ensure that management actions comply with policy and provides management with a reference point to check the reasonableness and practicality of company policies.

Effects on Outside Complaints and Litigation

Use of the *Resolution* process does not prevent an employee from filing complaints with federal or state agencies or from initiating lawsuits. *Resolution* was not explicitly developed to reduce the number of charges or lawsuits. Any reductions in charges or lawsuits is an indirect benefit of the process. We have been successful, however, in having the process recognized by a number of state agencies which have agreed to stay their proceedings until the *Resolution* process has run its course. Additionally, a number of plaintiffs' counsel have advised employees to use the process before initiating any legal action.

Resolution has provided management with early identification of potential problems and liabilities, and has permitted the company's legal counsel to be better prepared if legal steps are later initiated. In this respect, it has also saved time for department management, the Legal Department, and the Employee Relations

Department since the company's position can be easily articulated and most of the documentation is readily available. As of early 1987, only two of the ten Step IV cases have gone on to litigation. The company believes the employee claim in these cases is without merit and we are defending the company position in the judicial process.

As more and more employees are made aware of *Resolution* and the process gains more credibility, the company would anticipate fewer charges or lawsuits. A key factor is increasing the knowledge of *Resolution* for Aetna's field office employees. Field office employees account for two-thirds of Aetna's work force while composing only one-third of *Resolution* consulting cases. Since the field typically accounts for 75 to 90 percent of our formal charges, the company hopes that field office employees will use the internal *Resolution* process before initiating external complaints.

Effects on Employee Relations and Organizational Objectives

One of the key factors in approving the *Resolution* process was its explicit encouragement of the company's philosophy of responsive management, that is, a management style capable of making sound business decisions while communicating the rationale to employees. Our company chairman, James Lynn, firmly believes that employees and agents are the company's greatest asset. This philosophy is contained in the company's statement of principles. Not only is it a sign of enlightened management but it makes good business sense. The payoff in terms of increased productivity, improved morale, recruiting, and positive public relations is significant if somewhat difficult to measure.

Some observers might suggest that *Resolution* was initiated as a union avoidance technique. While it is hoped that a credible process would contribute to maintaining nonunion status, *Resolution* was developed as a way of providing management with a process to review supervisory decisions. It also provides a forum for employees without fear of retaliation or retribution to appeal decisions that they believe to be inappropriate. The process has served to emphasize the company's philosophy of fair treatment and encouraging problem resolution at the lowest level. This philosophy is best realized by having supervisors accountable for their decisions and responsible for creating a positive employee relations climate.

Resolution and Aetna's internal consulting services have led to refinements of company policies and procedures, specifically in the areas of progressive discipline and termination. The experience has been used to make the personnel manual a more effective resource for both employees and supervisors. *Resolution* has also served to emphasize the importance of documentation and the necessity for clear, concise communications to employees. In a small number of cases, *Resolution* has resulted in identifying the need for training of supervisors and/or better recognition of how their management style was affecting employees. In other cases, divisional consultants have been requested to provide management training on issues such as progressive discipline and termination.

Final Remarks

Aetna does not envision making any changes to *Resolution* in the near future. Any change, however, which may come will have to remain within the guiding principles underlying *Resolution*:

- The process should be consistent with Aetna's culture of fair treatment,
- The process should be so simple as to make employees comfortable using it,
- The responsibility for making and reviewing policy-related decisions should remain with management,
- Retaliation toward employees who use the system will not be tolerated, and
- The process must have the support of senior management.

So far, *Resolution*, based on these guiding principles, has been a success. The reception by both management and employees has been positive. Aetna's process, however, cannot be transferred to all companies. Companies contemplating use of an internal complaint process should take note of their management style and human resource philosophy before initiating an internal process.

One principal challenge awaiting Aetna is increasing the familiarity of field office employees with the process. In a company the size of Aetna, even the most elaborate communications program cannot ensure reaching *all* employees. Once that challenge is met, *Resolution* can be assessed in terms of meeting its goal of providing a credible, internal problem *Resolution* process.

The *Problem Review Procedure* at Citibank

*Joseph Fernandez**

Citibank is a wholly owned subsidiary of Citicorp, an international financial services organization that employs over 85,000 people in the United States and in 96 countries throughout the world. Citibank's employees number approximately 40,000 domestically. Roughly, 24,000 are grade-level or staff members, most of whom are office and clerical workers, and 16,000 employees are management/professional level or officers. Professionals include financial analysts, economists, accountants, lending officers, credit analysts, and experts in investment management and taxation. Professionals are also employed in support functions, such as marketing, advertising, public relations, personnel, and systems design.

Citicorp is organized into both line and staff functions. The line function is composed of its major banking groups, which are highly decentralized to allow for day-to-day decision making close to the customer and to provide operational flexibility close to the point of service. Staff groups provide for corporate control in the areas of corporate strategy, legal affairs, public relations, accounting and control, credit policy, economics, and human resources.

The personnel group is divided according to line and staff functions. Group personnel offices service the day-to-day needs of each of the banking groups. The corporate personnel divisions are responsible for corporatewide personnel strategy, programs, and policies. The group personnel offices' relationship to the corporate structure is a dual one, with reporting responsibilities to both line management and, through the personnel staff group, to the group senior personnel officer, who is located at corporate headquarters in New York. Each of the personnel divisions has a specialty function: compensation, education and research, medical, personnel

*Vice President, Division Head, Staff Relations, New York, New York.

processing, services and systems, recruiting, policy and communications, and staff relations. The division personnel professionals—or specialists—provide expertise to the group personnel offices in their particular specialty, when needed, and design, develop, and administer corporatewide programs. The divisional offices are all located in New York City, although the specialist is available for consultation worldwide. All group senior personnel officers and division heads are at the vice president level.

The staff relations division provides consulting services and problem-solving skills. It has five major subdivisions: Labor Relations, Equal Employment Opportunity, Affirmative Action, Communications, and Employee Relations. The last, Employee Relations, has four units, one of which—the Employee Relations Unit—is directly involved in Citibank's *Problem Review (Grievance) Procedure*. It is a corporate level unit independent of any of the banking groups.

The Employee Relations Unit is made up of three seasoned professionals, who serve as consultants and problem solvers on employee relations issues at all levels. In this capacity, they function principally to resolve disputes at the lowest possible level. Because they are consultants, they must, and do, have credibility with line management. All have had line experience and are thoroughly acquainted with policy. In addition, they have all demonstrated good judgment skills, an essential ingredient for a position that must handle an avalanche of questions from the line on numerous controversial issues.

Management Philosophy

In most modern corporations, almost all of which are organized along the lines of a chain of command, the tone of the organization is invariably set by top management. Corporate officers determine policy not only on the manner in which the company conducts its business, but also in the way it interacts with the employees. Corporate leadership may be sensitive to the problems, concerns, and needs of its work force—and establish a mechanism to address them—or it may not. The decision is a prerogative of management. Thus, the corporate officer's ideological view of the employees' role direction is crucial, since it sets the stage for the employer-employee relationship.

Citibank's dispute-resolution machinery grew out of management's conviction that controversial issues should be confronted

openly and objectively. Perhaps the best expression of the belief—
which is really the basis for Citibank's program—was made by the
bank's then president, William I. Spencer, before the Third National Seminar on Individual Rights in the Corporation, a meeting
conducted by the Educational Fund for Individual Rights in 1980:

> Today's workers no longer view employment as an extended
> period of involuntary servitude, after which they hope—in retire-
> ment—to enjoy the fruits of their long labors and leave something
> to their children. The modern trend is to view employment as one
> of many life interests—all serving the common purpose of self-ful-
> fillment, which usually includes a sense of social purpose. Thus,
> workers are more determined than ever to bring into the workplace
> the same values they cherish outside the workplace.
>
> This includes such intangible values as self-respect, dignity, and
> individuality. It also includes the particular values enumerated in
> the Constitution. Workers no longer consider the "Bill of Rights"
> something to be stashed out of sight, like a wet umbrella, when they
> arrive at work. They expect such guarantees as "due process," "pri-
> vacy," and "free speech" to follow them to their desks and work
> stations. After all, a right that doesn't apply through much of your
> waking day and which you can be fired for exercising, isn't much of
> a right.
>
> Today, an enlightened management recognizes that internal
> complaints and the procedures for addressing them offer positive
> benefits to both the individual and the company. The constant chal-
> lenge faced by business managers is how to maintain a continuous
> and fair balance between employee rights and corporate responsi-
> bilities.
>
> There is something to balance in every area of employee rights.
> The worker's right of privacy must be balanced against the need for
> work-related information. An employee's expectation of equal ad-
> vancement must be weighed against the company's need to recognize
> and reward outstanding achievers.
>
> A company that falls too far behind the rolling average of other
> companies in creating programs to enhance employee rights may
> save the costs of such programs, but that gain will eventually be
> offset by the stress and strain of increased dissent and the loss of
> public image and credibility. Conversely, a management that puts
> too much daylight between itself and the pack may get good marks
> for humanitarian pacesetting, but poor marks from investors and
> competitors who take advantage of their lower operating costs.
>
> In general, corporate experience indicates that recognizing in-
> dividual employee rights is good business.
>
> For one thing, not every program to expand rights proves to
> be a net cost. . . . One industrial company recently reported that it
> spent $300,000 on reemployment counseling for workers laid off by
> two plant closings. This "humanitarian service" saved an estimated
> $3 million for the company in unemployment compensation assess-
> ments. Even humanitarianism can reach the bottom line.

Origins of the *Problem Review Procedure*

Citicorp's avowed goal is to be the most competent, profitable, and innovative financial organization in the world. To achieve that objective, Citicorp relies upon the talents and contributions of its staff and their commitment to excellence. One way Citicorp encourages its staff to adhere to this high standard is through a document put out in 1976 called *The Citicorp Approach*. The set of principles enunciated in *The Citicorp Approach* is the basic covenant between the bank and its employees, and virtually all of the bank's personnel policies flow from the ideas expressed in it.

Citicorp's employee handbook, entitled *Working Together*, communicates these concepts to all employees, and makes it clear to them that *The Citicorp Approach* is the central policy statement on which all personnel decisions are made. *The Citicorp Approach* is:

- To provide the climate and resources that will enable all staff members to advance on merit as far as their talents and skills will take them, without regard to age, color, handicap, marital status, national origin, race, religion, sex, or veteran status.
- To offer pay and benefits that are fair and competitive.
- To make certain that ideas, concerns, and problems are identified and that two-way communication is effectively maintained.
- To provide an environment that identifies, encourages, and rewards excellence, innovation, and quality customer service.
- To remember always that respect for human dignity is fundamental to our success.

These are the operating philosophies that govern the relationship between Citibank and its staff. The *Problem Review Procedure*, by providing due process, serves as a protection of the rights of individuals implicit in *The Citicorp Approach*.

The Work Environment

The *Problem Review Procedure*, however, is only one among numerous programs designed around *The Citicorp Approach* that is geared to form the fabric of a total positive staff relations climate.

Before discussing the *Problem Review Procedure*, it is useful to examine both the channels available to employees for voicing their concerns and suggestions to bank management, and the resources that help them cope with personal or work-related problems that may affect their on-the-job performance.

Attitude Surveys

One channel for the expression of employees' opinions is called the Continuous Employee Reaction Surveys Program (CERS), which is conducted at the individual-business level. CERS was introduced in 1973 to create a structured and systematic method to measure staff member attitudes about working conditions, salaries, management practices, and other issues, on a continuing basis. CERS is a diagnostic tool for management. It is interested solely in investigating and analyzing important issues in the working environment. To that end, the entire survey process is designed to protect the anonymity of the individuals involved, so that an open contribution of ideas can take place. In a typical CERS program, the process works as follows:

- *Questionnaire Development:* A CERS survey is requested by management at any level. Managers are briefed on the process and a questionnaire developed.
- *Survey Administration:* The questionnaire is distributed to a work group in the area in question. Answers are never identified with an individual, and the work group must consist of at least seven people.
- *Results-Feedback:* The questionnaire responses are tabulated, and a summary of write-in comments is prepared by an outside firm, which sends it to Citicorp without the individual comment sheets. The work group then meets in a feedback session to discuss, analyze, and elaborate on problems in their work environment and to recommend solutions to these problems. The discussion is led by an independent feedback leader from another part of the organization, who is a staff member carefully trained for this role.
- *Management Action:* Work group recommendations are submitted to and reviewed by the appropriate management, which then informs the work group of its decisions.

The process has led to meaningful improvements in the work environment. Information provided by CERS, for example, was used to plan salary program revisions. Other CERS programs plumb attitudes over a larger cross-section of the staff worldwide. In some cases, confidential questionnaires are mailed to randomly selected groups of previously surveyed staff members. Through this technique, trends are measured and analyzed to determine appropriate courses of action.

Citiline

Citiline is a program that offers a direct route for an employee's questions, comments, suggestions, or complaints on any work-related subject. Boxes with *Citiline* forms are located in all Citibank offices and branches. If a staff member requests a personal reply, he or she can choose to put name and home address on the form. The message is handled in complete confidence by a *Citiline* administrator, who contacts the person best qualified to give an answer. The *Citiline* administrator mails the answer to the staff member's address. A staff member can also elect to remain anonymous, in which case a reply cannot be returned; however, the concern will nonetheless be carefully investigated. Since the program's inception in 1971 *Citiline* inquiries have led to the introduction of more detailed pay statements, a new system of performance appraisals, more flexibility in vacation scheduling, and an improved sick leave policy.

Personal Problem Counseling

The Staff Advisory Service (SAS)—a unit of the staff relations division—is available to assist staff in the resolution of personal problems. SAS is composed of a group of professional counselors, specially trained to help staff members with marital or family problems, financial problems, questions on housing, child-care centers, legal issues, substance abuse, and other personal concerns that may affect their work life. In addition to conducting one-to-one group counseling sessions on personal issues, SAS acts as a referral source for more in-depth legal, housing, and psychological assistance.

Medical Department

Citicorp's medical department provides free counseling and medical services for staff with health, emotional, alcohol, or drug problems. All discussions with the medical staff—which includes physicians, nurses, and a consulting psychiatrist—are kept completely confidential.

Line Personnel Function

When employees encounter work-related problems, Citibank encourages them first to seek out and discuss the problem with their supervisor. This is in keeping with the bank's basic philosophy that the responsibility for problem resolution and a healthy work environment is fundamentally that of line management. If a staff member does not feel that he or she can resolve a problem by working with the supervisor, then the bank encourages the staff member to call the local personnel officer for advice and direction. The personnel officer will then work with the staff member, the staff member's supervisor, and anyone else to find a solution to the problem. The staff member can also go directly to the employee relations unit in the corporate staff relations division. The employee relations specialist will discuss the problem confidentially with the staff member, or with the staff member and the supervisor. It is the employee relations specialist's function to ensure that personnel policies are administered equitably and consistently throughout the organization. If the problem cannot be resolved by discussion with the immediate supervisor, the personnel officer, or the employee relations specialist, then the staff member may resort to the appeal process offered by the *Problem Review Procedure*.

Disciplinary Procedure

We have discussed the positive staff relations climate that Citibank seeks to foster through its various programs. The discussion would not be complete, however, without mention of the bank's disciplinary procedure. In any healthy work environment, staff members must be made aware of an organization's expectations and how these expectations can be met. If a supervisor feels that a staff member's job performance is substandard, he/she may begin corrective action. The procedure is designed in steps to give staff members a chance to improve.

First, there is a discussion between supervisor and staff member identifying the performance problem and determining ways to improve performance. If there is no improvement, the supervisor can decide to complete a written warning that the staff member is asked to sign to show that he or she has read and understood it. The usual time limit set for improvement is three months. The next step is a final warning, which essentially means that the staff member may be released if no improvement is evident. The usual time limit under a final warning is six months. Here again, a staff member can use the *Problem Review Procedure* and appeal any step of the corrective action process.

History of the *Problem Review Procedure*

Ten years before launching *The Citicorp Approach*, in the mid-1960s, a grievance-resolution mechanism—the *Problem Review Procedure*—was successfully introduced into Citibank. In 1976, the staff relations division, concerned about the program's under-utilization, conducted a critical analysis of the procedure. As part of this analysis, questions pertaining to the *Problem Review Procedure* were included in CERS. Resulting statistics showed that 75 percent of the exempt staff members and 50 percent of the nonexempt staff members were unaware of the *Problem Review Procedure*'s existence. The analysis also revealed a number of other shortcomings, including undue processing delays and murky roles assigned to the participants.

On the basis of its findings, the staff relations division redesigned the *Problem Review Procedure* to meet four objectives:

1. To establish clearly the concept that staff members have a right to appeal an issue without reprisals by management;
2. To establish a structure encompassing the principles of due process;
3. To establish time limits at each step of the procedure to ensure a prompt resolution of each issue; and
4. To establish clearly defined roles for all of the principals.

Citibank's Appeal Procedure

As a result of the revamping of the *Problem Review Procedure*, a new appeal mechanism—the Problem Review Board—was developed and incorporated into it. This is an impartial body that recommends to senior management a final resolution of an employee's grievance. The bank's revised *Problem Review Procedure* provides every staff member or officer of the bank with the right to appeal any management decision. A grievant can utilize the procedure by collaborating with the supervisor, the local personnel manager, or an employee relations specialist. Any of these resources can provide a staff member with information about the process and how to use it. Furthermore, to ensure that all staff members are aware the procedure exists, the process is also described in two important bank booklets: *Seven Ways to Solve a Problem* and *Working Together*.

The *Problem Review Procedure* is a 4-step mechanism that follows sequentially and stops whenever the person with the problem accepts a decision at an interim step, withdraws the issue, or when a final decision is reached at Step 4. The procedure may be invoked by any staff member who is not satisfied with the resolution of an issue and who chooses to appeal that decision. Decisions concerning performance appraisals, terminations, salary, promotions, and discipline issues are typical of the types of decisions challenged by staff members through use of the *Problem Review Procedure*. They are not limited to these, however; the *Problem Review Procedure* is meant to be a recourse of appeal for any work-related issue.

The Four Steps of the Procedure

To understand the procedure in action, it is useful to examine the individual steps that it includes. Each step represents an effort to resolve the issue with the right to proceed to a higher level.

Step 1. The staff member's supervisor, in concert with the line personnel officer, prepares a written record of the facts of the dispute. This includes the supervisor's position on the issue, the staff member's position, and any Citibank policies, standards, and practices that apply. This record is then transmitted to the supervising officer for review. The supervising officer is required to gather any additional information, to meet with the staff member as necessary, and within seven working days, to make a decision and relay it, either orally or in writing, to the grievant.

Step 2. If the staff member is not satisfied with the decision, it can be appealed to the division head or equivalent. The human resources officer will compile a written summary, including an investigation of the circumstances leading to the appeal. Prior to providing the summary to the division head, it is reviewed with an employee relations specialist. In a consulting capacity, the specialist ensures that the facts are presented without bias and the summary is a clear-cut portrayal of the incident leading to the appeal.

The division head has seven business days to review the written summary and respond in writing to the staff member with a decision. If the staff member wishes to continue the appeal, the human resources officer will advance it to the Step 3.

Step 3. The staff member is provided with an opportunity to read the written summary, add additional pertinent information if required, and choose the Problem Review Board. The human resources officer is responsible for overseeing the grievant's selection of a Problem Review Board—that group of employees who actually hear the issue—as well as scheduling the board's meeting date.

The Problem Review Board is an ad hoc group convened by the only permanent board member, the vice president of staff relations, or his designee. To ensure objectivity, the grievant selects the remaining four members of the board from a random computer listing of staff from banking groups other than the staff member's group. One of the four must be at the vice president level. The remaining three members, may be either officers or staff members at the same or higher grade as the grievant. When an officer uses the Problem Review Board, the same guidelines apply: the officer may select a board that includes one vice president plus three peer level officers, or a board of all vice presidents. Service on the Problem Review Board is voluntary and confidential. The human resource officer is a nonvoting member of the board, serving as a technical adviser, responding to questions from board members and impartially elucidating the issues.

Prior to the Problem Review Board meeting, the human resource officer provides the written summary to all board members. This record typically includes statements submitted by the staff member, the supervisor, and the human resources officer; a review of the issue at hand and the background facts; and all appropriate exhibits, such as performance appraisals, written warnings, and memos. Within 10 working days, the Problem Review Board must meet to review the record and make a recommendation to the staff member's group or staff department head. (This senior line manager is usually at the executive vice president level and sits on the corporation's policy committee.) The recommendation by the board to the senior line executive need not be a unanimous one and will reflect any minority opinions.

Step 4. Within five working days, the senior line executive will review the entire record, including the recommendation of the Problem Review Board, and come to a final decision. In doing so, direct discussions with the principals may be arranged. The staff member is informed of the decision in writing directly by the senior line executive.

The Procedure in Practice

Now that we have described how the mechanism works, let us look at it in action. Although each individual case has its unique aspects, a few examples should be helpful to illustrate both the types of issues encountered and how determinations are reached. These examples are hypothetical to protect the privacy of people who have used the process, but they are based on actual cases.

The Counseled Employee. A management trainee who worked as a financial analyst had, among his job duties, the responsibility of preparing issue/risk analysis reports. He did them improperly, making mathematical errors repeatedly. In line with the disciplinary procedure outlined previously, the employee's supervisor instructed him to improve the quality, timeliness, and reliability of his work. After four months, the employee's performance had not improved. The supervisor issued the employee a written warning for continued lack of understanding of the financial process, for his mathematical errors, and for incorrect vouchers he had written. Another three months passed, the employee's work remained unsatisfactory, and the supervisor issued him a final warning covering the same deficiencies.

At this point, the supervisor interceded to ask the employee if there were any personal problems he was experiencing that were affecting his work. He replied that there were none. The supervisor advised him that he could appeal the warning through the *Problem Review Procedure*, and told him how to proceed. The employee appealed when he was terminated three months later for unsatisfactory performance. After reviewing the case, the Problem Review Board decided, and the group head agreed, that all possible corrective measures were taken before terminating the employee. The board found the employee's release to be equitable and consistent with corporate policy.

The Uncounseled Employee. A staff member did not follow instructions from her supervisor, neglected top-priority work assignments, and contrary to policy, accepted assignments from outside her department. The same employee had been overheard advising another staff member on "how to beat the system." In addition, the employee's behavior and work performance were generally unsatisfactory. As a result, the employee's supervisor gave her an unsatisfactory performance appraisal, and she was given a formal written warning. Three months later, the employee was given a final written warning for failure to follow prescribed work procedures in a timely manner and for lack of coooperation with department managers.

The employee appealed the final warning through the *Problem Review Procedure*. After considering the case, the board determined that the employee was not properly counseled about what would result if her behavior did not improve as the deadline for the first formal warning approached. The Board also agreed that management had not given her sufficiently precise information about her failure to improve to issue a final warning. The Problem Review Board recommended, and the group head agreed, that the final warning should be rescinded, and that management should spend more time with the employee to identify and correct specific problems.

The Discouraged Employee. An employee attempted to have certain personnel issues resolved to no avail over a period of years. Among the issues were management's failure to provide a timely job description; management's adding comments to a performance appraisal after the staff member had already signed it, a procedure strictly against bank policy; and the failure of management to provide meaningful work for her during a period of reorganization. The Board upheld some manangement decisions but noted the impropriety of others, with a recommendation that every effort be made to place the grievant in a position commensurate with her skills and abilities. The group head agreed.

As these cases illustrate, the Problem Review Board does not begin the dispute resolution process. It addresses specific employee issues that have not been solved at other levels. Much previous effort takes place in the line. Only when this effort fails or is unsatisfactory does the *Problem Review Procedure* provide the employee with a means of appeal.

It should be noted that the *Problem Review Procedure* does not function to alert management to important policy considerations. There are other channels for this, including surveys, and the suggestions and recommendations of staff members using staff meetings to inform management of concerns and problems. In addition, there is the policy and communications departments of Staff Relations which is specifically charged with the responsibility of examining the bank's policies continuously and to recommend changes in it.

Communicating Policy to Employees

One of the keystones of successful corporate management is its ability to communicate with its employees. Nowhere is this more crucial than in personnel management. Clearly, none of Citibank's personnel programs or policies could be effective if employees had no knowledge of them. We saw in our previous discussion, for example, that the bank's former appeal mechanism was underutilized because a large percentage of staff was unaware of its existence. Similarly, employees must know about corporate policy, or they cannot be expected to comply.

We have already referred to two important publications through which Citibank informs its staff members of personnel policies and programs: *Working Together*, the organization's employee handbook, and *Seven Ways to Solve a Problem*, the bank's guide to its dispute resolution machinery.

Working Together is a 50-page booklet designed to tell employees precisely what the bank expects from them and what they can expect from the bank in return. Written in a lively fashion, accompanied by whimsical illustrations to make comprehension more pleasant, the booklet covers Citibank's operational philosophy, job-related policies and procedures (such as IDs, personnel records, ethics, performance appraisals, outside employment, and political activities); financial concerns (such as merit increases, overtime, and expense reimbursement); holidays and leave (including maternity leave, jury duty, personal days, and sick days); employee benefits; problem-solving mechanisms; and policies on a staff member's leaving the bank. *Working Together* is revised whenever a major staff-related policy revision takes place.

Seven Ways to Solve a Problem is a 12-page booklet that is designed to augment the basic employee handbook. The booklet is laid out as a guide to staff who have a problem that they want Citibank to address in some way. Its design format follows a cartoon figure through each mechanism available to him until all seven alternatives for resolving the problem are explored. The booklet reiterates Citibank's underlying philosophy that it is natural for employees to encounter problems in their work life, and that these mechanisms should be used without fear of retribution, as its introduction demonstrates:

> *We've all got our problems.* Everyone has problems from time to time—and certainly, some are worse than others. But whatever their nature, most problems have one thing in common—a solution.
>
> Of course, it's not the same solution—that'd make things too easy. And no one ever said solving problems was easy—it's sometimes hard and painful work.
>
> *Some things help, and some things never help.* If you've got a problem there are certain things you can expect.
>
> First, you can expect the problem to remain a problem unless you do something about it. But just worrying about it doesn't count. That never helped anything.
>
> Second, you can count on getting help from people right here— if you're willing to give them a chance. And that's what this booklet's all about. Seven resources available at Citibank and Citicorp to help you solve job-related and personal problems.
>
> Why seven ways to solve a problem? Simply because no single approach is going to work for everyone, but everyone has several options to choose from.
>
> *It's confidential.* You can use any of the resources described in this booklet in complete confidence. No one else will be contacted in efforts to help resolve a problem unless you first give permission. And no one will try to get back at you for raising an issue or concern through one of these channels.

This sort of communication has been a vital element in Citibank's efforts to address concerns of its staff. There is also an added element. While a relatively small percentage of the work force actually brings a problem to the problem-solving programs each year, staff morale is elevated by the knowledge that the bank cares enough about its work force to develop such mechanisms, and that its stated concern for the individual is given more than lip service.

Problems of Conscience

Internal appeal procedures that have proven entirely adequate to handle conventional job-related complaints may be unable to respond to problems of personal conscience, which are often referred to as whistleblowing issues. The employer and employee who differ on the morality of a business practice or the social benefit of a particular transaction, are hard pressed to find a mutually acceptable yardstick to resolve the problem to one another's satisfaction.

Citibank's attitude toward the special difficulties that whistle-blowing situations pose was summed up by William Spencer in his 1980 speech before the Third National Seminar on Individual Rights in the Corporation:

> If it is good business to set up internal procedures for recognizing and responding to individual rights, in general, that applies even more to conscience issues, in particular. An industrial worker's anxiety over a possible safety defect in a product, if raised early enough through internal channels, can prevent a costly recall later. A potential environmental hazard or discriminatory practice flagged by employee complaints, can be corrected without the need for massive, costly regulatory agency intervention.
>
> Finally, a company's name and public image—its hard-won reputation earned by prior generations of employees and managements—have very real value. This intangible value is jeopardized when all internal dissent mechanisms have failed and a distraught employee feels there is no recourse but to express personal ethical reservations to a public that is often only too willing to hear and believe the worst. At this point the company incurs a very substantial loss—whether or not the employee's charge is verified by an impartial investigation of the facts.
>
> A company that has been deliberately concealing a known misconduct deserves this fate. For the rest, and particularly for those cases where everyone has acted in good faith—convinced that their own position best reflects the current state of social values—some better resolution is called for.

In recognition of this problem, Citibank created a special procedure in 1980 for its employees to use when a whistleblowing situation arises.

The policy requires each of Citibank's business units to communicate to employees the bank's existing guidelines on ethical standards and conflicts of interest, and its regular procedures for handling employee concerns over such matters. The policy also specifies that there can be "occasions when an employee may question or object to actions or decisions taken by the organization or by one or several individuals." This might involve actions that are viewed as being "illegal or against public interest, undermining the trust or rights of the organization's employees or customers," or "detrimental to the reputation, the profitability or the sound operations of the organization," such as "violations of corporate policies or practices" or "abuse or mismanagement of corporate resources, property, privilege, public influence or vested authority."

The policy statement recognizes that an individual concerned about such matters "may feel personally affected by the situation or feel compelled to act on it as a matter of conscience. . . ." This could lead employees "to challenge decisions or actions, or to bring to higher management's attention what they feel is a questionable practice that has gone unheeded or unnoticed."

When this occurs, though existing procedures may still be used if the employee wishes, the policy creates "a separate and distinct global corporate procedure for the internal disclosure and investigation of allegations of questionable practices." The policy specifies the reasoning behind it, and management's view toward its necessity:

- To allow such concerns to surface constructively and without fear of retribution or alienation;
- To provide a focal point where matters of this nature can be initially analyzed, evaluated, and differentiated from others (and) steered through a coherent institutional framework designed to ensure impartiality, confidentiality, and thorough investigation;
- To exhaust internal channels of discussion and resolution and protect the organization and all affected parties from what may be unwarranted public attention; and
- To ensure that our corporate commitment to integrity and respect for the individual is maintained in practice as well as spirit.

In accordance with these guidelines, employees may question any actions or decisions taken within the organization, whether or not they are personally affected in their jobs. They may, without fear of retribution or alienation, communicate their concerns to the Committee on Good Corporate Practice. This committee serves as the "last court of internal appeals" and the "last line of defense against the sad consequences of a public dispute." The Good Corporate Practice Committee comprises five high-level Citibank officers with broad, global career experience. Four are members of the larger policy-making body which directs the worldwide activities of Citibank and Citicorp.

The policy provides that the chairman of the Committee on Good Corporate Practice will consider the nature of the issue in question, then either retain jurisdiction or request a preliminary investigation and evaluation by the head of personnel. When the views of the employee have been fully explained and all relevant documents analyzed, the head of personnel may close the case, refer it to other jurisdictions such as the comptroller for additional review, or submit findings back to the Committee on Good Corporate Practice.

Depending on the degree of confidentiality requested or required, other senior officers and concerned parties may be consulted during a further investigation subject to specific time limits. For all issues brought to the attention of the committee, its chairman decides whether to accept prior recommendations, close the matter, investigate further, or convene the full committee. Once convened, the full committee reviews the matter and renders a decision that is communicated to all affected parties. The committee's responsibilities extend beyond particular cases, however. It meets regularly to reexamine existing policy, review conflict of interest questions, and formulate new policy, as appropriate. Each year it makes a full report to the board of directors.

Does It Do the Job?

A breakdown of the activites of the Staff Relations Unit in administering Citibank's interrelated programs from 1983 through 1985 provides the following picture:

Employee response mechanism	1983	1984	1985
1. Problem Review Board issues			
Termination	9	6	4
Discipline	1	3	—
Retirement	1	—	—
Job security	3	1	1
Transfer	—	1	—
Job reclassification	—	1	—
2. Benefits Appeal Board hearings	10	11	19
3. Work-related issues interventions	379	320	473
4. Personal problems (Employee Assistance Program)	869	900	850
5. Whistleblowing process	—	—	—

As for the *Problem Review Procedure*, most grievances are satisfactorily resolved by line management at the business levels, or in consultation with an employee relations specialist. Since the procedure is designed to support Citibank's line-driven organizational structure, it is the role of the employee relations specialist to work with the staff member and/or the line personnel officer to resolve a grievance before it escalates to the board level. Because Citibank is a highly decentralized organization, with personnel professionals sprinkled throughout the organization, referrals to the Board are not recorded and reported to corporate staff. Our personnel people earn their keep by resolving those local issues directly at the scene.

However, there are good indicators of the Problem Review Board's effectiveness as a "court of last resort." For example, the mere existence of review process serves as a deterrent to possible inequitable actions and as a spur to the resolution of issues at the lowest possible level and in the most expeditious manner.

More importantly, the Problem Review Board has established, by the nature of its decisions, a solid reputation as an equitable arbiter of disputes and an effective appeal mechanism. Between 1977 and August 1986, the board reviewed 72 cases. Thus far, every recommendation by a board has been accepted by the group or staff department head. One could leap to the conclusion that the boards are captive tools of management docilely handing down rubber-stamp decisions. On the contrary, boards have succeeded in reversing management decisions either in whole or in part. Without exception, board members have displayed an independent bent that allows them to vote based on their evaluation of the facts. Participation on the board is taken seriously and issues are argued fervently. As noted earlier, not all board votes are unanimous, and disparities are communicated in the board's recommendation to the senior line manager.

Because the procedure has produced equitable results supported by management, it has gained increasing credibility with the staff. Evidence of this can be found in a case load that is expanding both in type and in quantity. Before its revision in 1977, the procedure was limited almost exclusively to discharge cases. While these cases, for obvious reasons, continue to predominate, the board created by the revision has been exposed to a much broader range of issues.

In terms of number of cases, in 1977, only two cases reached the Review Board level, followed by an increase to eight in 1978. During 1979 we saw the number reach nine cases.

Since 1980, there have been an additional 53 cases, heard by the board, suggesting that the process is well entrenched in the Citibank milieu.

The success of the *Problem Review Procedure* and related dispute resolution mechanisms within Citibank can be attributed in large measure to the commitment by the bank's senior management to the objective resolution of issues through a system that ensures due process.

While the mechanisms do not always resolve issues to an employee's satisfaction, they provide an effective forum for the problems to be heard, and the issues raised by them to be considered. As Citibank President William I. Spencer noted in this 1980 speech: "We are under no illusion that any of our programs, or all of them combined, will eliminate employee dissent. An employee, who has used all these available procedures to get a fair hearing, and a decision from the Committee on Good Corporate Practice, may still go public with a complaint. That is the real world. So long as the issue is disputed in good faith by all parties, we have no complaint."

The availability of the *Problem Review Procedure* punctuates the operating philosophy enunciated in *The Citicorp Approach* and personifies the organization's commitment to the staff. Citibank management has always adhered to the belief that people make the difference in the success of a business. Having accepted this premise, the creation and preservation of a total work environment that allows individuals to perform at the highest level is a never-ending organizational quest. Although the *Problem Review Procedure* is no panacea, it is an important element in the achievement of that goal.

The *Formal Complaint and Appeal Procedure* at Michael Reese Hospital and Medical Center

*Jerry Sideman**

Michael Reese Hospital and Medical Center is a large urban teaching hospital located in Chicago, Illinois. With 1,000 beds, Michael Reese is one of the largest private medical centers in the United States. Patients are serviced by a professional staff that includes more than 700 full-time practicing physicians, dentists, and research scientists; 300 interns, residents, and fellows; and 1,300 nursing personnel. The total number of full-time employees is 3,800. Approximately 1,100 of these employees are covered by five collective bargaining agreements, which include grievance procedures culminating in binding arbitration. Bargaining units have been in existence since 1968.

Approximately 70 percent of the work force is female, 60 percent is black and other minorities, and 40 percent is over age 40. These are not startling statistics for this industry, for an inner city location, and for an institution that has been in existence for as long as Michael Reese. The Medical Center has a federally approved Affirmative Action Program.

In addition to direct patient care activities, Michael Reese is a major research center and has made several contributions to medical science and the health care industry, including invention of the modern incubator, development of the first nuclear accelerator designed for cancer therapy, discovery of the principal mechanism of insulin action, development of a vaccine to combat all three strains of polio, major advances in the treatment and understanding of arteriosclerosis and cardiovascular disorder, and development of the first successful artificial shoulder joint.

*Director, Employee Relations, Chicago, Illinois.

Origin

The *Formal Complaint and Appeal Procedure* was adopted at Michael Reese in July 1978. Its development occurred during the formalizing of institutionwide personnel policies and the publishing of the Medical Center's *Personnel Policy Manual*. Also the Medical Center had recently received federal approval of its Affirmative Action Plan, which included commitments for establishing internal resolution mechanisms of discrimination disputes. Several other communication programs were established during this period, including a job-posting/bidding procedure for nonunion hourly employees and development of the first performance evaluation system for all hourly Medical Center employees.

The establishment of the *Formal Complaint and Appeal Procedure* represented both faith in the development of supervisory staff to implement personnel policies correctly and equitably, and a commitment to employees of prompt, orderly consideration and definitive action at an appropriate management level concerning a complaint regarding terms and conditions of employment.

Also, immediately prior to development of this procedure, the Medical Center experienced a long organizing drive which resulted in approximately 350 clerical employees (one half of the clerical work force) being represented for collective bargaining under the relatively new Health Care Amendments to the National Labor Relations Act. Much of the union's appeal (and most of its literature) related to those elements of due process afforded to Michael Reese employees in bargaining units but not provided for nonunion employees. With several other large employee groups who are not organized who could potentially compose one or more bargaining units, the Medical Center chose to establish a formal due process mechanism for all Medical Center employees.

How the Procedure Works

The procedure has been designed to gain employee confidence that this procedure may be used to obtain prompt, objective consideration of a complaint and to gain redress, when appropriate, without jeopardizing personal dignity or employment security. Incorporated into the procedure are assurances of freedom from fear of retaliation in any form, availability of staff personnel to aid and advise, the opportunity to appeal unfavorable decisions to progressively higher levels of operating management, prompt consideration and decision making at each stage of the procedure, and

finally a review by an impartial outside arbitrator, whose decision
is advisory to the President of the Medical Center who makes the
final decision.

The procedure may be used by any nonprobationary permanent full-time or part-time employee. Employees who are members of recognized collective bargaining units are covered under
grievance procedures outlined in their agreements. A "complaint,"
eligible for review under this procedure, is defined as:

> any difference of opinion between an employee and a higher level
> of Medical Center authority regarding the interpretation and/or ap-
> plication of personnel policy or unambiguous past practice as related
> to the employees wages, hours, benefits, or other terms and con-
> ditions of the employment, or regarding any disciplinary action taken
> against an employee.

Employees are encouraged to first discuss any concern they
have with their immediate supervisor prior to initiating a formal
complaint. However, if this is not successful, a complaint may be
submitted in writing on a form designated for this purpose. The
steps of the review process, once a formal complaint is filed, are
as follows:

- Step 1: Written complaint to immediate supervisor;
- Step 2: Appeal to department head;
- Step 3: Appeal to Vice President, Human Resources; and
- Step 4: Appeal to advisory arbitration.

All complaint/appeals are to be presented in the sequence
indicated, except that suspensions or discharge appeals and charges
of discrimination are taken immediately to Step 3. A written response is provided to the employee at each step.

An employee initiating a formal complaint or pursuing an appeal may be assisted, accompanied, and/or represented in preparation and/or formal presentation by one other Medical Center
employee selected by the complainant. Attorneys are not permitted. Both employees receive full base pay for reasonable and approved absence from regularly scheduled work if it is necessary to
permit an effective presentation.

To ensure a prompt and orderly review process an employee
must initiate a complaint at Step 1, the immediate supervisor,
within 30 calendar days from the date in which the cause of the
complaint occurred or the date the cause should have been known
to the employee, which ever occurs later. If the complaint concerns
any type of disciplinary action, the complaint is to be submitted
within seven calendar days. Once a complaint is filed, specific time

limits are established for processing the complaint at each step and appealing the decision to the next step. These time limits are as follows:

TIME LIMITATIONS:

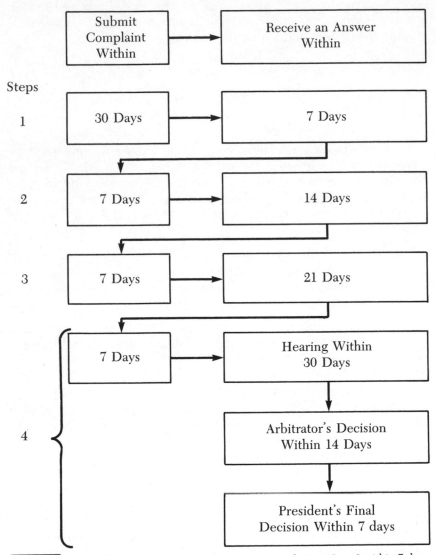

| Submit Complaint Within | Receive an Answer Within |

Steps

1 | 30 Days → 7 Days

2 | 7 Days → 14 Days

3 | 7 Days → 21 Days

4 | 7 Days → Hearing Within 30 Days → Arbitrator's Decision Within 14 Days → President's Final Decision Within 7 days

Note: If complaint concerns oral or written warning, submit at Step 1 within 7 days. If complaint concerns suspension or involuntary termination, submit at Step 3 within 7 days.

The *Formal Complaint and Appeal Procedure* is communicated to all new employees at employee orientation and periodically to all current employees through a brochure that describes the procedure, outlines time limits, and provides referrals if questions exist. On a day-to-day basis, the procedure requires that a supervisor advise an employee of the right to pursue a formal complaint if the employee continues to express dissatisfaction with an action of management.

Advisory Arbitration

Complaints that are not resolved through the first three steps may be appealed to external advisory arbitration. At this step (Step 4), a permanent arbitrator, selected by the Medical Center, makes advisory rulings to the President of the Medical Center. The arbitrator is a professional arbitrator, a member of the Federal Mediation and Conciliation Service arbitration panel, and is experienced in internal nonunion grievance arbitration mechanisms. He recognizes the Medical Center's interest in maintaining the concept and the perception of fairness by employee and line managers. The President has the authority to either accept, modify, or reject the advisory arbitrator's recommendation. The employee shares the cost of the arbitration process by paying 10 percent of the overall cost. The Medical Center pays the remainder. The employee's share is averaging $45.00 per arbitration.

There may be some who see this aspect as a potential weakness in the system, since the Medical Center is not bound by the arbitrator's decision. However, it is not believed that it is. Of the 52 complaints heard at Advisory Arbitration since 1978, the President of the Medical Center has accepted the advisory decision on each occasion. Understandably with this history, there has never been criticism of this feature or pressure to alter the procedure. This could well change if the arbitrator's decision is not accepted. The option therefore is carefully considered by top management.

In developing a complaint-resolving mechanism for nonunion employees at Michael Reese, it became clear that a procedure modeled after, but not necessarily identical to, the standard union grievance procedure would be desirable. One-third of the Medical Center work force is covered by labor contracts and grievance and arbitration procedures. A substantial portion of the nonunion employees at Michael Reese work in areas where unionization has expanded in the hospital industry, for example, nurses, licensed practical nurses, technicians, and clerical employees. Therefore, a complaint resolution system for nonunion employees modeled after a union grievance and arbitration procedure has been perceived as fair by employees, line managers, and top management. *And*, anything other than this, given the environment at Michael Reese, could well be perceived as *less* and therefore *unfair*.

With today's more independent, more educated work force, complaints are not always easily resolved. Many employee complaints just cannot be resolved, it seems, without the employee obtaining "a second opinion" from someone other than their immediate line manager. This sometimes can be the Vice President, Human Resources, at Step 3 of the procedure. If not, it is often the advisory arbitrator. For many obvious reasons, it is more desirable to provide this "second opinion" in a less structured review procedure than having the Equal Employment Opportunity Commission or the courts in this role.

Under this procedure using an external arbitrator, the employee has reason to believe that there will be an objective review of an adverse personnel action without the need to claim "protected status" or "wrongful discharge" (in cases of discharge).

From the standpoint of line management, use of an external professional arbitrator places management in a position of proving its case based on facts rather than relying on political or personal persuasion which often occurs in the review of line decisions by senior management. This has given decision-making authority at early steps greater importance and credibility.

Nature of Step 3 and Step 4 Meetings

Although the *Formal Complaint and Appeal Procedure* parallels the union grievance and arbitration model, there is a significant difference in the nature of Step 3 and arbitration meetings.

At the Step 3 meeting, emphasis is placed on fact-finding. In a union procedure, a union representative usually presents the grievance at this stage. Because of the adversary nature of this procedure, the union representative presents the information that he or she believes will be most persuasive and withholds information that is not helpful or detrimental to the case. Management often does the same, relying on the other side to discover and emphasize weaknesses.

However, under the Medical Center's *Formal Complaint and Appeal Procedure*, the Vice President, Human Resources, plays a more active role in ensuring that all relevant facts are presented. Since the employee does not have experienced assistance, what might be cross-examination of management witnesses is conducted by the Vice President. Through a thorough questioning of the employee, the employee's position can be more understandable and persuasive. A high premium is placed on fact-finding, at this stage, and less on eloquence, argumentation, or technicalities.

The meeting does not end without the employee being offered the opportunity to present additional information. The meetings average approximately two hours each, much of which entails general informal discussion designed to present the position of the parties in the most effective and efficient way possible.

This type of meeting can become uncomfortable at times for either line management representatives or the employee. However, at the conclusion, all parties generally agree that the facts are on the table. Employees and management realize that they have had a full hearing and the complaint has been given the closest scrutiny. Some issues are resolved before the hearing is concluded since each party has had an opportunity to consider more objectively the other party's arguments.

The Step 4 arbitration hearing is more formal and is structured more like a union arbitration proceeding. It includes formal agreement on the issue before the arbitrator, opening statements by each party, presentation of direct testimony by witnesses, formal presentation and marking of exhibits, and closing statements.

Not unlike the Step 3 meeting, the arbitrator tries to ensure that all facts relevant to the case are presented.

- The employee who is inarticulate is drawn out by the arbitrator through questioning to gain full participation.
- A particularly belligerent employee is steered in the proper direction through questions relevant to the specific issue.
- Management's witnesses are questioned by the arbitrator to clarify testimony and to complete discussion on the subject. Although done always with decorum and respect for the witness, the impact of the arbitrator can be as devastating to a weak case as probing cross-examination by a skilled union attorney.

The technicalities of the procedure, rules of evidence, or other trappings take a back seat to the full and complete testimony of the complainant and other witnesses.

TABLE 1.   SUBJECT OF CHARGES OF DISCRIMINATION

Year	Charges	Dis-charge	Disci-pline	Promo-tion	Retalia-tion	Harass-ment	Employee	Condi-tions	Resig-nation	Transfer	Salary	Demo-tion	Job Class	Retire-ment
1985	37	26	6	0	0	0	1	2	0	0	0	0	2	0
1984	31	20	3	4	0	0	0	1	0	0	0	1	0	2
1983	38	14	0	13	2	0	0	8	0	0	0	0	1	0
1982	19	11	2	0	1	0	5	0	0	0	0	0	0	0
1981	14	8	0	2	0	2	2	0	0	0	0	0	0	0
1980	20	6	0	5	0	2	2	0	0	2	3	0	0	0
1979	15	9	2	2	2	0	0	0	0	0	0	0	0	0
1978	13	11	0	1	1	0	0	0	0	0	0	0	0	0
1977	18	7	2	4	0	0	0	1	2	2	0	0	0	0
1976	39	13	3	7	0	1	11	0	0	2	0	2	0	0
1975	43	17	7	11	0	2	4	0	0	2	0	0	0	0
Total	287	142	25	49	6	7	25	12	2	8	3	3	3	2
		49%	9%	17%	2%	2%	9%	4%	1%	3%	1%	1%	1%	1%

The procedure is intended to provide a fair and effective review mechanism for employees wishing to challenge management actions. The decision at any step, including arbitration, is not intended to be based on the skill or experience in using the procedure, or on technicalities. This is an internal procedure and it is not intended that the determination of a management action as being either right or wrong be influenced by a complex procedure or by stringent rules of evidence beyond those minimally required to have an orderly process.

The meeting is conducted with the line managers and employee seeing each other as respected advocates for their respective positions. The way the arbitrator conducts both the hearing and himself is an important factor in maintaining this perspective.

Since the procedure was established in 1978, 320 complaints have been filed. Of these, 192 complaints have been addressed at Step 3. At Step 3, approximately 22 percent of the complaints have been sustained in whole or in part. Of the complaints denied at Step 3, 53 have been pursued to advisory arbitration. At this step, approximately 40 percent of the complaints have been sustained in whole or in part. In general, complaints have been filed by various employee groups in proportion to their representation in the work force. (See Table 1 above.)

Although the Michael Reese *Formal Complaint and Appeal Procedure* may not address all concerns relating to an effective dispute resolution mechanism, it is working effectively at Michael Reese. Changes have not been made, nor are any planned. The current system is achieving its desired result—it has gained the confidence of employees and line supervisors as a mechanism to obtain a prompt and objective review of a complaint and to gain redress, when appropriate, in a professional manner.

The Grievance and Arbitration System for Nonunion Employees at Northrop Corporation

*Lawrence Littrell**

Northrop: The Company and Its Business

On March 7, 1939, John K. Northrop and five colleagues joined together in Hawthorne, California, to create Northrop Aircraft, Inc. Their objective was to apply new technology in innovative ways to design and build better airplanes.

This sound concept, applied across an expanding range of technologies for a growing number of customers in the United States and abroad, helped mold the Northrop Corporation of today, a worldwide community of more than 40,000 skilled men and women. A diversified advanced technology company, Northrop operates primarily in the fields of aircraft, electronics, and technical and support services. Worldwide operations, which extend into more than 70 countries, are directed from corporate headquarters in Los Angeles, California. Sales in 1984 were slightly over $3.6 billion.

The company consists of two major operating units—the Aircraft Group and the Electronics Systems Group. Overall, the company has 15,267 production workers, 5,784 clerical and office workers, 15,550 workers in professional and sales positions, and 5,424 managers and executives. In equal employment opportunity categories, the percentages of minorities and women in these sectors are:

Work Force	Minorities	Women
Officials and managers	14.9%	13.2%
Professionals	25.04	21.3
Production workers	34.9	26.02
Office and clerical	31.12	77.5

*Corporate Director, Industrial Relations, Los Angeles, California.

Out of a total employment force of 42,025 in March 1985, 3,170 employees are represented by unions, primarily in production and maintenance work. This representation is divided among the Auto Workers, Teamsters, Machinists, Brotherhood of Electrical Workers, and an independent employee association.

The credo of Northrop appears on the opening page of the handbook that welcomes new employees. Over the signatures of our Chairman and Chief Executive Officer, Thomas V. Jones, and our President, Frank W. Lynch, we explain that the company stands for "challenging work, fair treatment of every employee, and respect for the dignity of the individual." This 64-page handbook not only describes the company, employee services, pay and benefits, the seniority system, performance reviews, and promotions and transfers but it also spells out attendance requirements, a detailed code of standards of conduct and progressive discipline, and general personnel and security practices. The final section of the handbook describes our *Grievance Procedure*, the oldest system of any American company providing arbitration as a final option for its nonunion employees.

We take the promise of individual fair treatment very seriously. It has been our philosophy since Jack Northrop founded the company and, despite the legal hazards it may pose today, it continues to be our policy. We expect that employees who have successfully passed their probationary period will be discharged only for good cause; that discipline short of discharge will be progressive, corrective, and fairly applied; and that employees will be properly classified and compensated. For hourly and salaried employees who feel they have not been treated in accordance with those company policies, we provide a formal grievance procedure through which they can seek redress.

The Evolution of Northrop's Grievance System: From Open Door to Formal Mechanism

In its earliest days, just prior to World War II, Northrop Aircraft, Inc., consisted of a small group of engineers and technicians headed by our founder John K. Northrop, who were dedicated to the development of aircraft of advanced design. Jack knew everyone and everyone knew him. He was immediately available to solve problems as they arose whether they involved an aircraft design, a policy dispute, or a personnel matter.

As the company's production activities grew during World War II, a personnel department was added to handle employment, draft deferments, recreation, Bond drives, war-time wage controls, and incidentally the day-to-day personnel problems that arose. Throughout this explosive growth, Jack Northrop made every effort to maintain the close relationship with the personnel that he had enjoyed in those early days and he was extraordinarily successful. He knew more Norcrafters by their first name than anyone else in the plant. His door was always open, and more important, people walked through it. It become common knowledge that if you could not get a problem resolved elsewhere, you could go to Jack and it would get fixed. So naturally the load got heavier. Many times the problems Jack handled dealt with employee discipline, and most often he would see to it that nothing really bad happened to anyone— he was that kind of person. However, some people who got favorable decisions from Jack Northrop really did not deserve his help, and others who did would not go or could not get to him in time. Inconsistencies grew, along with demands on his time, and it became apparent that a better way of handling personnel complaints and problems was needed.

Recognizing this need, Roger McGuire, a manager in what by then had become the Industrial Relations Department, proposed in 1946 that the company adopt a formal grievance procedure with arbitration as its final step. To suggest that a nonunion company adopt a formal grievance procedure was unprecedented at that time, and to propose that management expose its theretofore unilateral personnel decisions to the scrutiny of an outsider for validation or rejection was nothing short of revolutionary. To compound this madness, the procedure was to be made available not just to the production and maintenance personnel but also to all nonsupervisory employees, hourly and salaried alike.

For a nonunion company to take such a step required both sensitivity and courage: a sensitivity to the needs and desires of the people of Northrop and to the company's management climate at that time, and the courage to open up important internal judgments to outside decision makers.

In the usual case, the adoption of a grievance procedure with arbitration requires neither sensitivity nor courage, but merely a desire to obtain a no-strike clause in a union contract. In Northrop's case, the only negotiations were within the management structure of the company, and I am sure they were intense. The final result, however, was that Northrop became—we believe—the first non-union manufacturing company to adopt a formal grievance machinery for both hourly and salaried personnel which terminates in final and binding arbitration.

Now, lest I appear to be "the complete Northrop chauvinist" or extremely naive, let it be noted that our sensitive and courageous predecessors in management had had their sensitivity heightened and their courage bolstered by two union elections in 1945. While the employees chose not to be represented (the first time by an uncomfortably slim margin), it became clear that even though the company provided wages, hours, and working conditions as good or better than others in our industry, a significant gap existed in our procedure for conflict resolution, which required a new approach.

The grievance procedure adopted in 1946 is essentially the same as the one we have today and closely parallels the 4-step procedures found in many union contracts. It addresses not only the concerns of the employee who feels he has been unfairly terminated, but many other work-related problems. Our employee handbook, *Working with Northrop*, provides that nonsupervisory employees may file a grievance "when they feel they have not been treated in accordance with company policy." In actual practice, this language is interpreted quite broadly, and anyone with a real work-related complaint will get access to the grievance procedure.

The first step of the procedure, which must be taken within five working days of the event which precipitated the grievance, is an informal discussion between the employee and his immediate supervisor. Quite often, this step is initiated upon the counsel of an Employee Relations Representative to whom the employee has come with a problem or complaint. Most grievances are settled at this point and that is the goal of the procedure—to resolve problems at the earliest stage and within the organization in which the employee works.

If, after presenting his problem to his supervisor, often with the assistance of the Employee Relations Representative, the employee is not satisfied with the result, he or she (and with increasing frequency, she) may take the second step in the procedure by filing a written Grievance Notice. The Employee Relations Representative will assist the employee in writing the grievance and will then conduct a more formal investigation to ensure that all the facts are known and that the underlying problems which may have led to the stated grievance are discovered, if possible.

The Employee Relations Representative then acquaints the appropriate higher level of management, called the Administrative Officer, with the grievance and the discovered facts relating to it. The Administrative Officer may then make a decision or may call for a conference with the grievant, the supervisor involved, and the Employee Relations Representative, in an effort to resolve the grievance. In any event, the Administrative Officer must, within 10 working days after receiving the grievance, render a written decision.

If the Administrative Officer's decision is unacceptable to the grievant, the decision may be appealed within five days to the third step in the procedure—the Management Appeals Committee. This committee consists of the Division Vice President responsible for the organization in which the employee works; the Division Vice President of Human Resources; and the Corporate Vice President of Industrial Relations or his designee, selected by him from a panel of Corporate Directors and Vice Presidents of Human Resources from other divisions.

To assist the committee at the hearing and in its deliberations, the Employee Relations Representative prepares a folder for each member of the committee. The folder contains the Grievance Notice, the Administrative Officer's Decision, and the Grievance Appeal. It also contains a statement of the facts as determined by the Employee Relations Representative, the stated positions of the grievant and the management, an analysis of the case, and copies of any record or other documentation which bears upon the case.

On an appointed date, the committee meets with the grievant and the Employee Relations Representative. The facts are reviewed and the employee tells his side of the story. The employee may support his position by calling witnesses, if he chooses to do so. The immediate supervisor and any other management or staff employees who can add to a full understanding of the problem give the committee their views of what "really" happened.

This hearing with the Management Appeals Committee is conducted informally. The process is again one of fact finding, and the members of the committee participate directly by careful and thorough questioning of each witness. If need be, a hearing will be continued to develop additional facts or meet with necessary but unavailable witnesses. At the conclusion of the hearing, the committee members discuss and evaluate the evidence presented and reach a decision—often unanimous; occasionally two to one. This decision is then prepared by the Employee Relations Representative, reviewed by the committee members and, when acceptable to them, signed. Within two weeks of the hearing, the written decision is delivered to the aggrieved employee.

If, despite this application of collective wisdom by the members of the Management Appeals Committee, the employee's grievance is still not resolved to his or her satisfaction, it may be appealed to the fourth and final step of the procedure—final and binding arbitration.

The question of who shall arbitrate the grievance is decided by mutual agreement between the grievant and the company, represented by an Employee Relations Manager. If mutual agreement cannot be reached—this seldom occurs—a list of five qualified arbitrators is obtained from an appropriate source such as the State Conciliation Service. (The Federal Mediation and Conciliation Service has declined to provide lists to us for the past few years on the grounds that their charter limits their services to disputes arising between companies and their certified bargaining representatives.) The final selection is made by each party alternately striking names until only that of the selected arbitrator remains.

After agreement is reached, the selected arbitrator is contacted and a date set for the hearing. This alone has become something of a problem. The popularity of certain experienced arbitrators either makes them practically unavailable, in which case the selection process must be repeated, or, the date must be set weeks or sometimes months after the decision to arbitrate has been reached. As a result, we frequently select less well known arbitrators.

At this point, it should be noted that it is rare for the company to allow a case to go to arbitration unless it is convinced that its position is supportable, both on the facts and in its equitable aspect. All other cases are resolved at one of the earlier steps of the procedure. We are not always correct in this evaluation, however, because arbitrators do from time to time make decisions that favor Northrop grievants. Despite this, I have maintained that the company has never "lost" an arbitration case. The lessons learned are almost always worth the cost incurred. Arbitration keeps a dear school, but antediluvian supervisors will learn in no other—with apologies to Poor Richard and Dr. Franklin.

In the arbitration hearing, the company is represented by an Employee Relations Manager experienced in arbitration and familiar with the case. The employee may represent himself or may elect to be represented by counsel of his own choosing. If so, that is an expense that the grievant must bear. All other costs of arbitration and the grievance procedure preceding it are borne by Northrop, including the pay of all employee witnesses and that of the grievant (if he is still an employee) during the processing of the grievance.

Until a few years ago, the grievant could not ask for and have the Employee Relations Representative represent him or her in the arbitration. This limitation became of great concern to us. Throughout the processing of the grievance, up to the point of arbitration, the grieving employee has been counseled by an Employee Relations Representative who, by the time the grievance reaches arbitration, probably knows more about the case than the grievant himself. However, the grievant could not avail himself of this expertise in the arbitration, but was required, at that point, to seek his own paid counsel or represent himself against an expert.

The company's Employee Relations Managers felt that this was a weakness in the system which was manifested in a number of ways. Where the employee represents himself, lack of knowledge of the procedure often unduly delays the proceedings; the imbalance in the experience and skill of the grievant in relation to that of an employee relations professional forces the arbitrator to take a more active role than he might otherwise do; the arbitrator, if he feels that the contest is uneven, may unconsciously give the grievant the benefit of more doubts than the grievant is really entitled to; and finally, as in one case, an arbitrator may even refuse to render a decision due to the lack of advisory counsel.

To remedy this, a new policy was adopted in 1983. In addition to obtaining paid outside counsel or representing himself or herself, the employee is permitted to choose as counsel the Employee Relations Representative who has helped the grievant through the earlier steps of the procedure, or can choose a member of the Employee Relations staff of a division other than the grievant's own. If this option is exercised, the division in which the case arose will transfer funds to the division in which the selected counsel works to cover the preparation and hearing time. Knowing our Employee Relations people as I do, and based on experiences so far, this gives the grievant a real advocate working in his or her behalf.

As noted earlier, the arbitrator's fee and expenses are paid by the company. This particular feature of our plan has been criticized by some knowledgeable experts who seem to feel that, consciously or unconsciously, the arbitrator might be biased in favor of the party paying the bill. This has not been our experience and perhaps reflects a lack of faith on the part of the critics in the professionalism of the community of arbitrators. Be that as it may, we bear the cost of the arbitration for the practical reason that most of the employees who seek arbitration of their grievances could not afford it if we did not. We find that when we deserve to win, we usually do, and when we do not, we lose. But win or lose the existence of the final arbitration by an independent professional arbitrator demonstrates our intention to be fair to our employees, and to provide a system of due process which we believe validates that intention.

The Northrop System in Operation

To get a good feeling for the operations of the Northrop grievance system, we can look at its experience in the Aircraft Division in 1984. This is Northrop's largest operating unit, with about 14,000 employees. Its headquarters are in Hawthorne, California, and it designs and produces advanced military fighters, as well as portions of commercial aircraft.

In 1984, 145 written grievances were filed by employees in the Aircraft Division, or one grievance for every 96 employees. When the issues and frequency of these 145 complaints are broken down by type, it can be seen that the four largest categories are attendance (22 percent), substandard work (15.8 percent), classification (14.4 percent), and discrimination (8.2 percent).

Issue	Number	%
Attendance	32	22.0
Substandard work	23	15.8
Classification	21	14.4
Discrimination	12	8.2
Leaving workplace	7	4.8
Miscellaneous labor practices	7	4.8
Insubordination	6	4.1
Harmony and discord	5	3.4
Performance review	5	3.4
Loafing/sleeping	4	2.7
Safety violation	4	2.7
Drugs/alcohol	3	2.0
Overtime	3	2.0
Theft	3	2.0
Fighting	2	1.3
Horseplay	2	1.3
National origin	2	1.3
Negligence	2	1.3
Medical limitation	1	0.6
(Not in computer)	1	0.6
Total	145	100.0 (rounded)

The following five cases illustrate how the issues are framed and how grievances progress upward in the system. The first two illustrations are grievances in which management decisions were upheld, first in a case that reached the Management Appeals Committee (MAC) level, and the second a case that was taken by the grievant to arbitration.

Grievance that Reached MAC Level:

— First notice, excessive absenteeism, 8/25/82
— Second notice, unauthorized entry to premises, 4/11/83
— Final notice, substandard workmanship, 10/6/83
— Discharge, excessive absenteeism, 5/21/84

- Grievance filed 5/29/84, stating that grievant was undergoing personal as well as job-related stress which was causing him to drink heavily. Grievance requested a second chance and an opportunity to enroll in Employee Assistance Program.
- Denied at Administrative Officer level, 6/6/84.
- Appeal to MAC filed 6/20/84, stating that grievant had been denied opportunity for assistance program which was afforded other individuals. Grievant also contended that other employees with similar performance and attendance problems were not disciplined as severely as he was.
- Denied by MAC 7/18/84. Rationale included a check of discipline records of all employees in department; no disparate treatment evident. Additionally, grievant at no time mentioned a drinking problem prior to discharge, and in fact stated at the MAC hearing that he did not have a problem.

Grievance that Reached Arbitration Level:

— First notice, excessive absenteeism, 1/5/83
— Second notice, excessive absenteeism, 9/28/83
— First notice, substandard workmanship, 12/22/83
— Final notice, substandard workmanship, 1/18/84
— Discharge, substandard workmanship, 3/9/84

- Grievance filed 3/15/84, stating that grievant had been harassed by supervision and had been disciplined more severely than had others who committed the same infractions. Additionally, tools were claimed to be defective.

- Denied at Administrative Officer level, 3/29/84. Tools were checked out and found not to cause the hole elongations that resulted in grievant's discharge. Management had tried to work with grievant to correct problem; no results.
- Appeal to MAC filed 4/9/84. No new issues stated.
- Denied by MAC 5/15/84. Administrative Officer rationale reiterated and upheld.
- Appeal to arbitration filed 6/11/84. Hearing held 8/23/84. Discharge upheld. Arbitrator findings:

1. Evidence of poor workmanship well established.
2. Employee did not grieve any discipline other than discharge, therefore all prior discipline must be considered appropriate.
3. Progressive disciplinary policy was followed appropriately, leading to discharge as the only alternative.

The following two grievances in 1984 illustrate decisions that went in favor of the grievant. The first was decided at the Management Appeals Committee level, and the second in arbitration:

Decision in Favor of Grievant at MAC Level

Maria X was hired on March 27, 1978 as an Aircraft Installer Structures Trainee. She was promoted to an Aircraft Installer Structures on May 12, 1979, and to an Aircraft Assembler Structures on April 5, 1980. She held this classification at the time of her layoff on January 13, 1984. Maria X was eligible to be reviewed for the Aircraft Mechanic Bench classification between July and October 1981, but had active warning notices in her file at this time. She was therefore not promoted, but reclassified to an Aircraft Assembler Bench (same level job as Aircraft Assembler Structures) to better align her classification with her actual duty assignment. She continued to receive warning notices and was issued a final warning notice on August 11, 1983 for negligence. The performance reviews issued to Maria X generally indicated that her work was good, however.

Maria X claimed that she was not promoted to the A classification because she is Hispanic, and contends that she would not have been laid off had she held the higher classification. Management, on the other hand, maintained that Maria X's skill level and performance did not warrant her promotion and that she was properly laid off because she was appropriately classified as a B Mechanic.

— Step 1   Grievance Notice filed, 1/11/84
— Step 2   Administrative Officer denial, 1/24/84
— Step 3   Appeal to MAC, 1/30/84
— Step 4   MAC decision granted, 5/1/84

The MAC decision to reinstate Maria X and reclassify her to the A Mechanic included back pay retroactive to January 16, 1984. The committee based this decision on several factors. First, there was conflicting testimony from management as to whether or not they had ever recommended her for promotion. Secondly, she was advised that an evaluation would be conducted to determine if her skill level qualified her for the A position. This evaluation was found to be inconsistent with the gradual evaluation methods normally used in reclassification situations. There was also inconsistent testimony from management as to her promotability, and little documentation to indicate that her performance was not at a satisfactory level. The committee also felt that the final notice which Maria X received for negligence would have been more appropriately a first notice for substandard workmanship. Maria X was therefore reclassified and reinstated retroactive to January 16, 1984.

Decision in Favor of Grievant at Arbitration Level

Catherine B was hired on June 4, 1981 as a Standard Tool Store Worker and remained at this classification until her layoff on June 10, 1983. She contended that she had asked for and been denied a reclassification to the position of Standard Tool Store Attendant, and that she would not have been subject to layoff if she had been properly classified. Management, on the other hand, maintained that Catherine B was denied promotion due to her inability to perform at the higher classification. The poor performance level was, in management's opinion, a direct result of her excessive absenteeism. Catherine B claimed that her attendance was no worse than that of another employee who had recently been promoted.

Step 1   Grievance Notice filed, 6/9/83
Step 2   Administrative Officer denial, 6/20/83
Step 3   Appeal to Management Appeals Committee, 7/5/83

Step 4   Appeal to MAC denial, 9/29/83
Step 5   Appeal to arbitration, 9/30/83
Step 6   Arbitration decision, 1/16/84

The arbitrator ruled in favor of the grievant, awarding her the classification of Standard Tool Store Attendant, a recall from layoff, and back pay for the time spent on layoff. He based his decision on the fact that Catherine B was actually performing at the higher classification and had not been issued any discipline for her poor attendance. The arbitrator was careful to differentiate between a promotion and a reclassification, both as outlined in *Working With Northrop*. He concluded that good attendance/performance are necessary elements in the consideration of an employee for promotion, but a reclassification simply requires that the employee have the ability to do the higher level job. The fact that other employees with similar attendance records had been reclassified led the arbitrator to conclude that the company had acted arbitrarily in the case of Catherine B. She was therefore reinstated with full seniority.

The fifth and final example illustrates a compromise between the position of the grievant and management.

Decision of Compromise—Administrative Officer Level

Martin F was issued a final warning notice for threatening and intimidating his lead man while in the performance of his duties. A confrontation had occurred between Martin F and his lead man over the lead man's removal of Martin F's time card from the rack. Martin F had left the premises for a court appearance and had returned a few minutes later to find that his time card was missing. He confronted the lead man and a heated argument followed in which the lead man contends his life was threatened. Due to the fact that Martin F had been issued verbal warnings for previous confrontations with co-workers, his management felt that strong discipline was in order. Martin F had an active first warning notice for absenteeism in his file, and was thus issued the final due to the aggravated nature of this incident.

The Administrative Officer took into consideration Martin F's three years of service and previous history of substantially good performance in making his decision. He ruled that discipline was in order but felt that a final notice was overly harsh, so the final notice was reduced to a second notice. Martin F accepted this compromise and did not pursue his grievance to the MAC level.

Looking at the level at which written grievances were resolved in 1984 in the Aircraft Division, the following describes the outcomes:

Withdrawn by grievant	10
Settled at supervisor level	18
Settled at Administrative Officer level	36
Settled at MAC level	8
Decided at arbitration level	3
Appeal period expired, AO*	22
Appeal period expired, MAC**	3

*After an answer from the Administrative Officer, the Grievant chose not to proceed to the next step.
**Same as above, but after a Management Appeals Committee decision.

Finally, in terms of how the system renders decisions between grievants and management, the 1984 outcomes were as follows:

Withdrawn (13)

11 for management
1 for grievant
1 compromise

Settled at supervisor level (24)

2 for management
18 for grievant
4 compromise

Settled at Administrative Officer level (47)

10 for management
31 for grievant
6 compromise

Settled at MAC level (15)

2 for management
9 for grievant
4 compromise

Decided at arbitration (1)

1 for management

Appeal period expired, Administrative Officer (32)

31 for management
1 for grievant

Appeal period expired, MAC (4)

4 for management

I view those cases where the appeal period expired without further action on the part of the grievant as indicating a satisfactory conclusion to the grievance. However, in those cases where the grievance was denied by the Administrative Officer or the Management Appeals Committee, it would be difficult to say whether the *employee* was satisfied with the results, or merely felt that carrying it to the next step would be fruitless. I suspect that the latter is the case. However, the counseling that takes place at the various steps of the procedure must be considered as a valuable contribution to Employee Relations and if, in fact, the grievant has accepted the reasons for the decision, either by the Administrative Officer or the Management Appeals Committee, I would consider that to be thoroughly successful.

Conclusions About the Northrop System

The system of grievance handling and arbitration for nonunion employees now used by Northrop has been in effect for 39 years— and it works. Basically, it works because we want it to work and take pains to see that it does.

Our Employee Relations people are all degreed specialists with experience as industrial relations generalists. They are selected on the basis of their ability to communicate at all levels and to understand and apply Northrop's industrial relations philosophy in those many cases where the facts do not quite square with an established rule or policy. They serve the long-range goals of the company in maintaining fair and equitable treatment of employees by daily application of knowledge and mature judgment and I am very proud of them.

They serve as the counselor, shop steward, and business agent for the aggrieved employee. They are also the counselor and sometimes the conscience of management. They walk a thin line on a hard road and they do it very well. However, the thing that makes managers listen and employees believe is the existence of the grievance procedure and, most important, the potential that in any given case management's decision may be judged by an impartial arbitrator outside the influence of management.

I have come to believe that without final and binding arbitration, a system of internal grievance handling, whether it be a simple "open door" policy or a more formal system, runs great risk of losing credibility in the eyes of the employees.

A further and very practical benefit flows from a system which uses arbitration; it forces the establishment of written personnel policies, rules, and regulations which add certainty and consistency to the treatment of personnel.

Perhaps the most beneficial effect of such a grievance system is that it makes people think before they take actions that may result in a grievance. No system will ever substitute for good supervisory judgment, but it may help some supervisors to exercise it, knowing that sometime in the future an independent arbitrator may be asked to judge the propriety of the action taken.

This then is Northrop's way of providing due process in a nonunion industrial environment, and I recommend it for your consideration. I do not believe that it is the only way, but I do believe it has significant advantages over the creation of a new judicial or regulatory-agency bureaucracy to further reduce the nation's productivity by ensuring—without understanding—that every "i" is dotted and every "t" is crossed.

It has been suggested that a unique corporate culture or ethic is necessary for the success of our system, and this I will not argue. I do know that, to be successful, such a system must have the support of top management and at least the acceptance of every other level of management. It must be a formalized procedure designed to discover all of the facts important to the equitable resolution of the grievance and to reveal those facts to those who have authority to make decisions. And those decisions must be based on sound written policies and standards of conduct which have been effectively communicated to all personnel.

It also requires an organization of professional and experienced employee relations people who have the skill, independence, dedication, and support required to make it work.

Finally, such a system must have the confidence of the employees it seeks to serve, and ensure that their expectation of fair treatment will not be disappointed.

Arbitration for Employees at Life Savers*

Evan J. Spelfogel**
and
James J. O'Kane***

Introduction

The Squibb Corporation is a diversified pharmaceutical concern engaged, through subsidiaries, in the production and sale of professional products including ethical pharmaceuticals, household products, surgical instruments and sterilization monitoring systems, medical systems, consumer products and confections, and fragrance and cosmetic products. Health-care products are produced by wholly owned E.R. Squibb and Sons, Inc., and its subsidiaries. Fragrance and cosmetic products are made by a wholly owned subsidiary, Charles of the Ritz Group, Ltd. Confectionary products are manufactured by a wholly owned subsidiary, Life Savers, Inc.

Squibb, through its subsidiaries, owns or operates plants throughout the United States and in 30 foreign countries. It employs 27,000 people worldwide. Its consolidated sales in 1980 were approximately $1.7 billion. International operations accounted for approximately 43 percent of net sales and 34 percent of profit. The company's corporate headquarters are located in New York City, where it also maintains the headquarters of its Life Savers and Charles of the Ritz subsidiaries.

Life Savers operates plants in Holland, Michigan; Canajoharie and Port Chester, New York; Las Piedras, Puerto Rico; and in five foreign countries. It was incorporated in 1899 in New York as the Beechnut Packing Company and has continued since then (under

---

*Squibb closed the Port Chester, New York, facility of Life Savers in 1983, for business reasons. However, the experiences and successes of the fair procedure system at the plant warrant its inclusion in our profile series.
**Burns, Summit, Rovins, and Feldesman, New York, New York.
***Senior Vice President, Personnel, Life Savers, Inc., New York, New York.

various names) to manufacture Life Savers and Beechnut roll candies, Lollipops and mints, and Pine Brothers and Beechnut Cough Drops. More recently, it has manufactured Bubble Yum, Carefree Gum, Breath Savers, and Sweet Nothings candies and mints.

The Port Chester, New York, Life Savers plant, the original Life Savers factory, turned out Life Savers from 1919 until it closed in 1983. Its five-story stone and tile facility is a landmark on the edge of the Port Chester suburban community. The factory for years had been the village's largest private employer.

Many of the plants and facilities of the Squibb subsidiaries are unionized or have been so in the past. The Holland, Michigan, and Canajoharie, New York, Life Savers plants are presently unionized. The Port Chester plant, as described in more detail below, was unionized, and its 500 production and maintenance workers were represented by the Candy and Confectionary Workers, an AFL-CIO affiliate, until 1973.

Squibb and its subsidiaries are committed to the principle of social responsibility within the communities served by plant facilities and within the plants themselves. The company is in the forefront of programs designed to ensure equal opportunity for all employees. It recognizes that the company's future depends upon the continued effort, dedication, and creativity of the tens of thousands of its employees in whose hands the company's long-term future rests.

Background

From 1967 to 1973, the 500 production and maintenance workers at Life Savers' Port Chester facility were represented by the Candy and Confectionary Workers, and the employees had high hopes for this union when they elected it as their collective bargaining agent. After six years of experience with it, however, most of these employees came to regard the union as ineffectual. The union appeared to them to be unaggressive, both in pushing employee complaints through the 4-step grievance system provided for by the contract then in force (which included binding arbitration as a final step) and in achieving significant wage increases. By late 1972 there was a widely shared feeling among the Port Chester employees that their union was not doing its job. Employees wondered if the local had made some "sweetheart" deal with management. All around the plant employees could be heard asking, "What's the matter with our union? They're collecting our dues and initiation fees, and we're not getting anything for our money. The wage increases we're getting are token increases, and our battle is not being fought for us."

In early 1973, Local 91, an independent union in the New York City area, began an organizing drive at the Port Chester plant in an attempt to replace the Candy and Confectionary Workers as the bargaining agent for the employees. Under National Labor Relations Board (NLRB) rules, competing unions are allowed to run organizing campaigns like these at the end of the term of the incumbent union's contract. If the competing union gets 30 percent of the employees' signatures on authorization cards, the NLRB rules provide for an election at which the employees may vote for their incumbent union, the new union, or "neither."

When Local 91 got the requisite number of signed union-authorization cards in early 1973, management at the Port Chester facility was faced with a dilemma in dealing with the upcoming election. There was little quesiton that the incumbent union had not met employee expectations, and that it was likely to be voted out. At the same time, Local 91 was affiliated with organizations which had the reputation of being "crooked," and whose officials were involved in a variety of criminal proceedings. Life Savers management opposed Local 91's organizing effort, but it felt it could not support the incumbent union, both because it had lost credibility with the employees and to do so would appear to validate Local 91's allegation that the incumbent had a "sweetheart" deal with management.

Instead, Life Savers management opted to wage a vigorous campaign against both unions. In effect, management said that it could do a better job than either union in providing employees with a viable grievance system and adequate wage increases. "We can sympathize with you and appreciate your predicament," management told the employees at a preelection meeting. "The incumbent union did absolutely nothing for you. But don't go running away with Local 91 because you'll be repeating the same mistake. Give management a chance. Let's see what management can do without a union dictating to it."

When the election was held, the Candy and Confectionary Workers received only 10 votes out of the approximately 500 votes cast, a total repudiation of this union's performance at Port Chester. Local 91 received 245 votes. The "neither" line on the ballot received one vote more than the combined total of the two unions. By that slim margin, which was certified by the NLRB, the Port Chester Life Savers plant became a nonunion facility.

Until the 1973 election, management at the Port Chester Life Savers plant was fairly traditional. After the deunionization vote, however, the company was presented with an opportunity to experiment with innovative labor relations policies. Indeed, management became committed to such a course to fulfill the expectations of the majority of the plant's employees who had voted for deunionization. The responsibility for living up to that commitment fell to James O'Kane, Life Savers' vice president for labor and employment relations.

Following the 1973 election, O'Kane put into operation a set of policies that kept the salaries and benefits of the 500 production and maintenance employees at the Port Chester plant competitive, provided them with job security based on seniority, adopted much of the pre-1973 collective bargaining contract as the official *Handbook of Rules and Procedures* for the Port Chester facility, and established a grievance procedure for the nonunionized work force. As O'Kane put it, "We recognized that if we were more able to satisfy our employees and make them happy, the more productive they would become." These policies reduced turnover at the plant, enabled the company to hire and keep the best people, and helped it to remain competitive.

Before going on to a more detailed discussion of the grievance system at Port Chester since the deunionization vote, it should be pointed out that, since 1973, there were seven NLRB elections at the plant, involving three or four different unions. (Unlike 1973, however, each of these elections involved only one union at a time.) In each instance, the Port Chester employees voted against rejoining a union, every time by increasingly larger margins. Management's position at each of these elections was to say, "Look what we've done for you up to now. Give us the continuing opportunity to build on that." The employees voted for that option, but with the knowledge that any time management failed to live up to its commitment, a union was standing by ready to organize to fill the breach.

The Port Chester Grievance Procedure, 1973–1979

Establishing in-house grievance and complaint procedures for unorganized workers has become an important concept in modern employee relations. Usually, these in-house procedures provide for three or four steps through which an employee can take a complaint or unresolved problem to a company's highest echelons, often a vice president or even chairman of the board.

Following the 1973 election at the Port Chester plant, a grievance system based on this model was instituted. Under the first
step of the procedure, an employee could express his or her grievance to the immediate line supervisor. If the supervisor's response
was unsatisfactory, under Step 2 the employee could appeal to the
plant manager. If a satisfactory response was still not forthcoming,
the employee could reduce the grievance to writing and submit it
either to the vice president for manufacturing or the vice president
for personnel at the corporation's New York City headquarters.

This grievance system essentially was a continuation of the
system in place under the 1967–1973 collective bargaining agreement, without the fourth step of that procedure, which called for
binding arbitration. The scope of the post-1973 procedure was left
quite broad. Under the 1967–1973 agreement, the scope of griev-
able issues was defined as "any dispute, question, or controversy
involving interpretation or application of any term of the collective
bargaining agreement." After the deunionization election, this was
modified to include "any term or condition in the employee handbook," which, as mentioned previously, incorporated most of the
essential points of the 1967–1973 contract.

The important difference in the new procedure was that the
individual employee controlled how far a grievance would be pursued. Under the old agreement, and indeed under virtually all
such contracts, access to grievance machinery is a prerogative of
the union. While individual employees may initiate the grievance
process at Step 1, the decision to appeal the result is left to a
succession of union officers, usually a shop steward at Step 2 and
moving upwards in the union hierarchy as the grievance progresses.
The 1967–1973 incumbent union's failure to pursue most grievances was one of the principal reasons that it lost the 1973 election
so overwhelmingly.

After several years' experience with the new grievance procedure, however, it became apparent that this system was not
working as well as management had hoped. O'Kane found that the
procedure "wasn't receiving enough complaints," and came to believe that this reflected either that employees were fearful of complaining or were being discouraged from appealing their complaints
to a higher level. Either way, employee complaints were being
suppressed and this was hampering productivity and employee job
satisfaction. Employees seemed to be reticent to write to headquarters, afraid that they would be labeled as troublemakers. Few
appealed to the Port Chester plant manager, either, reluctantly
resigning themselves to a "company decision" against them. The

number of complaints that were processed to higher levels was inconsistent with the nature of 500 people working together.

In 1975 an attempt was made to deal with this problem. The Port Chester employees attempted to establish their own independent plant committee to deal with management with respect to working conditions and grievances. That effort was aborted as a result of an unfair labor practice charge filed against the company by an outside union involved in one of the annual NLRB election campaigns. Without admitting any wrongdoing, the company agreed to withhold recognition from the employees' grievance committee until it was certified as the majority representative by the NLRB in a formal proceeding, something the employees were unwilling to do. Thus, although wages and benefits generally had been improving significantly over the years, employees still felt a lack of an adequate and fair method for addressing their grievances.

O'Kane recognized that it was far better to get these differences out in the open and resolve them quickly for everyone's sake, than to let them fester and develop into more significant problems. He believed that employees might be more comfortable and more encouraged to complain if they knew: (1) that an outside neutral party would be the final appeal step, and (2) that this neutral party's decision would be binding on all sides. So, with the backing of the company's labor attorney and the assistance of the American Arbitration Association (AAA), a unique procedure was developed providing for final binding arbitration of grievances at the company's expense for the Port Chester plant's workers.

Internal debate at the plant level and at the company's corporate headquarters over the proposed new grievance and arbitration mechanism was intense. Local plant management questioned the need and advisability of such a procedure. First-tier supervisors feared loss of control and loss of "face" if employees were routinely to take their grievances over their heads and, indeed, outside the plant. It was one thing, they pointed out, to communicate with corporate headquarters with respect to an unresolved plant grievance; it was wholly another matter, however, to go to a "neutral" who had no appreciation of the problems and peculiarities of the Port Chester plant. Plant management also pointed out that the creation of an outside arbitration procedure could be turned against the company by unions seeking to organize. They contended that it could provide a ready-made mechanism for diehard militant employees seeking to embarrass the company. O'Kane and other labor-relations professionals within the corporation also recognized that a union could use the arbitration machinery to conceal a slow-down or work stoppage and to obstruct production. And a union could appeal to employees as the proper party necessary for their representation at the arbitration hearings.

All of these considerations were debated at the highest level within the company. Despite the misgivings expressed by various sectors of management, the new arbitration plan was announced in April 1979.

The New Arbitration Procedure

Life Savers' revised grievance procedure gave the nonunion employees at the Port Chester plant the option of arbitration as the final step in the dispute resolution process. The arbitration, which is final and binding on both the employee and the company, was conducted by the AAA under its Expedited Labor Arbitration Rules—a streamlined process adopted by the AAA in 1971 designed to cut arbitration costs by scheduling and completing arbitrations promptly. The procedure had several essential elements:

- The company bore the total cost of the arbitration;
- The company appointed a representative, at no cost to the employee, to help present his or her case before the arbitrator;
- The company advised the AAA on a monthly basis of grievances to be submitted to arbitration; the AAA then appointed an arbitrator from its National Panel of Labor Arbitrators for Expedited Arbitration to conduct the hearing(s) in those cases;
- Hearings were scheduled for the second Wednesday of each month at the Port Chester plant or in the nearby vicinity;
- Employees did not lose pay for time spent in an arbitration hearing;
- In accordance with the AAA's Expedited Rules, no recordings or transcripts were made at the hearing and no briefs were filed;
- The arbitrator was to hand his decision down within five days of the close of the hearing;
- Finally, the decision was posted on the plant's bulletin board (unless the employee requested that it not be posted).

The new arbitration step supplemented the original three steps of the grievance procedure. The process after 1979 took the following progression:

Step 1: Within five days after an employee became aware of events giving rise to a grievance, the employee discussed the matter with the immediate supervisor, who was obligated to provide a verbal answer within two working days.

Step 2: If the employee was not satisfied, within two working days of receiving the supervisor's answer, the employee could request a grievance form, write out the grievance, and present it to the same supervisor, who would provide a written answer within two working days.

Step 3: If the supervisor's written answer did not resolve the problem, the employee could present the grievance to the plant personnel manager within two working days. After consultation with the plant manager, the personnel manager would provide the employee with a written answer representing the final management position, within three working days. If the personnel manager's decision was not satisfactory, the employee could within two weeks from receipt of the personnel manager's written decision, request an arbitration hearing on the matter.

Step 4 (Arbitration): The request for arbitration had to be in writing, signed by the employee on the form provided by the personnel office. It had to be delivered to the plant personnel office for processing. The request included the following information: employee's name, job classification and department, home address and telephone number, and whether or not the employee wished a company-supplied representative to help prepare and present the employee's case at the hearing. The form contained space for a brief description of the grievance. Employees were asked to enclose a copy of their original grievance and the written answers received from the supervisor and the personnel manager. The personnel office was available to assist employees in completing the grievance form and in compiling the necessary papers.

As noted previously, the arbitrator was appointed by the AAA and the hearing (except as expressly modified by the company's procedure) was held in accordance with its Expedited Labor Arbitration Rules. Copies of those rules were available in the company's personnel office and were also attached to an announcement of the new procedure which was distributed to all employees when the program was first implemented (and to new employees when they began their employment).

Upon receipt of a timely request for a hearing on a matter covered by the employee arbitration procedure (i.e., within the scope of the *Employee Handbook*), the personnel office would appoint a representative to help the employee prepare and present the case (if the employee so requested). Usually, this was done by the personnel manager suggesting to the grieving employee one of several people within the plant—generally middle management—whose skills, familiarity with the operations of the plant, and communications ability would be helpful to the employee in presenting his or her case at a hearing. The employee was under no obligation to choose one of the people suggested by the personnel office, however. Anyone employed within the plant, from top to bottom, could be selected, if amenable, to aid the grieving employee.

The personnel office compiled a list of timely requests for arbitration hearings during each calendar month and, on the last day of the month, sent the list to the AAA, together with copies of the employees' "request for arbitration hearing," original grievances, the company's written responses, and a copy of the *Employee Handbook*.

Requests for arbitration received between the first day of the month and that month's scheduled hearings were normally held over for the next month's hearing (unless all parties and the arbitrator agreed to move the case up for immediate hearing). The AAA notified all grievants and the company in writing, and the personnel office reconfirmed verbally with employees, the dates, approximate times and location of the hearings, and the name of the arbitrator appointed.

The arbitrator conducted hearings on the second Wednesday of each month (or next scheduled workday if the plant was closed the second Wednesday). Hearings were held at the plant, at the nearby White Plains, New York, office of the American Arbitration Association (or anywhere else in the Port Chester, Rye, White Plains, New York area the parties agreed on). To help expedite the proceedings, there were no recordings or transcripts made at the hearing and no briefs were filed afterwards. The arbitrator handed down the decision within 5 working days after the hearing, mailing copies to the employee's home and to the plant personnel manager. Copies were also posted on plant employee bulletin boards (unless the employee requested that the decision not be posted).

The company and the AAA agreed upon a $150 fee, which covered the appointment of a single arbitrator to hear and determine all requests for arbitration received during a given month, and all normal AAA processing and servicing incidental to them. The fee of the arbitrator appointed by the AAA for a given month's hearing was set at $200 for each day of actual hearings, regardless of the number of cases heard that day. The arbitrator was required to make every reasonable effort to complete hearings on all scheduled grievances in one day. There was no additional fee for time of the arbitrator spent "in consideration of the case" or "in writing the decision." The fees of the AAA as well as the fee and expenses of the arbitrator (e.g., travel, food and lodging, and stenography) were paid for entirely by the company.

The grievants could request from the personnel office that other Life Savers' employees testify at the hearing as witnesses. The company made very reasonable effort to grant such requests. Employees did not lose pay for regular time lost from work to prepare for or attend a hearing, either as the grieving party or as a witness for another employee (provided arrangements had been made in advance with the personnel office).

The arbitration procedure was available to employees in all cases of grievances involving discipline and discharge, benefits, job bidding, seniority rights, plant and safety rules, and the interpretation and application of all other provisions of the Life Savers *Employee Handbook*. Copies of the *Handbook* were available in the personnel office. In all other grievance situations (those not involving the interpretation or application of provisions of the *Employee Handbook*), employees were afforded the opportunity to appeal the personnel manager's third-step written decision to the company's vice president for confection operations at the company's New York City headquarters. Employees also had the option of electing to appeal to the vice president of confection operations instead of requesting arbitration in *Handbook* grievance cases.

The award of the arbitrator was final and binding upon the employee and upon the company, notice of which was printed on the form on which the employee requested arbitration. The form also provided that neither the employee nor the company would be represented at the hearing by an attorney, and that no person who was not an employee of the company (except the arbitrator) should be present at the hearing. Both the employee and the company signed this Request for Arbitration form.

Finally, in its agreement with the AAA, the company acknowledged that the AAA was not responsible for the acts or determinations of the arbitrator or for the legal enforcement of awards under the procedure.

Development of the Arbitration Procedure

There was substantial soul-searching concerning the kinds of disputes that should be subject to the grievance arbitration procedure when the process was established, and whether attorneys or other representatives should be permitted in the arbitration hearings. It was quickly decided to make the procedure applicable to the widest range of grievances possible. Only in this way would the "pressure safety valve" objective of instituting the procedure be met. As for the appearances of attorneys or outside representatives at the hearings, the original policy did not expressly negate the possibility.

In the midst of a union-organizing campaign, a prounion employee attempted to bring his union representative and attorney into an arbitration hearing. Company officials intitially refused entry. The AAA took the position that under its Expedited Labor Arbitration Rules, an employee had the right to be represented, absent an express negation of that right. Negotiations, discussion, and argument over the problem led to a compromise in that one instance, permitting the employee to have his private attorney represent him (but not the union representative or union attorney). At the same time, a written clarification of the procedure expressly barring attorneys or other nonemployees from hearings in the future was distributed to plant employees. The company and the AAA signed an amendment to their initial agreement excluding attorneys, notices were posted on employee bulletin boards covering the point, and the forms upon which employees requested arbitration were revised to reflect the clarification.

The decision to clarify the exclusion of attorneys and representatives was not an easy one. Employees often feel they are an inadequate match for the company, particularly in an "adversary" situation, like an arbitration hearing. Employee resistance, however, was countered by clarifying the role of the personnel office in the arbitration procedure and hearing.

The personnel office at the Port Chester plant—which consisted of only four people—did not take an adversarial position in an arbitration but rather made itself available to assist the grievant in compiling and presenting the necessary facts, materials, and other evidence to the arbitrator. Although the personnel manager sat in on the arbitration hearing, he did so only in the capacity of "master of ceremonies," explaining the facts of both sides to the arbitrator, but then leaving the defense of the company's position to the supervisor involved, who presented his or her own case without outside help. The personnel manager, moreover, had instructions to prompt an employee if he saw a good point that the employee has overlooked. Both the employee and the supervisor were to base their case on the company's *Handbook* or prior interpretations or modifications of the *Handbook*.

This accommodation appeared to have resolved the problem of potential disruption by outsiders and the possibility of labor organizations using the procedure for their own purposes. At the same time, it appeared to have satisfied employees that they would receive competent representation and a fair hearing.

Arbitration Cases Under the New Procedure

From the initiation of the arbitration procedure in September 1979 until 1983, arbitrators heard more than a dozen cases. In one case, an employee complained about a change in work assignment that reduced the employee's pay by 25 cents per hour. The supervisor had taken the position that he had the absolute right to reassign a maintenance employee to any job in any department for which the employee was qualified. He argued that within the maintenance group, employees were not assigned to a single area as they were in production. The employee argued, successfully, that the reassignment should have been based on seniority and that, alternatively, he should carry his higher rate of pay in the reassignment. The arbitrator ordered that the employee be reinstated to his former position and that a less senior employee be moved to the other area. The employee was awarded back pay.

In another case, an arbitrator upheld the method used by the company for calculation of two percentage pay increases which, by coincidence, occurred at the same time for the same employee. The employee argued that the company should have applied the second percentage increase to the amount resulting from the first increase. The company chose to calculate both percentage increases upon the employee's preincrease rate. The arbitrator upheld the company's method of calculating the pay increase.

Other cases that went to arbitration included interpretations of the company's bereavement-pay benefits and the company's bumping procedures. In addition, there were a half dozen cases concerning disciplinary matters. One arbitrator ordered the language of a written warning modified to reflect an absence without permission, but not insubordination. Another arbitrator sustained an oral rebuke, but directed that a written warning on the same matter be removed from an employee's personnel folder "in view of the employee's good employment record and unusual circumstances of the case."

Several of the cases which alleged improper discipline also challenged the discipline on the grounds of protected union activities; another involved an allegation of racial discrimination. All three of these cases went to outside regulatory agencies after a ruling unfavorable to the employees in arbitration. In each instance, the NLRB and the New York State Human Rights Agency gave great weight and deferred to the decision of the arbitrators in dismissing the actions, finding "no probable cause" for intervention by them. In one case, the NLRB expressly noted, "This is a case that the employee has taken through the grievance procedure for a fair hearing. The matter was determined by an impartial arbitrator, and there's no reason for us to proceed further on the matter."

The Benefits of the Procedure

A major result of the Port Chester plant's unique arbitration procedure—and the result most desired—was happier employees. Although this was one result, the best benefit from management's point of view—and one that was not anticipated—was that supervisors at the plant learned to make decisions affecting employees in a more rational, objective, and mature way. Supervisors realized they would have to defend their decisions before an arbitrator. Few were willing to put themselves in the position of being defeated. When supervisors disciplined employees, recommended promotions, or made job assignments, they thought the situation through and projected themselves into a possible arbitration. They asked themselves, "Could I handle any objections? Could I defend my decision according to company policy and practice?" In short, supervisors hesitated and made certain of their positions, rather than making emotional or arbitrary decisions that might not be defensible before an arbitrator.

The results were remarkable. Disciplinary problems were substantially reduced; the company was required to discipline fewer and fewer employees. The quality of supervision and plant morale continued to improve as supervisors acted more reasonably and more consistently in accordance with established, understood, and accepted company policy. Supervisors were less anxious to "shoot from the hip." The feeling at the plant was that supervisors were far more reasonable and slower to anger.

One indication of the improving climate and morale at the plant was reflected in the "annual" NLRB union elections. The company won these elections by greater margins in the last two years of the plant's operation than ever before.

Another important aspect of the arbitration procedure was its minimal cost. Even if hearings were held every month during a year (and this was not always the case), the monthly cost to the company for the AAA fee and the arbitrator's fees and expenses was approximately $400. Aside from the value of the time of employees and company management personnel, the actual cost of this valuable fringe benefit was only about $5,000 per year. Even if the arbitration procedure had cost double this amount, it would still have constituted one of the least expensive fringe benefits available.

This is not to say that the arbitration plan had not been a sore point for both management and some employees to a degree. As management anticipated when it began the plan, unions tried to turn the procedure to their advantage, and recalcitrant, militant, prounion employees attempted to disrupt production and to embarrass the company in the exercise of their rights under the procedure. In the most recent NLRB election, in fact, the provision that attorneys and outside representatives be excluded from arbitration hearings became the focal point of the union's organizing drive. One union flier said, "The company is giving you this big, fancy arbitration procedure, but what good is it to you if you can't have your representative present?" The company countered that argument by pointing out that its own attorneys were excluded from the hearings as well, and that in the hearing itself, the supervisor alone had responsibility to defend the action that led to the arbitration. The best measure of these attempts to use the arbitration procedure as an organizing tool was the last election, which the company won by a 70 percent vote, its biggest margin ever.

Despite the fact that supervisors considered their decisions concerning employees much more carefully and there was other objective evidence of the benefits of the procedure, some Port

Chester management, at the top level as well as the immediate supervisory level, continued to be less than enthusiastic about the plan. In this view, which was in the minority, the arbitration was just another impediment to management doing its job.

Nevertheless, the overall results far exceeded the hopes and expectations of O'Kane and corporate management at the outset. The pressure building up from unresolved, festering grievances was eased. Supervisors realized that first-line decisions on discipline and day-to-day operations could be subject to review by an outside arbitrator. Consequently they became far more objective, consistent, and reasonable. Employees armed with the weapon of an outside neutral appeal at no cost to themselves more readily accepted supervisory and managerial decisions. Communications between the rank and file and supervisory levels improved demonstrably. Morale—and productivity—were way up.

Conclusion

Of course, a good grievance and arbitration procedure is not the panacea for all plant problems. It is also not the answer for every company. Life Savers management had constantly and continuously reviewed wages, benefits, and working conditions. It constantly searched for ways to continue its policy of enlightened employer-employee relations. Wage rates at the Port Chester plan were *higher* than union rates; fringe benefits were *better* than union contract benefits. Once employees and supervisors alike knew that there was an outlet for employee feelings and frustrations, everyone was more willing to accept the decisions, assignments, and, where necessary, disciplinary actions of management.

Each company must tailor its procedures to its own needs. Arbitration will not work unless there is first a good employee communications base and strong promanagement feelings. Given the proper framework, however, such a procedure may provide a major breakthrough in peaceful and productive labor relations. Even though the Port Chester facility was closed in 1983 for business reasons, the success of the grievance and arbitration system there was clear.

The EEO Complaint System at Chicago and North Western Transportation Company

*Robert W. Russell**

Organizational Profile

The Chicago and North Western Transportation Company is the oldest of all railroads that were founded in Illinois. It was originally known as the Galena and Chicago Union Railroad, chartered in Illinois in 1836 for the purpose of building a railroad from Chicago to the lead mines of Galena in the northwestern corner of the state. It became operational in 1848 when the first train operated over the Galena and Chicago Union tracks from Chicago to a point approximately 10 miles west of the city. In subsequent years the line extended westward, not to Galena but across Iowa and Nebraska and north into Wisconsin, Minnesota, and the Dakotas.

In 1958, the North Western acquired the Litchfield and Madison railroad which gave it a direct link to St. Louis. In 1960 the railroad acquired the 1,500-mile Minneapolis and St. Louis Railway, which was followed in 1968 by the merger of the 1,500-mile Chicago Great Western Railroad. This merger gave the railroad access to Kansas City. On June 1, 1972, the railroad assets of the North Western were acquired by the Chicago and North Western Transportation Company, in which the employees were the stockholders. The approximately 4,000 employees who invested in stock in the new company established the largest employee-owned enterprise in the United States, and the first U.S. railroad ever to be owned by its employees.

Today, the railroad operates approximately 9,300 miles of road in 11 midwestern states. It is the only railroad in this region that directly serves every major midwestern railway interchange point,

*Senior Vice President, Administration, Chicago, Illinois.

called gateways—namely, Chicago, Peoria, St. Louis, Des Moines, Kansas City, Omaha, Council Bluffs, Sioux City, and Minneapolis-St. Paul, as well as major western ports on the Great Lakes.

The North Western is one of the nation's largest haulers of grain and grain products. The company also is a major carrier of coal, iron ore, paper and paper products, steel, manufactured items, cement, automobiles, and auto parts. To move these products safely and efficiently, the company has over 38,000 freight cars and 1,000 diesel locomotives to operate over 115 scheduled freight trains daily. In addition to the movement of products, the North Western operates the largest commuter railroad service in the Metropolitan Chicago area, carrying more than 100,000 riders daily on three lines. The company maintains sales offices in major cities throughout the United States and Canada.

To provide effective management, the North Western is organized into the following departments: Administration, Corporate Communications and Secretary, Executive, Finance and Accounting, Government, Quality Improvement and Materials, and Traffic. Each of these departments is under the supervision of a Senior Vice President.

Ninety percent of the approximately 12,000 employees are unionized and governed by the standard rules and grievance procedures used in the railroad industry. The majority, 65 percent, of employees are skilled or semiskilled workers, 18 percent are clericals, 7 percent are service workers, with managers, officials, professional, and sales workers combined representing 11 percent of the work force. The largest number of employees are found within the Chicago metropolitan area. Similarly, most minority and female employees work within Chicago locations or other facilities near metropolitan centers.

Origins of the Present EEO Complaint System

The present internal EEO complaint system was formally introduced on May 13, 1979. This system was preceded by a quite unstructured process which did not adequately produce either the statistical data needed to periodically evaluate the effectiveness of methods used or the follow-up measures necessary to ensure satisfactory long-term resolution of specific complaints.

Three very elementary factors suggested the usefulness of creating an internal EEO grievance process. First of all, top-level

management sincerely wanted to eliminate any type of discriminatory employment practice within the company and minimize the
involvement of governmental agencies. Management believed that
a significant number of employees who did file external complaints
would prefer to settle differences with the company internally, if
there were a viable, safe means for doing so. Secondly, having
historically been subject to governmental regulations and guidelines, top management was well aware of the excessive delays,
adversary relationships, and monetary losses which could result
from dealings with a frequently understaffed bureaucracy. There
was a similar concern that loyal employees would not want to
"publicly attack" the company by filing an outside complaint, in
that these individuals were likely to be long-term employees who
had or were willing to passively accept the "status quo." Management feared that their grievances and misunderstandings would
remain unheard and unresolved if there were no option other than
seeking relief through regulatory agencies. Management also felt
that this group of employees, because of their experience and job
knowledge, could greatly assist in the identification and correction
of subtle potential problems in the day-to-day work environment
which might otherwise remain unreported to management. Finally,
the company wanted to handle EEO complaints promptly, in contrast to the union appeal process which is very structured and can
require many months for final disposition. As the concept of equal
employment/affirmative action was still novel to many of our employees outside large metropolitan areas, it seemed necessary that
such claims be handled as rapidly as possible so employees could
see that the company was, indeed, serious about affirmative action
and equal employment.

The development and initiation of the system was the responsibility of the Manager of Equal Employment who reported
directly to the Vice President of Personnel. Once the rationale for
creating the system had been formalized and approved by the
Senior Vice President of Administration, the proposed procedures
were circulated to the Law and Labor Relations departments for
comments or identification of areas which could result in legal
problems or conflict with the various collective bargaining units.
This process began in the latter part of 1978 and was submitted to
the President for final approval in March 1979.

During the period between March and May 1979, discussions
were held with the division's Labor Relations and Personnel officers

to familiarize them with their role in the process. It was believed that these officers who were trained in both personnel and labor relations functions, and who had experience in the investigation of external EEO complaints, would be the most appropriate officers to become involved initially in a complaint. These officers also were likely to be viewed positively by employees since they were not normally a part of the supervisory command and may have been the first officer the employee encountered in the hiring process. This group of officers were additionally responsible for informing their management staffs of the internal procedure, and the company's expectation that management would adhere to the guidelines described in the system.

On May 13, 1979, the booklet, *Affirmative Action and Complaint Procedure* was included with each employee/officer paycheck for that period. Each facility widely posted the booklet and maintained additional copies to be provided to employees.

Overall Description of the Current System

Who is Covered

The internal EEO complaint system can be used by any employee, regardless of their job category, union status, grade, or position.

What Issues Are Covered

Issues covered by the procedures include disciplinary actions, demotions, promotions, training, or any other employment practice or activity.

How and When System Communicated to Employees

The procedures were initially provided to employees with their regular paychecks for the period. The system is periodically covered in the company newspaper, posted on all bulletin boards, and summarized in the company's handbook for new employees. In addition, each facility maintains copies of the procedures to be provided to employees upon request or if the officer believes the system may be helpful to the employee.

Mechanics of the System

An employee who encounters what he or she feels is discriminatory treatment should:

1. Attempt to work out the problem with the immediate supervisor. If this is not possible,
2. Employee and supervisor consult with the Labor Relations and Personnel officer;
3. The Labor Relations and Personnel officer will attempt to develop a fair and just resolution of the problem. In instances where there is no local Labor Relations or Personnel officer the employee and supervisor should contact the Manager of Equal Employment directly.

If a satisfactory solution cannot be worked out, the Labor Relations and Personnel officer is required to submit a written report to the Manager of Equal Employment detailing the nature of the problem, steps taken to remedy the problem, reasons for the failure of the informal resolution effort, and recommendations proposed to resolve the dispute. A similar report is prepared in instances where the informal approach was successful.

There are no boards, committees, outside mediation, or arbitration. The Manager of Equal Employment investigates all unresolved complaints and attempts to work out a resolution if the complaint has merit. In cases where resolution fails, the Manager of Equal Employment submits to the Vice President of Personnel a written report, including recommendations for resolution which will conform to Title VII or other applicable civil rights laws. The final decision is made by the Vice President.

Role of the Personnel Department; Legal Department

The Personnel Department is solely responsible for the function of the internal EEO procedures. As of mid-1987, there have been *no* cases that warranted the involvement of the Legal Department.

The System in Action

A total of 41 internal EEO complaints were filed in 1986. Of this number, the largest majority (29) was based on race or color, followed by sex (8), national origin (2), and age (2). Included in the race and sex categories were 6 whites and one male. Issues cited in the complaints were harassment, threat of disciplinary action, terms and conditions of employment, that is, job assignments, disqualification from a specific job, letter of warning, and failure to promote. Approximately 83 percent of the complainants had not suffered any monetary loss, but typically alleged some type of verbal harassment by other employees or different treatment in regard to the usual conditions of employment.

None of the complaints were resolved at the first step or with the immediate supervisor. Instead, 31.7 percent were settled at the second step (department or division); 61 percent at the third step (the corporate EEO office); and 7.3 percent were referred to Labor Relations, as involving contract-covered issues. In 1985, none of the decisions were appealed past the third step (Director of Equal Employment) or resulted in official external EEO charges. In 1986, three decisions were taken to outside EEO agencies and were pending in early 1987.

All charges filed in 1986 were closed by the end of that year. Resolutions were quite rapid, with two days as the average length of time required to reach a final resolution. This speed reflected the lack of severity or complexity of the issues as well as the low monetary liability involved. Most cases resulted in supervisors being warned to adhere to company and government EEO policies or in clarifying a specific issue of concern to the employee.

The following charts provide a more detailed description of the complaints received during 1986.

CHART I. BASIS OF COMPLAINTS

Basis of Complaint	Number of Cases	Percent
Race (black)	21	51.2
Sex (female)	7	17.1
Race (white)	6	14.6
National origin	2	4.9
Color	2	4.9
Age	2	4.9
Sex (male)	1	2.4

CHART II. ISSUES RAISED

Issue	*Number of Cases*
Harassment	18
Failure to promote	5
Letter of warning	4
Suspension	4
Attendance	3
Loss of seniority rights	2
Denial of telephone use	1
Work conditions	1
Denial of overtime	1
Forced resignation	1
Job abolishment	1

CHART III. LEVEL OF RESOLUTION

Step	*Percent*
Step 1: Immediate supervisor	0
Step 2: Department or division	31.7
Step 3: Corporate EEO office	61.0
Step 4: Vice-President Personnel	0
Referred to Labor Relations	7.3

CHART IV: OUTCOMES

	Percent
Resolved favorably for employee	48.8
No evidence to support case	43.9
Not related to Title VII	7.3

Examples of Cases Resolved

As Chart 2 above shows, 44 percent of the 1986 internal EEO complaints involve some type of harassment. These cases concern derogatory statements or jokes about the complainant's race, sex, or religious affiliation. The typical offender is a long-term contract employee who feels that ethnic or sexist jokes are harmless and in no way intended to offend the female or minority individual. Frequently, other employees are witnesses to such incidents; thus, the offender very seldom denies making the statements.

The investigation of these complaints is fairly clear-cut. Once the matter is brought to management's attention, the alleged offender is ordered to immediately report to the Labor Relations/Personnel officer or Manager of Equal Employment, depending on the location. If the employee denies making the comments, witnesses, if any, are contacted and questioned. If there is any indication the incident occurred as reported, the offender is issued a severe verbal warning, including the advice that a similar incident will result in actual discipline. A formal letter of reprimand is also entered in the employee's personal file. In the few instances where witnesses were not present, the accused denies making the statement, and there is no evidence to support either party, the company has adopted the practice of advising both of the Equal Employment/Affirmative Action Policy. They are informed of the seriousness of such allegations, the company's unwillingness to tolerate this type of behavior, and that the incident will be recorded, not in their personnel file, but as a reminder to the manager if a similar incident takes place in the future.

To date, there have been *no* second violations by employees. Although the letter of reprimand is not actual discipline, it can be taken into consideration in a subsequent violation where actual discipline is warranted. Then, too, the alleged offender realizes that he is now negatively "known" to management, has been embarrassed, and may not enjoy his previous popularity with his peers.

The following case exemplifies the nature and resolution of the typical internal charge of racial harassment:

Mary, a black seven-year track laborer, and other employees were performing their assigned duties in a location several miles from the Yard Office. During a rest break, the accused employee, Joe, initiated a conversation with co-workers in which he used a term derogatory to blacks. When one of the listeners reminded Joe of Mary's presence, he immediately apologized and promised Mary he would never again use such a term. However, Mary refused the apology and reported the incident to the Manager of Equal Employment.

The resolution of this case was similar to the procedures previously described. Joe was verbally advised by his supervisor that he would be severely disciplined if a similar incident occurred in the future. He was also issued a formal letter of reprimand and ordered to review the company's Equal Employment and Affirmative Action Policy.

The second most frequently raised issue in internal EEO claims involves some form of disciplinary action. This type of complaint can result from the employee receiving a deferred suspension (where no actual time is served if the employee has no other infraction for a 12-month period) or dismissal from employment. The typical complainant is an employee with less than five years of service. He/she is not likely to be one of the department's "good" employees. Usually, the most recent discipline is the last prior to dismissal under the progressive discipline system, that is, 60 days' suspension, and the employee attempts to use the EEO complaint system as protection against further disciplinary actions. This employee will probably not agree with the resolution of his/her case and will eventually file an external complaint. The following typifies what could occur in this sort of case:

Henry began employment with the company in 1979 as a trackman. He had been furloughed several months in each subsequent year, but had established a record of poor attendance early in his employment. In 1983, Henry failed to report to work on several different occasions. His last absence resulted in an investigation and the issuance of a 60-day actual suspension. Within a few days, Henry filed an internal EEO complaint with the Manager of Equal Employment.

According to Henry, his suspension was based solely on his race, as white employees were not disciplined for being absent. Henry added that he was one of only a few blacks reporting to his supervisor, who had stated he did not want blacks in his crew.

Discussion of these allegations with Henry's supervisor, Jones, indicated that Henry was a fairly good worker whenever he reported to work. However, Henry was often tardy or absent—most of Henry's absences had not resulted in discipline. Jones stated that he could not continue to operate his crew efficiently if he did not have dependable workers, and felt that Henry's attendance would improve once he realized he would lose his job if he did not change his attendance pattern. Jones added that nearly one-half of his crew was black and denied ever stating he did not want blacks in his crew.

Review of Henry's work record showed he had received five letters of reprimand for attendance infractions. He had been issued two different deferred suspensions, two actual suspensions, and the recent 60-day suspension. During a relatively short period of actual employment and work, Henry had served a total of 105 days in suspensions.

A similar review of the work records of other employees, black and white, under the supervision of Jones showed that none had been disciplined as much as Henry in a comparable length of time. The actual attendance records indicated Henry was indeed absent or tardy more than his co-workers, regardless of race. It was also correct that Henry, just as others in the crew, was not disciplined for each instance of tardiness or absence. Furthermore, interviews with the crew failed to support Henry's allegation regarding Supervisor Jones' unwillingness to have blacks in his crews. Jones' crews were 36 percent Hispanic, 35 percent white, and 29 percent black.

When Henry was informed of these facts, he accused Jones of changing the records. Within 2 weeks he had filed an external complaint, which was dismissed when the agency reviewed documents contained in the internal investigation.

The failure to be selected for a higher level position or promotion can cause hostile reactions from some employees. This is especially true for those minority employees who *expect* that their race will be the primary factor considered in the selection process. This view is greatly intensified when some form of written test procedure is a part of the system. Quite often the minority's perception of any testing device is influenced by the common misconception that such tools automatically have an adverse effect upon minority groups.

For example, Joan had been employed with the company for six years when she applied for a supervisory position in her department, and was not selected because of low test scores. Joan discussed this matter with her supervisor, and was advised that the selection was made from a list of qualified employees. Joan argued that she had been in the department four years—two years longer than the selected employee—and thus had more experience and should have been promoted. When Joan's supervisor repeated her position, Joan contacted the Manager of Equal Employment.

According to Joan's complaint, since entering the department, she had received a Bachelor of Arts degree, and had acted as supervisor in the absence of her immediate supervisor. The white employee selected did not have a degree, nor had she acted in the supervisory position. Because of this, Joan felt that her race must have been the only reason for her nonselection.

Investigation of the records showed that Joan had received a Bachelor of Arts degree, letter of commendation for exceptional work, and had no apparent problems which would interfere with a managerial promotion. However, the company had introduced a new validated selection procedure for officers and near-officer positions. This system required employees desiring promotion into the managerial ranks to complete an Interest Skills Inventory and specific tests which, in addition to education, experience, and years of service resulted in an overall battery score. The battery score, along with the employee's stated interest area, were entered into the computer system, with selections being made from these data. Employees not in the system would not be considered for promotions.

Although Joan had been advised that she had to complete the above battery, she had failed to do so. At the time of her promotional request, Joan still had not completed the required documents even though letters (including the Inventory) describing the new computer system and its impact on future promotions had been mailed (in stamped return envelopes) to minority employees. Joan stated that she refused to complete the battery because all tests discriminated against blacks or, at least, were fixed. She further claimed that she was aware of the fact that white supervisors either had not taken the tests or had failed to pass them.

Review of the department's work force revealed that blacks represented nearly 40 percent of supervisory personnel. Furthermore, all supervisory staff had successfully passed the test battery. Therefore, no racial basis existed for Joan's allegations in regard to the test battery or selection process.

In Joan's view, the resolution of her complaint was mixed. As her basic allegations were without merit, Joan was advised that she should update her test scores, if she was serious regarding promotions. Having previously filed an unsuccessful external EEO complaint against the company, Joan was quite familiar with outside investigatory rules concerning evidence. Joan agreed to complete the battery.

The placement and accommodation of the disabled employee is of prime concern to all members of the railroad industry. Throughout the years, the Chicago and North Western has taken a leadership role in developing and validating physical standards for the industry which can be utilized in the placement of handicapped individuals, and are acceptable to government agencies.

In a work setting that is typically heavy duty and potentially dangerous, the accommodation of a disabled employee often requires sensitive, as well as pragmatic negotiations between the Personnel Department and the specific location. However, the company has eliminated much of the misunderstanding and financial liability which can result from the mishandling of such cases by establishing a strong, cooperative relationship between the EEO and Medical and Rehabilitation departments. The following illustrates some of the adjustments which could be required in the resolution of these complaints:

Paul, a 17-year mechanical employee was bumped from his position during the 1982 reduction in force. He subsequently exercised his seniority to temporary jobs until he was able to bid on and receive a permanent job. Shortly after, Paul advised his supervisor that he was having difficulty hearing and was referred to the Medical Department for evaluation. Based on this evaluation and that of his personal physician, Paul was restricted from positions where a good sense of hearing was required for safety and satisfactory performance.

Subsequently, Paul requested a leave of absence because his seniority was not sufficient to allow him to hold a job which conformed to the restrictions prescribed by his physicians. The leave was approved, and he was referred to the Rehabilitation Department. Nonetheless, Paul contacted the Manager of Equal Employment because a co-worker and his union representative advised him to do so.

Discussion of the case with Paul's Rehabilitation Counselor indicated that he had not been fully cooperative, feeling that the division was not interested in assisting him. Paul believed that there was an open, nonunion clerical position he could fill if the department were willing to provide written instructions to him, and give the heavy typing duties to another employee. The department, however, was strongly opposed to adjusting the job's responsibilities, or taking any actions which could lessen the area's overall productivity. This position was maintained until the officers were reminded of the company's legal and moral obligations to attempt to accommodate employees such as Paul. They were requested to take several days and objectively consider how to accommodate Paul's disability, without decreasing the area's efficiency.

The case was resolved with the department's decision that the typing requirement could be somewhat lower without decreasing productivity. Because written instructions to Paul would be time-consuming for all involved, the company agreed to purchase an appropriate hearing aid for Paul. In addition, Paul agreed to enroll (at the company's expense) in a refresher typing course held at the local junior college. Within a relatively short period of time, Paul was satisfactorily performing all aspects of his new job.

Attitudes toward the System

In general, the attitude of officers and management toward the internal EEO complaint system have been very favorable. This is particularly true with those officials who at some time have had to become involved in the investigation of an external EEO case. To them, the internal system serves as a type of warning flag that possible, unrecognized, problem areas may exist. In addition, the system is timely and provides the officer with a nonthreatening, objective environment for settling differences with the employee.

Any negative reaction toward the system is most likely to come from the first-line supervisory level. Quite often this group of employees are contract workers who have received the supervisor/foreman position through their seniority status. They are not subject to the standard officer appraisal procedures, nor has management had any input into their selection. Thus, their basic loyalties, in some respects, remain with the bargaining unit. Yet, this problem is minor and has not influenced the overall effectiveness of the system due to the strong support given the procedure by the Chief Executive Officer and other members of top management.

Effects on Outside Complaints and Litigation

During the first six months of 1984, 21 EEO charges were filed with outside agencies, compared with 23 filed under the internal system. Although 3 of the 23 internal cases were subsequently filed externally, all 3 were dismissed, due primarily to the evidence contained in the internal investigation. In 1986, the number of charges filed with outside agencies was slightly lower than the number filed internally, and only three of the charges filed inside resulted in an outside filing by a dissatisfied employee.

Our records indicate that the internal complaint system has a direct impact on the number of cases filed with our regulatory agencies. Prior to the full implementation of the system in 1979, external complaints filed averaged 4.5 claims per month in the first six months of each specific year. Since 1979, this figure has decreased to an average of 1.83 cases per month within the same time frame. While the number of complaints filed externally or internally is likely to vary during specific time periods, there is no question that the internal system results in an overall decrease in the number of complaints filed with regulatory agencies.

Effects on Employee Relations and Organizational Objectives

To date, there has been no employee or general survey performed specifically on the internal EEO procedure. The company's belief that the system offers employees a prompt and fair opportunity to resolve their EEO-related concerns without outside influence is supported by employee use of the system. Indeed, over 50 percent of the employees with such problems chose to file their grievances internally rather than seek the assistance of an outside agency.

Ours is a 90 percent unionized work force. As a rule, the internal EEO system involves issues not typically addressed in the union grievance process. While the EEO procedure can deal with such matters as race, sex, religion, and comparative data, the union investigation and/or appeal process is normally confined to the interpretation and administration of contractual rights.

In practice, the company has discovered that the internal EEO complaint system can be compatible with the union grievance process. In some instances, employees seeking to file an EEO claim have been advised that a more appropriate remedy may be found in the Labor Relations/union area. On the other hand, several union representatives have established a practice of advising members to schedule appointments with their EEO officer. However, if necessary, the company would not hesitate to remind union officials of their individual obligations. Because the majority of the company's jobs are unionized, it can be helpful to have the cooperation of the various bargaining units, particularly in matters of employee accommodation.

The weakest application of the system occurs at the first step and in those cases where the supervisory staff consists of union-covered employees. Our data indicate no complaints have been resolved at that level. Employees seem not to be discouraged but to simply proceed to the next step in the process.

Changes Under Consideration

There are no basic changes in the system under consideration. However, there are discussions under way with our Labor Relations/Personnel officers concerning a standardized method for the maintenance of second level complaint resolution. Due to the deliberate informality of the procedures, some resolved complaints are not recorded as such. The system is actually more effective than our statistics portray. For example, an employee may visit or telephone the Labor Relations officer and state a problem he/she is encountering with a supervisor. The officer simply telephones the supervisor, informs him/her of the problem, a resolution is proposed, and the matter is over when the employee agrees to the settlement. This process may be completed in less than an hour, and may go unrecorded mainly because it did not require the normal resolution time.

Conclusion

Overall, we believe our internal EEO complaint program is doing the job. It is contributing strongly to helping us become the company we want to be—fair, open, and trustworthy.

The *Intercom* System at Chemical Bank

Edward F. McCabe*

Chemical New York Corporation, operating through Chemical Bank and other subsidiaries, is a diverse organization that provides financial products and services to individuals, financial institutions, governments, and corporations. In size, according to assets, it ranks seventh in the United States and sixth in New York City. The company employs more than 20,000 people worldwide.

The Chemical Bank is the largest subsidiary of the Chemical New York Corporation, employing 15,000 persons, in 13 separate operating divisions. Division employees work throughout New York City, New York State, and parts of New Jersey. No employee of the bank is represented by a labor organization.

Pattern of Organization

Chemical Bank is organized according to a chain of command. At the top of the bank's management structure are the chairman, presidents, vice chairman, and senior executive vice president. Each division of the bank is led by a person of at least senior vice presidential rank; most are executive vice presidents. The division heads report to the top management group on both organizational and functional bases. Under each division head is an array of officers, managers, or supervisors who, in turn, oversee the work of line employees.

The human resources division, which oversees the bank's *Intercom* program, is composed of five separate groups: compensation and benefits, staff planning and development, employment and training, affirmative action, and employee relations. Functionally, *Intercom* is part of the division's employee relations group, which also oversees general employee relations, discrimination cases, official staff concerns, employee services, financial counseling activities, the suggestion program, in-bank seminars on employee

*Senior Vice President, Human Resources, New York, New York.

relations, outplacement, communications, and the regional human resources offices. On a day-in and day-out basis, *Intercom* is supervised by an assistant vice president.

History of *Intercom*

In late 1969; the senior management of the Chemical Bank began to explore through contacts with outside directors, customers, and client companies, how they might improve employee relations. Senior management had come to believe that clerical employees needed some means, apart from the normal supervisory chain of command, to express their concerns, problems, and needs to top management. There was some evidence that the chain of command was not always successful in communicating the problems of the clerical staff to senior management, and that a supervisor could, if he or she so desired, short-circuit this important communication. The bank began to explore a number of vehicles that could serve this function. The bank subsequently retained the firm of John Sheridan Associates, Inc., a management consulting firm, specializing in employee relations to assist the bank toward this objective. The consultants learned that the bank was poised to institute a system for handling employee concerns that relied heavily on a "write-in" format. They persuaded management to hold off on this system until the consultants had completed their initial study of Chemical's employee-relations policies and practices.

Ultimately, the consultant's study revealed that Chemical Bank was a "warm and personal" organization; further, that it was an organization that went to unusual lengths to show concern and respect for its employees. In addition to their many other recommendations, the consultants suggested that the bank install a system for addressing employee concerns which would operate on a *warm, person-to-person basis*, rather than a cold and remote "write-in" or "Dear Miss Lonelyhearts" system. *Intercom* was the result of that recommendation.

The *Intercom* Program

Intercom was not designed to be a substitute for or to replace Chemical Bank's chain-of-command for dealing with employee complaints, which today remains the primary dispute-resolution mechanism within the organization. Instead, it was intended to be an adjunct to it by providing clerical workers with a "safety valve" or "escape hatch" in case the other system failed or broke down.

Intercom is made up of eight *Intercom* staff representatives, all of whom are officers of the bank, supervised by a manager who is an assistant vice president. The eight *Intercom* representatives are the core of the program. These individuals are officers who have demonstrated an aptitude for employee relations work. They field problems and concerns from clerical employees in the departments to which they are assigned, which generally are the most labor-intensive areas within the bank.

A clerical employee who wants to express a concern to *Intercom* may do so in two ways—through a phone call to the *Intercom* office or in person when the *Intercom* representative visits their department or bank branch. All contacts are confidential. Once an *Intercom* representative has heard a complaint or concern, he or she then contacts the appropriate supervisor to get the other side of the story, and consults any relevant documentation. The representative then arrives at an appropriate resolution, and engages to "sell" it to both sides in the dispute.

The *Intercom* representative first tries to resolve the dispute at the lowest level of management, but he or she has the authority to follow the chain of command until a resolution is achieved. In the 14-year history of *Intercom*, disputes have occasionally risen to the division-head level. At this point, the *Intercom* representative is usually accompanied by his or her manager, and possibly the vice president for employee relations—who help to facilitate the process.

As we shall see, *Intercom* also plays an important proactive role within the bank. When employee complaints and concerns cluster around new problems or issues confronting the organization, *Intercom* can step in and make recommendations to top management that often result in policy changes that deal with them in a way that is both direct and immediate.

Intercom was introduced on a pilot basis in the operations division of the bank in April 1970. After its initial success there, it was successively phased into the bank's other divisions until December 1972, when it became operational throughout the organization.

Intercom—Its Planning, Its Philosophy

In most planning sessions for concern-handling systems, planners will indulge in gratuitous speculation about the concerns or complaints that are never expressed, for lack of a formal system. Such tangents argue that it might be possible to construct the "perfect" system, wherein each and every concern, however tentative or embryonic, would be heard and resolved successfully, to the mutual satisfaction of all parties. These considerations usually arise because human resources or personnel executives report to hard-headed, bottom-line oriented, line management. They know that someday, down the road, they will be asked to *quantify* the program, to list its successes and failures and above all, to be able to prove that it is cost effective.

The Sheridan consultants were quick to point out that there was no such thing as a perfect system. Thereafter, every effort was made to design one which would *work* as well as could be expected, albeit imperfectly. An *Intercom*-type system, like many others that handle employee concerns and complaints, must, of necessity, measure its achievements in terms of "what might have been" rather than real outcome. Many transactions result in quiet and relatively unnoticed resolutions rather than explosive and showy confrontations. Indeed, avoidance of the explosive confrontation should be one of the objectives of any system of this kind.

Because senior-management commitment and involvement was so important to *Intercom's* success, the Sheridan consultants insisted on the following "contract" between Chemical's senior management and their human resources division:

> First, that INTERCOM was *forever*. It was to become a permanent fixture of the bank's human resources program, rather than an "experiment" or a "Band-Aid" which could be peeled off later;
>
> Second, no employee could be penalized, threatened or subjected to recriminations for utilizing the services of INTERCOM. As a corollary, employees and their concerns would remain anonymous, unless the employee gave his or her permission for the concern to "surface" or be made more public;
>
> Third, senior management must not pressure the INTERCOM program for *numbers* of concerns (i.e., a "more is better" approach); rather, the emphasis was to be placed on *type* and *quality* of concerns being handled. Instead of asking, "How many are we getting?"; ask, "What are we *learning* from the concerns we get?"
>
> Fourth, INTERCOM must be sold as a line program, rather than as something cooked up by the human resources division to justify its existence;
>
> Fifth, and last, senior management was asked to provide, year after year, the funds necessary to operate INTERCOM.

What were the reasons for these stringent and binding commitments? Let us look at them, one by one.

1. *"Intercom* was *forever."*

One could easily imagine a scenario where a new management team took over, a team less employee-relations oriented than the one in power in 1970. As part of its "new broom" image, it might suggest wholesale cuts in employee relations services, including the abolition of *Intercom.* What would be the result?

Certainly, employees who had become accustomed, over a period of years, to a "Cadillac" system for handling their concerns and complaints, might now be compelled to ask, "If not *Intercom,* then . . . what?" If *Intercom* were abolished, the bank might be very hard pressed to present the employees with an alternative. The consultants said that if *Intercom* was not going to be a permanent fixture, then the bank should not bother with it.

2. "[N]o employee could be penalized . . . for utilizing the services of *Intercom.* . . . concerns would remain anonymous. . . ."

Every organization has some managers and supervisors who developed their employee-relations philosophy under the tutelage of Attila the Hun. Employees have readily identified them and indeed, it is often such a harsh and unforgiving supervisor who is the very target of many employee complaints. *Intercom* would never work, it was felt, if the employees viewed it as a direct pipeline to such a supervisor, or as a way of "getting into trouble." *Intercom* had to develop the image of a "safe house," a place one could go and "unload" without fear of discipline or discharge.

3. "[S]enior management must not pressure . . . for *numbers* . . . ; rather, the emphasis was to be . . . on *quality.* . . ."

The Sheridan consultants viewed the bank as a vertical, almost military organization, in which many layers of management and supervision separated the rank-and-file clerical workers from the senior management. The problem posed was how to get information from the very bottom to the very top of the organization, without subverting middle management.

Actually, the head of *Intercom,* along with members of the *Intercom* staff, meet on an informal basis with senior management to discuss what they are doing. In the early days of *Intercom,* these meetings were primarily to give senior management a flavor of the countless types of concern being expressed by employees. Gradually, a very subtle change began to take place. The senior management came to realize that people working in the *Intercom* program had direct and daily access to the lowest level of their organization.

Now, *Intercom* is used not only as an auditor (in the original sense of the word—"listener") but also as a sounding board. Senior management often throws out, on a confidential basis, plans and ideas that are in the works but as yet unannounced. It asks the *Intercom* personnel to predict employee reaction to these still germinating plans.

4. "*Intercom* must be sold as a *line* program. . . ."

Often, personnel programs are introduced into line organizations by personnel people, rather than by line people. Just as often, they are suspect. Line managers are suspicious of "those guys up in personnel who've never had to prepare a budget." At best, they are going to ask, "What's this program going to do for *me*?"

Intercom provided an answer to that question. It said that the program would give the line manager immediate feedback as to what his employees were thinking, on a daily basis. Further, it promised that the *Intercom* staff and, indeed, all of the resources of the human resources division, would be at his elbow to help him cope with the concerns when they started to flow. Finally, it promised that the supervisors, and not *Intercom*, would receive the credit for the resolution of the conflict or concern.

As a result, more and more managers and supervisors have called upon *Intercom* to survey situations prior to or shortly after implementation of new policies, procedures, or programs. In turn, *Intercom* plays a major role in "heading off" potential problems by uncovering difficulties in early, less critical stages and enabling management to deal with them effectively.

5. "Senior management was asked to provide . . . the funds. . . ."

Intercom is expensive. Because it employs eight staff relations consultants, many of whom have offices and cars, its budget for 1984 was $400,000. Since its inception, the bank has spent $3,000,000 to maintain the *Intercom* program. Most future senior managers of the Chemical Bank will probably be tempted, at some time in their tenure, to discontinue *Intercom* because it could save some money that might be quickly reflected in the balance sheet. It is hoped that they will resist this temptation and remember the bank's original commitment.

This level of commitment was reiterated recently by Chemical Bank's chairman, Walter V. Shipley: "The Bank's philosophy has always been one of encouraging a close partnership between managers and their staffs. This has never been more important than it is today as we chart a course for doing business in an increasingly competitive, deregulated industry."

Intercom—Its Operation

The cutting edge of the *Intercom* program consists of the eight staff-relations consultants (who are also referred to as *Intercom* representatives).

Until recently, the consultants rotated assignments every year. The initial theory behind this was to provide employees with a new person to approach with their concerns, as well as help the *Intercom* representative remain fresh and objective. Through the experiences of the consultants, however, a new procedure has been implemented. Many consultants felt they had just "broken the ice" and were really making progress when their one-year rotation was up. Because of this, the length of each consultant's assignment to any given area was extended to three years. The result has been the establishment of stronger working relationships, with management utilizing the consultant more readily.

The bank's official job-posting system is used to hire staff relations consultants. All are hired internally and a number are officers with line supervisory experience. The qualifications for an *Intercom* representative include supervisory experience, ability to communicate both upwards and downwards, willingness to work irregular hours, a high level of maturity, and the ability to work independently.

Once a new staff relations consultant has been recruited, he or she goes through a process more akin to "orientation" than "training," since there is minimal introduction to new techniques. On the contrary, the new *Intercom* representative will be utilizing previously displayed good supervisory skills, such as effective listening, counseling, and communicative techniques, as well as the qualities of sound judgment, common sense, and initiative—the very qualities and skills that prompted the choice of the individual for the *Intercom* staff.

The primary focus of the orientation is to develop a complete understanding of the role, philosophy, and approach of the *Intercom* program, and the second is the development of an individual style, specifically tailored to, and making maximum use of, the new staff relations consultant's personality and capabilities. Since the representative is widely viewed as an "emissary" for the human resources division or as a personnel generalist, particular attention is paid to the rapid development of an in-depth knowledge of the organization and its functions.

A new staff member spends at least one full day with each of the experienced *Intercom* representatives. Additional time is spent with the consultant he or she is replacing, for greater familiarization with the new assignment. He or she observes the *Intercom* approach in the assigned line areas, observes the handling of concerns, participates in a supervisory meeting, and becomes familiar with internal *Intercom* administration and recordkeeping. The new staff member is also scheduled for two to three one-hour sessions with former staff relations consultants, for a retrospective insight into *Intercom* and its development.

In addition, new staff members are scheduled for informal one-hour sessions with key spokespersons for the major human resource division functions, and for one or two days' orientation in the metropolitan division for familiarization with the organizational and functional relationships of the branches, the divisions, and metropolitan division personnel, and with the work flow and jobs found in various size branches. Periodically, during their careers staff members attend workshops or seminars conducted by the bank's outside consultants, John Sheridan Associates, Inc., on such subjects as employee relations, labor relations, and labor law.

Solving a Concern

Before an *Intercom* representative can solve an employee concern, he or she must understand something about the nature of it. Chemical Bank defines a concern as anything about his or her job which an employee feels is unsatisfactory or unfair. This may manifest itself through the application, interpretation, or violation of a policy or procedure, or, it may be present as a personal concern. General types of personal concerns include feelings against one's supervisor or the bank (of being discriminated against, picked on, or ignored), feelings about physical conditions or environmental factors (e.g., heat, cold, light, dark, machines, and cafeteria), and feelings about working conditions (e.g., benefits and hours).

The ultimate goal of the *Intercom* concern-solving process is to "sell" the resolution, whatever it may be, to the parties involved—usually employee versus management. The promotion of the resolution's acceptance often takes place in a highly antagonistic setting, and the importance of an amicable settlement looms large when one examines the reasons.

The most obvious is *Intercom's* primary purpose in being on the scene in the first place. The normal employee/supervisor problem-solving mechanism has reached an impasse. Day-to-day department efficiency has been disrupted and productivity has deteriorated. *Intercom* intervenes as the last workable alternative to lingering resentment or hostility. In addition, the *Intercom* program itself is at stake. *With each concern and subsequent resolution*, the credibility of the *Intercom* representative and of the entire *Intercom* program is enhanced or diminished. This credibility survives only through mutual acceptance of the *Intercom* representative as an objective, independent third party. Therefore, the resolution is synthesized and marketed to reflect that image.

Having stated the goal, let us take a look at the concern-solving process. It begins when an employee voluntarily enlists *Intercom's* aid. *Intercom* acts primarily through an invitation of this kind that grows out of prior contact with employees before they express concerns such as periodic visits (generally every five or six weeks) by the *Intercom* representative to the working areas, cafeterias, and lounges. The initial step of the *Intercom* process utilizes the rapport or familiarity built up by those contacts to create an informal and comfortable interview environment. On a subtle level, it takes the form of a peer-seating arrangement, contrary to the traditional across-the-desk, superior/subordinate setup, which conjures up images of management disciplining labor, or management meting out unquestioned judgments.

Intercom is designed to listen to employee concerns, unlike line management, to whom complaints are often bothersome intrusions. This "willing ear" serves as a safety valve for the pent-up pressure of an employee's emotions and frustrations. In the context of concern-solving, an *Intercom* representative's questions during the interview must be both sensitive and impartial. The *Intercom* representative's questioning should project the feeling that judgment is being deferred and no conclusions have as yet been reached, while at the same time eliciting and clarifying as many pertinent facts as possible.

Also, at some point during the interview, the representative should ascertain whether the employee has attempted to solve the problem through his supervisor or, if not, whether there is a valid reason for not doing so. If this criteria is not met, *Intercom* then encourages the employee to attempt "normal" resolution, careful to make it clear that *Intercom* is very much available, should that attempt fail. This is extremely delicate action, because if ill-timed or ill-stated, the employee can be completely discouraged from communicating and pursuing the resolution through *any* of the available means.

Once the interview is completed, the *Intercom* representative usually asks the employee to what extent he wishes it to be pursued and which facts can be disclosed. At the same time, the employee is assured that during the course of the concern-solving process, the *Intercom* representative will do nothing without the employee's prior knowledge or consent. All of this is done with the implicit understanding that at this point, only one side of the story has been heard. As an objective mediator, *Intercom* is obliged to hear the other side as well.

Before approaching management, *Intercom* checks the available documentation such as personnel profiles, folders, attendance profiles, and the *Personnel Policy and Procedure Manual*. Once that is done, the appropriate line of supervision must be contacted in order to attempt to solve the problem on the lowest level and in the least controversial manner.

The basic techniques used in the interview with management parallel those of the employee's interview. First, listening; second, reinforcement of *Intercom* as the objective third party, primarily through judgment deferral and impartial questioning. However, one point is made abundantly clear: *that it is local management's primary responsibility to resolve the problem and that it is* Intercom's *job to consult, aid, suggest, and recommend toward that end.*

Now, the actual problem-solving process begins. Having uncovered and weighed as many facts as possible, *Intercom* finds solutions which, while not violating principles and policies, reflect a reasonable flexibility in application of those principles and policies to live people in a real workplace. At the same time, *Intercom* must identify underlying, sometimes camouflaged, problems and pursue those resolutions through supervisory training, changes in policy, and others.

Intercom promotes the mutual acceptance of resolutions and agreements once they have been achieved. *Intercom* has the authority to go to any level of the bank to solve a problem, but this authority is tempered with the wisdom and foresight to know when it is not in the best interest of the participants to escalate the matter further. Having achieved a resolution through management, *Intercom* is then charged with the periodic follow-up of the situation primarily to insure that the employee is not penalized, or suffering for having used *Intercom*. This is to ensure the integrity and continuity of the program.

Intercom's Impact

Bankwide statistics have been kept on *Intercom* on an annual basis from January 1973 until the present. *Statistics have been kept only where an actual transaction and resolution took place.* Obviously, *Intercom* representatives have a multiplicity of informal contacts which are impossible to log and run well into the thousands, over the life of the program.

From January 1973 until December 1985, *Intercom* has participated in 15,000 recorded transactions and resolutions. Nearly 20 percent of the transactions have occurred in response to policy clarification inquiries. Benefits and services questions and personality conflicts accounted for about 15 percent (each) of the total, followed by salary and termination related problems (10–12 percent each) and advancement/mobility counseling (8.5 percent).

As stated previously, it has never been *Intercom's* objective to deal in quantity or to indulge in a "numbers game." Rather, the emphasis has been on quality and on discerning what really underlies the displayed concerns, problems, or complaints. Early in the program, this was described as the "Iceberg Effect." Time and time again, *Intercom* representatives have found that as people "opened up" to them, they revealed more than they had expressed in their original complaint.

The litmus test of *Intercom*, or indeed, of any concern-handling mechanism is: "What effect does it have on policy? Can it affect or change policy? Can it help make new policy?" In this area, *Intercom* has shone. A quick look at the chronological record will show that through *Intercom*, Chemical's employees have truly participated in the management decision-making process over the years. The examples listed below are by no means complete or definitive, but are only meant to give a flavor of what *Intercom* is really about.

Policy Change—"Special" Days

In the pre-*Intercom* days, confusion had existed within the bank over how to handle employee absence in connection with religious observances (e.g., Passover and Good Friday). *Intercom* recommended that *all* employees be given two "special" days per year, which they could use in any way they wanted. Such days could be used for a dental appointment, motor vehicle registration, or religious observances.

Relocation to New Operations Center

Until 1972, the bank's operations functions had been scattered throughout Lower Manhattan in various rented facilities. In 1972, they were all consolidated at one location—55 Water Street. This move, though strategically sound, necessitated the physical relocation of 7,000 employees. *Intercom* was closely involved in dealing with many employee problems caused by the move. The problems inherent in any new building (e.g., inoperative rest room facilities, inadequate lighting, partial cafeteria facilities) were brought to *Intercom* and were quickly "fixed." Certain individuals found the commute to a downtown location a hardship. Through *Intercom*'s efforts, those employees were transferred to other departments, branches, or divisions of the bank, in order to make their commutation easier.

Reorganization

In 1973, one of the major areas of the bank underwent a reorganization, which resulted in a reduction in force of approximately 400 employees. *Intercom* intervened to protect the jobs and job security of these employees. An Employee Reserve Pool was instituted. Employees who had been displaced were placed in the Reserve Pool, which in turn made these employees available, on a trial basis, to other departments in the bank with vacancies. Because of this plan, all 400 employees were absorbed, over time, into other areas of the bank.

Acquisition of Another Bank

In 1975, the Chemical Bank acquired the Security National Bank, an organization with operations on Long Island and in certain areas of Manhattan. Security National employed 3,000 people, whose first and understandable reaction to being acquired by a large New York bank was fear and suspicion. Through *Intercom*, these new employees soon came to learn about Chemical's dynamic personnel policies as well as the basic human dignity that all Chemical employees enjoy. They learned that they too could use *Intercom* to provide them with quick and accurate answers to the many questions they had about their new employer. Today, it is difficult to tell a former Security National employee from a long-time Chemical staffer, because the process of integration has been so complete.

Cost of Living

In 1979, many Long Island employees were concerned regarding cost of living and wage differentials that existed between themselves and their New York counterparts. *Intercom*'s feedback was instrumental in initiating a wage and salary study which resulted in adjustment that would ultimately bring the Long Island employees into competition with the New York labor market. Over 2,000 salary increases were processed and many employee concerns were alleviated.

Dealing with the Deaf

One of the areas of the bank employs a high percentage of deaf persons. This group came to *Intercom* and made it known that they felt excluded from many of the services which were taken for granted by the nonhandicapped employees. *Intercom* coordinated a benefits presentation, utilizing the services of a sign language interpreter. In addition, many of the deaf reported that it was extremely difficult for them to communicate notice of absence or tardiness to their supervisors. Many of these employees have special teletype machines in their homes by which they can converse with hearing and nonhearing people. *Intercom* arranged for a relay service to accept calls from deaf employees via teletype machines and forward messages to supervisors.

Robberies

From time to time, New York City is prone to a rash of branch bank robberies. One such period was in the summer of 1979, when the news media's treatment of the subject inspired fear and anxiety in Chemical's branch employees. *Intercom* has made it a practice to visit a branch, as soon as a robbery has occurred there, to help employees cope with an unpleasant and traumatic situation. This shows them that the bank really does *care*. Also, *Intercom* was instrumental in getting the bank to construct bullet-proof shields to protect tellers from armed robbery.

Installment Loan Policy

In late 1980, the bank changed its installment loan policy. In effect, the new policy stated that nobody, customer or employee, would qualify for an installment loan, unless they earned at least $15,000 per year. This had the effect of disenfranchising some employees who earned less than $15,000. *Intercom* presented the employees' concerns to the human resources division. The policy was modified to reflect the employee's length of service and his or her ability to repay.

Supervisory Training

Intercom representatives have been holding supervisory meetings and documentation seminars for 10 years. Also, with the assistance of Chemical's Training Department, *Intercom* has created a Supervisory Development Program. This popular program does not deal with current fads. Instead, it teaches basics, such as "how to handle a concern," "how to discipline an employee," "how to conduct a review," "how to document the discharge of an employee," and most importantly, "how to *talk* to an employee."

Intercom holds monthly meetings with supervisors, in groups of 10. Supervisors chosen for these meetings are those most closely in contact with the clerical staff. The meetings are chaired by an *Intercom* representative. The meeting agenda deals with, for example, employee concerns, complaints, problems, and questions. It also covers difficulties with present bank policies, proposed bank policies, and recommendations from supervisors on how best to deal with day-to-day problems they encounter in supervising their departments.

Intercom *"Hot-Line"*

In 1981, *Intercom* introduced a 24-hour "hot-line" telephone number. This number is available to all employees to be used for any reason. As their objective, *Intercom* representatives hope to be able to respond to such calls on a "next day basis." Calls can be about interpretation, concerns, or emotional or financial counseling, or indeed, about anything else the employee might wish to discuss.

The Supervisor and *Intercom*'s Credibility

Elsewhere in this chapter, reference has been made to "supervisory meetings." In the earliest days of *Intercom*, the Sheridan consultants suggested that *Intercom* representatives hold frequent meetings with supervisors. Orginally, the purpose of those meetings was to review unresolved employee concerns and to provide feedback—both to and from the supervisors. Very quickly, these supervisory meetings developed into a supervisor's "forum." In such meetings, which are held on a regular basis today, supervisors are encouraged to discuss anything related to their own positions, to those they supervise, or to the bank in general. It is through these meetings that *Intercom* builds and reinforces its credibility.

Individual *Intercom* representatives bear the greatest responsibility in projecting the positive role of the program. The supervisory meetings have developed into an important arena in which the *Intercom* representatives, through positive rebuttal to various negative perceptions of the *Intercom* program, have been able to correct inaccurate views of it and to reinforce *Intercom*'s role as a neutral, third-party intermediary. The following examples include the most common inaccurate perceptions of *Intercom*—both from supervisors and clerical staff—and how *Intercom* representatives are geared to deal with them.

1. *The line supervisor does not view the* Intercom *representative as an objective, impartial representative but rather as an exclusive representative of the clerical employee.* In this instance, *Intercom* representatives will generally hold frequent meetings (two to four per month) with the supervisors in question to discuss career paths for supervisors (mobility), salary, supervisory status (e.g., authority, value to organization, and self-esteem), and *Intercom*'s *advisory* role. These meetings will also stress anecdotes and stories about specific concern resolutions which reinforce *Intercom*'s objective third-party image.

2. Intercom *does not support or upgrade the supervisor. Intercom* representatives draw upon their observations throughout the bank to make fair assessments of supervisory responsibility and performance. *Intercom* representatives isolate topics in supervisory meetings that deal with supervisors' needs. Supervisors are shown actual cases of how their input has been channelled to appropriate

management for consideration in successive meetings. Actual concerns are used in a workshop environment to demonstrate *Intercom's* interest in their development as managers.

3. *Clerical employees generally view* Intercom *as a representative of "management"; employee rights are therefore compromised.* This attitude is minimized by the *Intercom* representative making a visible and concerted effort to win the respect and confidence of the employee—selling himself or herself. One technique for accomplishing this objective is making informal visits to work areas where discussions draw on actual involvements, demonstrating *Intercom's* objective, third-party role. *Intercom* representatives might also request individual interviews with the disgruntled employee away from work areas, on lunch hours, coffee breaks, or, by request from management, during working hours in a private area.

4. Intercom's *low profile has created various erroneous impressions, such as: outsider, spy, inactive, compromising, ineffectual, or noncontroversial.* The *Intercom* representative sells *Intercom's consultative* role, and makes every attempt to close the communication gap. Managers, officers, and supervisors are interviewed regularly with specific topics in mind—for example, work management, performance evaluation, and operational problems. The primary role of these interviews is to gather information for advisory feedback to the appropriate officer-in-charge. During the interview process the *Intercom* representative reiterates that all information will be held in strict confidence. He or she tries to assume the role of confidant. Any rumored or real information is followed up and weighed in terms of possible staff relations impact.

5. *Many employees feel that in some way they will be discriminated against for using* Intercom. This is a serious threat in *Intercom's* viability, since the credibility of the program depends on confidentiality and nonretaliation for using *Intercom.* In such situations, the *Intercom* representative explains *Intercom's* responsibility to follow up, assuring fair treatment. Specific concern situations are cited, to reinforce the idea that results will be nondiscriminatory.

Conclusion

Since 1970, *Intercom* has functioned as a voice of participation for the clerical work force of the Chemical Bank. *Intercom* has not been pretentious. It recognizes that there are probably hundreds of concerns it has never heard. It has never sought publicity, notoriety, or visibility. Indeed, this chapter is the first time *Intercom* has "gone public" in its history.

Intercom was designed to support management—not to replace it. As organizations grow, their senior managements find it increasingly difficult to maintain close personal contact with their employees. *Intercom* is only one of many ways to maintain such contact. In today's litigious society, where employees who feel threatened, alienated, or misunderstood do not hesitate to use formal legal means of recourse, a service like *Intercom* offers an attractive alternative to such actions. It is difficult to account for lawsuits or legal fees which have not materialized, but *Intercom* representatives frequently find that "threats" of outside intervention disappear following counseling or active assistance. Chemical Bank believes that *Intercom*'s "talk to the person" philosophy makes for good preventive medicine as well as good employee relations.

The *Counselor* System at National Broadcasting Company

*Roberta V. Romberg**

Introduction

In November 1920, the returns of the Harding-Cox presidential election were broadcast over the air. It was the first prescheduled radio program ever broadcast. Network radio—the broadcasting of a program simultaneously on a number of stations connected by telephone lines—came in 1923, and was recognized instantly as an unparalleled medium for education, entertainment, and information of all types.

The National Broadcasting Company was formed in 1926 and employed 195 people. Its purpose was network radio broadcasting as a service of the Radio Corporation of America. It continued to be a wholly owned subsidiary of RCA until RCA merged with General Electric in 1986. NBC started television broadcasting as a public service in 1939. On the day commercial television was authorized in 1941, NBC went on the air with its first television station—WNBT in New York.

Today NBC is one of the three major commercial broadcast operations in the fields of both television and radio. It operates radio and television networks with hundreds of affiliated stations, and owns stations of its own. It manages a worldwide news organization with bureaus around the globe. It produces, purchases, and distributes entertainment, sports, and news programming for use both by affiliated network stations and its owned stations.

The NBC Climate

NBC is almost a household word, yet it is actually a comparatively small company, employing only about 8,000 people on a

*Former Vice President, Personnel Administration, New York, New York.

regular basis. Because of the nature of its business, the relatively small size of its work force, and the attraction that it seems to hold for so many, its employees tend to be very competitive, well educated, highly motivated, and very individual. All but 2 percent of the population graduated from high school, over 40 percent have college degrees, and almost 10 percent have done graduate work. The competition for positions is extremely high. Those selected tend to be high achievers accustomed to succeeding. It is also, however, a friendly and personal environment. Good communication and interpersonal skills are essential for internal success.

Not surprisingly, the jobs at NBC tend to cluster at the upper end of the scale. Of all positions, almost 20 percent are in management, while only 6 percent could be categorized as hourly positions. Just under 30 percent are technical positions involved in broadcasting operations per se—for example, camera, audio, equipment maintenance, and radio frequency engineering. Almost one-quarter of all positions are categorized as professional, such as news producers, lawyers, auditors, financial analysts, and human resources professionals. Clerical positions, such as secretary, researcher, and financial clerk, represent just over 20 percent of all NBC jobs. Slightly more than 40 percent of all jobs are represented by a union, including broadcast technicians, newswriters, producers, television directors, and on-air talent. Some of those union agreements are negotiated on an industrywide basis, while others are negotiated locally. There are more than 120 different labor agreements affecting different segments and locations of NBC's work force.

The participation of women and minorities at NBC generally tends to be higher than in some other industries, and has increased substantially at the higher levels in recent years. For example, women and minorities represent more than one-third and one-fifth, respectively, of NBC's overall work force, while almost one-third of the management staff are women, and minorities represent more than 20 percent of all technical positions.

Affirmative Action at NBC

In 1976, NBC adopted a comprehensive corporatewide Affirmative Action Program. The basic strategy for the program was aimed at eliminating obstacles to free and open competition, enhancing employees' capacities to compete, and establishing numerical targets to measure progress. To implement that strategy, NBC adopted a series of programs broadly designed to:

- assure objective, formalized, and visible business procedures to improve the general environment for open competition;
- improve the management skills and awareness of supervisory employees whose day-to-day decisions greatly affect the business lives and careers of employees; and
- provide special efforts on behalf of minorities and women to enhance their capacity to compete.

Part of the approach to improve the general business environment was to introduce formalized *job evaluation systems* whereby the grades of all jobs are established by systematic examination of a series of factors; formalized *performance appraisal systems* whereby employee performance is measured against established standards; formalized *job posting* whereby open positions are posted for open competition by employees; formalized *auditing and reporting systems* to monitor the employment activity of each division; a system of *career counseling* to enhance the likelihood of career success; and a system of *grievance counseling* specifically to intercede to resolve conflicts or grievances.

The *Counselor* System

In response to the two counseling elements, the position of *Employee Counselor* was created in 1977. NBC initially assumed that the *Counselor* would be used by employees more as a grievance system to help resolve complaints than as a counseling system to enhance career development, but it recognized that those two orientations frequently overlap. NBC also assumed that the bulk of the grievances heard would be related to equal employment opportunity, (EEO), although the *Counselor* would be available for *any* work-related issue. The position resided in the Affirmative Action Department and reported to its Vice President.

The availability of this new resource was communicated to employees in several ways. The vice president issued a memorandum to all employees describing the *Counselor* and its role. The *Counselor* held a series of employee meetings introducing herself to employees and essentially making herself available. Whenever other professionals in the Personnel Department encountered a matter which seemed more appropriate to the *Counselor*, it was referred there. All of these approaches were conducted simultaneously, to provide maximum exposure to the concept of a counselor and enable her to generate her own credibility.

The *Counselor* was available to *all employees*, at whatever level, both union and nonunion; would discuss *any work-related issue*; and would maintain *confidentiality*.

The position of *Counselor* was not an independent decision-maker, not an arbiter, and not an ombudsman. It had no authority of its own to overrule a management decision or to substitute its own judgment. Its authority derived from its own management structure, reporting to the Vice President of Affirmative Action and ultimately to the Executive Vice President of Personnel and Labor Relations.

While it had no independent decision-making authority, the office of *Counselor* was an active rather than a passive participant both in the counseling and the resolution process. The trigger for its activity was an employee coming to it. Once that happened, the *Counselor* took the initiative to find the information necessary to make a reasoned judgment regarding an appropriate course of action.

The *Counselor* functioned in a variety of roles depending on the employee's need: as an *"intervenor,"* when the employee needed help in dealing with the system; as a source of *advice and counsel*, when the employee needed help in sorting through a problem; and as a *source of information*, when the employee was confused or uncertain about a work issue, such as how a personnel policy might affect him or her.

In addition to the impetus provided by the commitment under the Affirmative Action Program to establish some form of "grievance" counseling system, there were other reasons why NBC chose to establish such a system at that time. While there was no hard evidence to support the view, several key members of management believed increasingly that providing a visible avenue to air concerns might reduce employees' recourse to outside resources, particularly for matters which were frivolous, or clear-cut, or otherwise easily resolved. Moreover, NBC management believed that failing to provide an avenue to legitimately express concern encouraged some employees to make too much of things while inadvertently causing others to suppress or abandon concerns that might be legitimate.

Having decided to adopt some type of complaint resolution approach, NBC considered a variety of possible methodologies before finally creating a single position of *Employee Counselor*. It was decided very early on that a traditional, formal grievance procedure with steps and hearings was neither appropriate nor desirable. The corporate style at NBC tends to be informal, and NBC wanted to establish a system consistent with that style so that employees would feel comfortable using it. Second, it wanted a mechanism that would be seen as totally distinct and different from a union grievance procedure. NBC thought that a union-style procedure might be intimidating to the nonunion population as well as discouraging to the union population. Union members already had a grievance procedure, but members tended to use it only for specific contract complaints such as wage rates and assignments, not for EEO concerns. Third, NBC wanted to avoid a mechanism which, by its very nature, tended to define concerns in adversarial terms. They wanted the mechanism to focus on counseling and resolution rather than controversy.

Having committed to a counselor system of some type, NBC considered but ultimately decided against the notion of a series of "lay" counselors in favor of a single, professionally trained counselor. A professionally trained counselor would be competent to provide certain counseling assistance that lay counselors could not. Moreover, as a professional member of the Personnel Department rather than fellow employees designated as counselors for some period of time, the *Counselor* was recognized by management as a legitimate intermediary and questioner of management decisions. The *Counselor* was also allowed access to any type or level of management information. "Lay" counselors or fellow employees could not be.

A critical decision in establishing the *Counselor* system was *not* to limit access to the system to any particular type of problem or concern. The system had emerged initially out of a heightened sensitivity to EEO, it was established as part of the Affirmative Action Program and Department, and NBC fully expected most people to use it that way. Nonetheless, NBC specifically did not require employees to characterize a problem as an EEO problem in order to reach the *Counselor*. The reason, obviously, was that if an employee were required to define a concern in EEO terms in order to see the *Counselor*, all problems would automatically, by definition, become EEO problems. In keeping with the informality of the system, there was also no requirement that the concern be expressed in writing, that it be brought within any particular time frame, or that there be a response in writing.

As described, the *Counselor's* authority was quite broad in terms of issue, access, and scope of recommendation, but it had no authority residing in itself to change or overrule a management decision. If the *Counselor* concluded that a decision complained of should be changed in some individual way, the *Counselor* would review the suggestion with the manager involved. If the manager agreed, the decision was changed. If the manager disagreed, it went to the next level of management. Having no actual authority of its own, the *Counselor* had to rely on his/her own skill as an intermediary to influence others and affect change. If that was not sufficient, he/she used the strength of his/her own management chain to modify an individual management decision or to change a management policy.

The disadvantage of a system operating in this manner was that it was not, and did not appear to be, a completely separate and therefore completely independent system. The advantage was that it was able to accomplish some significant adjustments to management decisions as well as retain personnel policies that would have been difficult if not impossible to change otherwise. And it did so in a manner that was much less threatening, and certainly less disruptive to the management structure, than a more formal and adversarial system.

Experience

During the first three years of operation, the *Counselor* system produced results that were both anticipated and unanticipated. NBC had expected, for example, that the vast majority of those using the system would be clerical employees. It was assumed that clerical employees would likely have felt that they were without resources to challenge or complain, and therefore were more likely to use a system that had been made specifically available to them. While more than one-half of the employees using the system in the early years were nonexempt employees, a large segment were also professional level employees concerned with career mobility, and another significant number were midmanagement employees seeking help in dealing with difficult management issues. In 1985 this population composed more than 10 percent and 19 percent of the users, respectively.

The most surprising finding, however, was the *type* of problem brought to the *Counselor*. While NBC had specifically made the system available to respond to other than EEO complaints, it fully expected that the vast majority of concerns raised would involve EEO. It found, however, that less than 20 percent of the matters could be defined in EEO terms, even in the mind of the employee. By far, the vast majority of the issues were generic ones, relating primarily to career mobility.

NBC also anticipated that many more women than men would use the system, as well as a high proportion of racial and ethnic minorities. Experience proved that women did tend to use the system proportionately more than men, but not simply because clerical employees tended to be heavier users of the system. Women in professional positions, for example, tended to appeal to the *Counselor* more than men in professional positions. On the other hand, minorities initially tended to use the system less than their proportionate numbers in the work force, although that trend has now shifted and minorities, particularly minority women, tend to use the system somewhat more than their proportionate representation in the work force. In 1985 minorities represented 39 percent of the users, while minority women accounted for 70 percent of that figure.

One could speculate about the reasons for these trends in usage, but it still is not known for certain. For example, did women tend to verbalize their concerns more than men, or rather did they believe that in general they had access to fewer other, less visible resolution techniques and therefore needed an alternate system? Did minorities tend to verbalize their complaints less than majorities? If so, why? Is it possible that the minorities who joined a company like NBC earlier on in fact needed less help than the average NBC employee and therefore had less reason to seek out a *Counselor*? Is it that minorities tended to have less confidence in any internal system and therefore tended to utilize it less, a trend which has recently been reversed?

Whatever the reasons, NBC decided after the first three years that, since the vast majority of issues being brought to the *Counselor* were really generic issues of career growth and mobility, two major adjustments were appropriate. First, the reporting relationship of the *Counselor* was moved from the Affirmative Action Department to the Organization Development Department, in recognition of the nature of the issues with which it was dealing primarily. Second, and within the next 18 months, the focus of the Organization Development Department was adjusted to deal more broadly and more programmatically with career issues from the perspective of the employee.

The title of the department was changed from Organization Development to Counseling and Development; training and development staff was added; and a series of programs were designed and developed directed toward generic career growth, including career assessment, skill enhancement, and career pathing.

Over time, what emerged were actually two, and eventually three, parallel counseling systems, depending on whether the employee defined the issues strictly in terms of EEO, or in some more generic, or some personal way. Employees now had the option of seeking the resources of the Affirmative Action Manager, residing in the Affirmative Action Department, the *Employee Counselor*, residing in the Employee Counseling and Development Department, or the Employee Assistance Program. If, after consultation and review, the Affirmative Action Manager believed that the problem was more of a generic nature, involving career mobility, for example, it would be referred to that department. Similarly, if the employee sought out the Counseling Department first, and after consultation they considered the issue more properly belonged with the Affirmative Action Department, it was referred there.

Whether a concern was brought to the Affirmative Action Department or the Counseling Department, the process used in response was the same: namely, collecting information and then, if the employee consented, intervening with the employee's management.

It might be helpful at this point to describe a few of the cases handled by the Counseling Department and the Affirmative Action Department, to illustrate the types of issues raised and how they were approached and resolved.

Case Examples

Case 1. A white male professional in the Finance Department in his late thirties had been employed by NBC for 12 years. He came to the Counseling Department complaining that he had not been selected for a job for which he believed himself to be very well qualified. On five prior occasions as well, job openings had been posted, he had applied, and he had not been selected. He complained that the company was "unfair," and that jobs were obtained on the basis of favoritism and politics rather than on merit. The *Counselor*, in discussions with the employee, asked his permission to interview some of the people with whom the employee had worked over the last 12 years, to obtain some feedback. The condition was that the *Counselor* would provide only a consensus response, without identifying precisely who said what. The employee agreed, and the *Counselor* interviewed six people with whom the employee had worked closely over the 12-year period, including both supervisors and peers.

The consensus was that the employee was a "pain in the ass." Descriptive examples were provided in behavioral terms. This information was fed back to the employee, who at first denied it vehemently, challenging everyone, including the *Counselor*. The latter explained that the real issue was not so much how the employee saw himself, but how others saw him, based on his behavior. He could ignore the feedback and do nothing, he could try and change his behavior, or he could leave the company and start anew. But he could no longer say candidly that the selection process was based solely on politics, rather than on something which he could affect, namely, his own behavior.

Since the counseling process, the employee has been less openly negative about the company, and a little bit less of a pain in the ass.

Case 2. A relatively young white female came to the *Counselor* complaining of sexual harassment by a fellow employee. The harassment involved making suggestive comments and occasionally touching her in an offensive manner. She explained that she had not approached her supervisor directly with her complaint, because she was a little afraid of him and was not certain how he would respond. The approach agreed upon by the employee and the *Counselor* was to have the latter meet with the supervisor. The *Counselor* thus served first as an intermediary between the employee and the supervisor. The *Counselor* then became an advisor to the supervisor in terms of what behavior was encompassed in the definition of "harassment," and what potential liability could flow both to the company and to the supervisor from his failure to respond appropriately to the issue. Thereafter, the *Counselor* served as a counselor to the supervisor in devising a strategy for approaching the co-worker who was the subject of the complaint.

The supervisor handled the discussion with the co-worker effectively, reassured the complaining employee about the kind of work environment she could expect, and also had the co-worker attend the company's Affirmative Action Management Awareness Workshop, to reemphasize the supervisor's message as well as the company's position on such matters.

Case 3. A black female engineer came to the Affirmative Action Manager complaining that she was not being given opportunities for upgrades within the department. She also complained about the manner in which her supervisor dealt with her personally. The complainant, in her midfifties, said that her supervisor, who was almost 20 years younger and white, behaved in a manner which she considered disrespectful if not downright racist. The supervisor, she said, did not consider her for higher level positions, nor give her assignments to equip her for higher positions. The employee demanded a written list of the criteria to be used in making decisions about upgrades, and also demanded to be addressed in a proper manner. Several days later the company received notification that the employee had also filed a charge with the Equal Employment Opportunity Commission (EEOC) essentially making the same complaints.

The Affirmative Action Manager got from the employee several specific behaviors to use as examples of less than respectful behavior on the supervisor's part, and then went to see him. In discussing the matter with the supervisor, the Affirmative Action Manager found him to be quite resistant, defensive, and personally not very mature. He had not been a supervisor for long, and appeared a bit ill at ease in the role. His response was to be dogmatic. He almost resented having to discuss the issue at all, and certainly did not think it necessary or appropriate to discuss, much less to challenge, the criteria he used for making decisions about upgrades.

In this case, the Affirmative Action Manager decided to call upon the supervisor's own management, as well as the Personnel Director for that division and the Director of Management Development. Together they developed a strategy, supported by the supervisor's management, to educate the supervisor on his responsibilities and to provide him with certain resources to improve his supervisor performance. Jointly they devised a list of broad criteria which the supervisor should use in making upgrade selections, regardless of whether they would ultimately pass that list along to the complaining employee. The Affirmative Action Manager also notified the EEOC of what was being done. In this case, the EEOC seemed quite pleased to have the company resolve the matter if possible to the employee's satisfaction, and then either have the employee withdraw the charge or incorporate any resolution into an EEOC settlement agreement.

The case was resolved by improving, at least to some degree, the supervisor's performance and certainly his understanding of what the company expected of him as a supervisor, by providing the employee with the general list of criteria to be used in making upgrade decisions, and by having the EEOC accept a very generally worded settlement agreement. The employee ultimately balked at signing any agreement, and at withdrawing her charge, and the issue has not proceeded any further, either by the EEOC or by the charging party.

Case 4. A white female secretary went to the Affirmative Action Manager complaining that her new supervisor's style was so disorganized and erratic that she could not perform effectively as his secretary. She also considered him arrogant, and was therefore fearful of providing even constructive suggestions. After further conversation, the Affirmative Action Manager concluded that this was primarily not an EEO issue, but that the secretary was intimidated by the supervisor, and therefore reluctant to seek clarification of ambiguous instructions. The Affirmative Action Manager then called upon the services of the Counseling Department, and together they practiced a dialogue which would allow the employee to bring this to her supervisor's attention in a constructive manner. The following day she attempted the discussion, only to find that the supervisor was also concerned about his own behavior. He attributed it to the anxiety of a new position. They agreed that it was all right for her to give him constructive feedback, even to the point of sounding stern.

The working relationship became visibly more comfortable and effective for both parties.

Revisions in the System

Over the last three years, the clientele of the *Counselor*, and to some extent of the Affirmative Action Manager, has shifted a bit. It is quite likely that such a shift has more to do with the establishment of additional programs and resources which have been made available to the work force than with any change in the actual areas of need within the work force. For example, NBC has developed and put in place a sophisticated management development program to enhance the job skills of its managers. While one would hardly claim a perfect management environment as a result, this program has done much to improve the management climate from the perspective of subordinates. Moreover, this program provides a forum beyond the *Counselor* for managers to seek advice about how to deal with individual situations. Many of these questions had previously been directed to the *Counselor*.

Secondly, NBC expanded and reorganized its Personnel Department to provide greater resources to employees and managers on a divisional basis. Many issues that previously had been brought to the *Counselor*, because that person was seen as the only resource available to employees, are now being brought to the divisional personnel staff. Third, NBC established a formal Employee Assistance Program (EAP) to assist employees and their families with personal problems, many of which have work-related consequences. It is impossible to know how many personal problems now brought to EAP might otherwise have been brought to the *Counselor*, but they are believed to be considerable.

In terms of who within the work force tends to make use of the counseling process, it depends somewhat on whether the first approach is made to the Counseling Department, to the Affirmative Action Manager, to EAP, or to some other person within the Personnel Department. Of those seeking out the Counseling Department, more than half are women, more than half are white, and the vast majority are nonexempt, although relative to their population, minority women tend to use the system more than any other single group. The issues focus primarily on career mobility. Subsidiary issues include conflict with the supervisor, performance problems, interpersonal problems, and personal problems.

Of those who approach the Affirmative Action Manager, slightly less than 50 percent are clerical employees, almost 25 percent are technical employees, and the remainder are split between management and professional employees. Of the issues raised, more than 50 percent involve race, 25 percent involve gender including harassment, and 8 percent involve physical handicap. Within those breakdowns, complaints involve denial of training, imposition of discipline, terms and conditions of employment, selection for promotion, and termination.

Evaluation

NBC had several broad objectives when it established its *Counselor*-type system. Those objectives fell generally into two categories: helping to create an environment conducive to growth and development and providing a mechanism to respond to problems. It is not possible to evaluate the effectiveness of its system with mathematical precision, either in terms of promoting a more positive environment or in reducing the number of problems. NBC considers the system to be quite successful, however, and comes to that conclusion on the basis of several indicators.

First, in terms of hard indicators, the rate of externally filed charges has not increased over the last several years, despite heightened awareness among employees in the workplace generally. Moreover, few employees who seek the services of the *Counselor* subsequently seek outside resources. Not surprisingly, given the several roles that the *Counselor* plays, many more employees seek the aid of the *Counselor* and/or the Affirmative Action Manager than resort to outside agencies. In addition, there have been several major union drives within the last several years directed at the clerical work force. None of those drives has been successful. While there are certainly a variety of reasons for this, one may be the availability of a counseling process which is both confidential and perceived as interceding on behalf of employees.

Second, in terms of softer indicators, the fact is that employees do use the system. If asked, most employees would say that there is a place for them to go to ask questions, seek advice, and get help. Moreover from a management perspective, the counseling process is in a position to identify weak or untrained supervisors, as in the case example described above. Having the opportunity to identify management weaknesses early on enables higher level management to respond together with the Personnel Department before too much damage is done.

Similarly, the ability of employees to come to a *Counselor* in confidence tends to uncover cases where personnel policies are not being applied properly. Such an example was the *Counselor*'s discovery, in response to an employee's complaint that he felt that assignments were given out unfairly, that assignments generating overtime *were* being used as a personal reward system, without regard to merit or performance. If that employee had not had the courage or interest or presence of mind to raise the question, that problem would have remained invisible. Because the *Counselor* speaks with so many employees in the course of a given year, he is also in a position to identify policies that do not work out as planned, and which should therefore be modified.

Conclusion

NBC introduced the concept of a *Counselor* nearly ten years ago. Since that time, it has expanded significantly from an EEO complaint based system to a broad career development approach. It is also no longer limited to a single point of entry in gaining access to counseling services. Employees can approach the Affirmative Action Manager, any one of several professionals in the Counseling and Development Department, or any other professional within the Personnel Department with whom they feel most comfortable, who will then refer them to the proper resource.

The issues that are raised, the informality of the process, and the multiplicity of points of access to it, seem to suit NBC's environment quite well. What has emerged, however, is a process in which the level of comfort for employees using the system is tied more to the individuals within it than the system itself. For a few employees, that process is so flexible that it becomes too diffuse, and is no longer identified as a system so much as a particular person whom you seek out when you have a problem. For most employees, however, it provides a healthy balance between people and process, and continues to serve the purposes for which it was established.

The *Upward-Feedback, Mediation Process* at Massachusetts Institute of Technology

Mary P. Rowe, Ph.D. *

The Massachusetts Institute of Technology is a research university centered in Cambridge, Massachusetts. There are five major schools: Architecture and Urban Planning, Engineering, Humanities and Social Sciences, Science, and the Sloan School of Management. There are also several dozen laboratories and centers. MIT's mission is "to provide the highest quality programs in education and research, with a strong commitment to public service and to diversity of backgrounds, interests and points of view among the faculty, students and staff."

MIT is in fact diverse. There are about 1,000 faculty, about 10,000 undergraduate and graduate students and postdoctorals, and about 8,500 other research staff, visitors, support staff, and administrative staff. Ten to 20 percent of the community is foreign-born, about one-third are women, about one-eighth are minority. Fewer than half of the Ph.D.s on campus are on the faculty. About one-eighth of the total staff are in bargaining units; all other staff and all other students and postdoctoral employees have a nonunion grievance procedure.

The nonunion complaint system at MIT is in many ways similar to those of several hundred universities and corporations. In particular, MIT shares with some other employers and educational institutions the provision of several different options for people with problems. At MIT this is called "redundancy": provision of simultaneously available channels for complaint so that most people will find such a channel easily. One of these channels, the ombudsmanlike offices of the Special Assistants to the President, is a special focus for this article.

The MIT complaint system is also a mediation-oriented service, available with many other helping services to all students and

*Special Assistant to the President, Cambridge, Massachusetts.

to all nonunion employees including faculty and managers. The emphasis is on communication, counseling, fact-finding, conciliation, and mediation, with adjudication where necessary. The complaint structure also serves as an explicit "upward-feedback" channel, designed to help bring information to line managers in an orderly, timely, and supportive fashion. This article sets forth elements of the policy and a discussion of the origins, structure, functions, and performance of the MIT complaint system.

Origins

The present complaint system evolved into its current form steadily over the years. The ethos of "design the future" (an emphasis on upward-feedback and constant evolution) is part of the science and engineering tradition; it has had an effect on MIT's complaint system as on the rest of the institute. Emphases on "redundancy and options," and on problem-solving rather than adjudication, probably also derive from the engineering and scientific tradition and date back many years.

The present Special Assistants assumed their jobs in 1973 and 1974, reporting to then-President Jerome B. Wiesner and then-Chancellor Paul E. Gray. These Assistants were originally hired with a focus, respectively, on women and work and on minority affairs but always received concerns and visits from the whole community. When Paul Gray became President in 1980, the Special Assistants' titles were simplified, to recognize the generality of their complaint handling.

Complaint policies at MIT have developed in a slow, community-based consensus-building fashion. Many employees, personnel managers, and other senior administrators have shaped and now shape the system. A particular emphasis on having Special Assistants work closely with senior officers began in 1976, made explicit by Jerome Wiesner. A particular emphasis, developed under Paul Gray, aims at giving support to people with problems, who can then go back and work on their concerns themselves.

As the system has developed, there has also been an emphasis on supporting people to be able to use regular channels. The availability of "options" is meant to affirm rather than to replace line supervision, the personnel structure, and student academic and support services. Thus, with the advent of "options," it is still the case that most complaints and concerns go through traditional channels.

Structure

The major elements of the system at MIT are these: Various channels allow for both informal concerns and formal complaints, with particular emphasis on informal problem-solving. Redundancy and multiple options for help are major features at every stage of the complaint process, except at the end of the line. One option is available to everyone at MIT who is not in a union. This general option is represented by the Special Assistants to the President, who are designated (in-house) neutrals, or "quasi-ombudsmen." (A "pure" ombudsman is paid outside the institution or the community over which he or she has oversight.)

Confidentiality and privacy are meant to be protected throughout the complaint system. Rights of both offended persons and alleged offenders are explicitly safeguarded. The complaint system is designed to be used only so long as people keep their complaints in-house.

Redundancy and Options Within Formal and Informal Structures

Any student with a formal or informal complaint may bring it up either through the Dean for Student Affairs Office or the Dean of the Graduate School (hereafter the Deans for Students), or through the appropriate academic or administrative hierarchy, or both.

Every student therefore has at least two complaint and appeal channels that are usually simultaneously available. There are, in addition, many other channels for students, including the Office of Minority Education, the housemaster and tutor systems in living groups, in-house judicial procedures in living groups, and the Committee on Discipline. Serious complaints against students (by anyone at MIT) may go to the Committee on Discipline. Complaints by students against others at MIT may go upward within the relevant academic or administrative hierarchy.

Any employee or manager or faculty member with a formal or informal complaint may bring it up either through the line of supervision or the personnel structure, or both. Every employee, including faculty and managers, therefore usually has two possible complaint and appeals channels, which are usually simultaneously available. There is, in addition, a Faculty Administration Committee to which the faculty and academic staff may appeal on faculty-administration matters. Faculty appeals about negative promotion decisions go up the academic hierarchy, usually to the appropriate academic Dean or the Provost.

There are many other services for the whole community that receive complaints and concerns. People bring complaints to the Campus Patrol and to the wide range of health care practitioners and employee assistance people in the Medical Department. There are also religious counselors, the student-run Nightline, and dozens of networks of special interest groups. Some areas of the Institute also have special complaint structures like the Patient Advocate and Medical Advisory Board of the Medical Department and the Safety Coordinators at Lincoln Laboratory. Discrimination complaints may be brought through general complaints channels or to designated Equal Opportunity officers or both. Safety problems go to the Safety Office and through the general complaints channels.

Finally, there is one general option available to everyone at MIT not in a union, whether they are faculty, managers, employees, or students. The two Special Assistants to the President serve as designated neutrals who will hear or help with any kind of concern within the MIT community. They usually see people on an informal, problem-solving basis, but occasionally serve at the "end of the line" to make formal recommendations to the President. It is very common for several offices to work together, with the permission of the complainant.

Nearly all complaints and concerns at MIT are heard and resolved informally within the relevant academic or administrative hierarchy, within the Offices of the Deans for Students and within Personnel. In the rare case of a formal (usually written) complaint, the complaint must go into the appropriate line management channel, and may also go up through the channel of Personnel or of the graduate or undergraduate Deans for Students.

The tradition of "redundancy and options" serves many purposes. In this context, redundancy is seen as necessary, in the engineering sense of fail-safe and backup. It provides a safeguard against the subjectivity or coopting of any one complaints handler. It provides backup in cases of conflict of interest, illness, vacation, or overload. It provides a potential, where permission has been given, for collegial counsel. Options are equally seen as necessary. The most important problem of any complaint system is how to get people actually to feel free to use it. The MIT complaint structure includes, in its different offices, older and younger people; technical and nontechnical people; people of formal and informal demeanor; minorities, men and women, nonminorities. At the end of this procedure and as a general, informal option for everyone are two Special Assistants to the President, currently one black male, the other white female.

Confidentiality and Privacy

Everyone in the complaint system is required, if asked, to keep confidential whatever concerns may be brought to him or her. Of course a supervisor or counseling dean or personnel officer or Assistant to the President may not be able to act on a concern brought in by someone, if the individual requests confidentiality. Often the complaint handler can, however, provide information to respond to a concern. Or the grievant can be helped to resolve a problem on his or her own. Sometimes a complaint handler will wish to ask permission to speak to others to resolve a complaint. Except in the rare case when there is a "duty to warn," it is expected that confidentiality will be observed.

All offices of MIT observe strict privacy codes with respect to records. In addition, the office spaces of the Special Assistants are especially private. Many people with concerns may feel freer to come to the Assistants' offices because these officers are down a small corridor and out of the way.

Protecting the Rights of All Concerned: "Neutrality"

A complaint system could be devised on the principle that such a structure should strive to be perfect—to make no errors. The system at MIT is designed a little differently, on the principle that mistakes and partial mistakes will occur despite the most dedicated efforts to the contrary. The process is then guided by the principle first of all to do no damage. In a context where it appears that there will always be some errors of omission (too little being done), or some errors of commission (too much being done) there is an expectation that mistakes, if they occur, would be of the first type.

The complaint system of MIT explicitly seeks to protect the rights of alleged offenders as well as of offended persons. The Deans for Students and Personnel officers and Special Assistants are frequently asked, "Whose side are you on?" The MIT complaint system does not specify advocacy, either for MIT or for a grievant. MIT believes that the institution has a common interest with people who have been wronged. The complaint handlers' role is to ex-emplify this common interest with those who have been wronged. Or, in the case of people who have wronged each other, MIT may have a partial interest on each side of a question.

Complaint handlers are expected to seek to illuminate and to support the common interest of MIT with those who have been wronged, in whole or in part. This very frequently means endeavoring to improve a situation as well as the condition of an individual. A steadfast refusal to be drawn into simple polarization frequently leads to third alternatives. Although many people feel strongly that "he who is not with me is against me," the refusal to permit simplistic polarization appears in the long run to bring people the greatest sense of relief. For people who see themselves and everyone else as having many different motivations, the opportunity to see a problem in a balanced way may permit a grievant more comfort and more room to grow, and may help to protect the rights of those against whom a complaint is brought.

It is unusual for anyone in the complaint system to listen to a third-party complaint. The Special Assistants in particular do not play the role of inspectors-general. One may, of course, suggest to a third party that people with problems be referred in, to talk about their problems themselves. By and large, however, complaint handlers do not seek out concerns. Complaint offices, especially those of the Special Assistants, are "consumer-driven" on a first-party basis.

This principle extends also to relations between senior administrators and the Special Assistants. Obviously senior officers regularly express concerns to the Special Assistants. They do not, however, "assign" problems and conflicts to the Special Assistants. They may instead refer people with problems to the Assistants, but support the right and privilege of such people to come in or not, as they themselves choose.

People may present concerns or complaints accompanied by any MIT colleague. There is an expectation of reasonable speed in responding to complaints. MIT formally proscribes reprimand or punishment for raising a concern or grievance.

MIT complaint handlers will not ordinarily agree to see people accompanied by their lawyers. People with problems may often wish to consult with their lawyers on the outside. But offices in the complaint system, and especially those of the Special Assistants, are meant to stand free of polarization as much as possible. For the same reason this complaints and mediation process is usually available only so long as members of the MIT community stay "in-house," and not during or after formal application to outside agencies or courts. (An exception could occur where a criminal matter has been taken outside.) Once a specific problem has been dealt with outside, the Special Assistants in particular will no longer deal with that question, although different questions from the same person may be brought in. MIT people who choose to go to outside agencies or the courts without having exhausted the internal complaints procedure, and those who choose to be represented by counsel rather than by themselves, deal primarily with a different office at MIT (e.g., the Director of Personnel) or with MIT's law firm.

Functions

Complaint systems should perform at least the following functions: communications with individuals; counseling; fact-finding, conciliation and mediation; adjudications; and "upward feedback" to the employer as part of the management information system.

Communications and Counseling

All channels in the MIT complaint system are engaged in one-to-one communications and problem-solving counseling. This is usually on a confidential basis. The goal is, if possible, to help people help themselves, through listening to problems, helping to deal with anger, providing data, helping to frame a problem, and possibly extensive role-playing. Most people enter the system with "inquiries and concerns," rather than complaints; this is much encouraged. In the offices of the Special Assistants in particular, visitors are offered whatever seem to be all the reasonable options for the "next step." Most people choose the option of learning, with support, how to go back and deal with problems at the appropriate level, on their own. And sometimes people can, thereby, learn a process of problem-solving as well as an answer to a specific problem.

Many problems are resolved with confidential (and responsible) access to appropriate information. An MIT employee can find out in confidence, for example, whether the Wage and Salary Office believes she or he is being fairly paid. A student may talk with a department head about the fairness of a grading system in a given class. Often some information, and discussion with an objective person, will resolve a concern. This is especially true, for example, in times of inflation, budget crunch, and adjustment to regulation, when the complaint system serves an important information disseminating function. Sometimes a complaint handler can help just by listening, especially where an employee or student is extremely angry. The "individual communications" function goes two ways.

Fact-finding, Conciliation, Mediation

Fact-finding, conciliation, and mediation are found in all channels of the MIT complaint system and at all levels up to the top. In these functions the complaint handler, having been asked to intervene, has received permission to talk with other people. If nearly all "inquiries and concerns" are resolved by providing information and counseling, nearly all complaints and grievances are resolved through some brief or extended conciliation or mediation.

Because the complaint process is designed to be consumer-driven, and to help people who can do so to help themselves, the Special Assistants rarely fashion a unique remedy by themselves for someone else. Through listening, negotiating, and exploring all reasonable alternatives, the Special Assistants seek to illuminate new possibilities for people with problems. Often, however, people with problems will choose an alternative an Assistant might not have chosen had this been an arbitration situation. People often appear to seek less redress, or less of a specific settlement than an arbitration might have determined. (A few people appear to fight for more.) The hope is that this procedure provides people with more control over their own lives. It may also permit them to evaluate "subjective" considerations (such as the feelings of co-workers), in a way which may minimize damage and lead to a better solution in the long run.

Adjudication

Adjudication is the province of the complaint and appeal channels: supervision, the Personnel Office, the Offices of the Deans for Students, and some specific judicial bodies like the Committee on Discipline. Following the rule of ombudsmen, the Special Assistants do not normally adjudicate, although they often make informal recommendations and may be asked to make formal recommendations to the President.

Upward Feedback

Upward feedback is part of the role of all complaint handlers at MIT. In fact the principle of upward feedback is consonant with the general ethos of the Institute. It is deeply rooted in a general MIT commitment to "design the future."

The Special Assistants in particular have two explicit charges: They are to help each individual visitor as well as they can and they are to seek ways to reflect to line management, in a supportive way, data which came to the Assistants which would be useful to managers to run their areas effectively and humanely. This "upward feedback" must be done with a high degree of sensitivity to the privacy of people who raise problems and of line managers. For example, sometimes a Special Assistant will receive permission from a visitor to repeat an illustrative problem to a manager or department head. Sometimes confidentiality and privacy can be protected by raising problems in a generic way rather than by using individual stories. For example, where sexual harassment has been alleged, a department head may not need to know the identities of individuals to institute an apparently "routine" departmental discussion of harassment that will eliminate the problem.

Often data can be brought to a line manager in such a way that the manager can improve a process, without being embarrassed or exposed, and in such a way as to (rightfully) receive credit for progress in the system. This expected contact with line managers also serves on occasion to help keep open the lines of communication with a department where there have been unusual problems.

How Does It Work?

The complaint system and relevant MIT policies are publicized in employee and student handbooks and policy manuals; in the Affirmative Action Plan, which is widely available; in special resource materials given to students, for example, at registration; in the MIT newspaper; in various supervisor and employee training programs; at ad hoc meetings of any MIT group, on request.

Little is known about the total volume of complaints and concerns brought throughout the MIT complaint system. Most inquiries and complaints go to academic and administrative supervisors, to the Dean's Offices, and to Personnel. Most academic problems are resolved within academic structures and most appeals are resolved within the appropriate academic and administrative hierarchies.

The Special Assistants receive calls and visits and letters from 30 to 100 people a week, from a nonunion community of about 16,000. (This has been a relatively steady case load since 1973 when these offices began.) Many questions can be answered quickly; many visitors need appropriate referrals. Most of the rest can be rather quickly helped to go back to work on a problem directly by themselves. In any given year there are a few hundred more serious cases leading to conciliation and mediation.

Most university ombudsman offices receive more students than employees. The MIT Special Assistants' offices tend to receive more faculty, staff, and support staff. Among employee groups, visits to the office generally reflect the kinds and numbers of faculty and employees at MIT. Middle level and senior administrators and faculty are heavily represented; research staff come in proportionately less often. Among students, graduate students come in more frequently than undergraduates.

Because so many contacts with the Special Assistants are brief and informal, it is difficult to categorize types of concerns, and prevalent complaints change from year to year. For example, in 1973 the first Special Assistant got almost daily salary equity complaints. These are now very uncommon, due to changes in wage and salary administration. On the other hand, disagreements about scientific attribution, for example, problems of plagiarism, are more commonly reported than in 1973. On the whole the Special Assistants appear to get "new cases"—that is, whatever is a new kind of problem. Their offices tend to receive people who for one reason or another do not trust other services, who are particularly anxious about confidentiality, who particularly want their problems "heard at the top," who see themselves as whistleblowers, who have very bizarre problems, who do not know where to go and how the system works. Some visitors are extremely angry; an important function of the offices is to deal with rage.

Success of this complaint system may be seen to lie in the eye of the beholder, but some data may be useful to the reader. In the past 10 years there have been about a dozen nonunion complaints a year carried out of house. Most of these did not exhaust internal complaint services. No complaints in the past 10 years have gone to trial.

In the past 10 years there have been hundreds of small and large changes in policies and procedures and structures as a result of concerns and inquiries and complaints. These range from building improvements to improvements in information materials, to a change in the pension plan, to numerous changes in policy, to procedural changes brought about by the Safety Office.

Some kinds of complaints seem to come in now much sooner after a precipitating incident, for example, in harassment cases. Some kinds of problems have all but disappeared. There are very few reports of attempted or actual retaliation for a person's bringing complaint. Most department heads have become very adept at complaint handling. On the other hand, unexpected problems continue at the same pace. And some problems, like the "loneliness and isolation" of graduate students, are reported more frequently, perhaps as proxies for other underlying issues.

It is particularly difficult to gauge user satisfaction throughout the system. It is typical of mediation-oriented services that they are much more popular than systems oriented toward adjudication, so it is difficult to know how to judge MIT's largely favorable data. On the basis of anecdotal information from similar institutions, it appears that MIT may have a higher reporting rate of "concerns and inquiries" and a lower incidence of the most serious problems. This appears particularly true with regard to all kinds of harassment. It is fair to say, however, that from the complaint handlers' perspective much improvement is possible, especially with regard to making the complaint system better known in the community and more widely trusted.

With respect to managerial satisfaction there are no firm data. Over the years the complaint system use rate by managers (as employees and as supervisors), has risen sharply. Concerns and inquiries come in, in fact, disproportionately more often from managers. One may guess that supervisors in general are cautious about the complaint system until they have contact with it. Thereafter a small proportion dislike it.

An unknown percentage of the MIT community would prefer more emphasis on formal adjudication. This point and the constant need to do better in helping people understand the system, mean that there are always ongoing discussions at MIT about how to revise and improve the handling of complaints and concerns. In a real sense, the complaint system at MIT is just a process; next year it will and should be different. It reflects its home. As Paul Gray sees it, "MIT is simply an idea—one which has drawn together and sparked the imagination of countless faculty, staff and students."

The *Corporate Ombudsperson* at American Telephone and Telegraph-Information Systems

*Martha Maselko**

American Telephone and Telegraph-Information Systems (AT&T-IS) is a subsidiary of AT&T. Its mission is to develop, retail, and service leading-edge communications products, information management systems, and enhanced services for business customers. It also distributes products for residential and small business customers.

AT&T-IS comprised three divisions: Services, Marketing and Sales, and Product Management and Development. Of 93,000 employees, 66,000 are in the Services Division, 23,000 in Marketing and Sales, and 4,300 in Product Management and Development. AT&T-IS was formed with people transferred from various organizations across AT&T. In particular, Product Management and Development is composed primarily of scientists and engineers formerly at Bell Laboratories.

The Customer Systems division, of which the Office of the Ombudsman is part, is within the Product Management and Development organization. Headed by Lee S. Tuomenoksa, vice president, it has 1,800 employees at four locations—in Holmdel, Lincroft, and Morristown, New Jersey, and in Denver, Colorado.

Origins of the Function of Ombudsman

Throughout the transition from Bell Labs to AT&T-IS, the traditional procedures for handling employee complaints and problems were in existence and functioning, namely: Labor Relations, Affirmative Action Counselors, and Employee Counseling Service. There were also clubs within the Labs which responded to the

*Currently, Ombudsperson, Bell Labs, Lincroft, New Jersey; formerly Ombudsperson at American Telephone and Telegraph-Information Systems, Holmdel, New Jersey.

201

organizational need of particular groups as well as broader, more global issues facing groups such as Asian-Americans, blacks, Hispanics, and women.

On February 6, 1981, several Bell Labs employees wrote a letter to their vice president, Lee S. Tuomenoksa, describing the value and need for the function of an ombudsman in the organization. Their letter stated: "Problems resulting from a changing environment can be handled in many ways. An ombudsman provides an opportunity for informal, private discussion regarding a problem. Many times simply discussing the problem with an uninvolved person provides the perspective that enables the individual to solve the problem himself or herself." The concept appealed to Mr. Tuomenoksa, and he paid a visit to his alma mater, the Massachusetts Institute of Technology, to explore the role of ombudsman with Dr. Mary P. Rowe, Special Assistant to the President at MIT. After these discussions Mr. Tuomenoksa decided to explore the possibility of having this type of function in his area of responsibility. He started a search for a person with the special abilities to fill this role. He hired Martha Maselko, then the Group Supervisor for Affirmative Action Training at the Affirmative Action Center in Bell Labs, to start in November 1982. Tuomenoksa charged Maselko to explore the concept of ombudsman and to develop the concept so that it would be appropriate and effective in an organizational environment like that of AT&T.

The process of developing and installing the function of ombudsman was critical and had much to do with its current effectiveness. The concept of ombudsman existed in the public sector in Europe and in the United States. But what about organizations in the private sector? There are always differences between what is effective in the two sectors, and there was a need to determine what would make it work in industry in America. Therefore, the first task in developing and implementing was to learn just what the concept really was and how it worked or did not work in American business organizations. Maselko did an extensive search of the literature on the concept and application of ombudsman to business. She also located organizations where the function existed (sometimes by a different name) and also those that had experimented with the concept but no longer endorsed it. In addition to studying the literature, Maselko personally contacted several organizations where the function existed, including IBM, Xerox, General Electric, and Anheuser-Busch. She also contacted other organizations where the concept failed. This was to ensure a greater possibility of success by avoiding the pitfalls experienced by others.

The failures, it seemed, resulted from several consistent themes:

- The lack of commitment from top management.
- The distrustful culture of an organization.
- The ombudsman reported to a lower level manager and was not viewed as having sufficient influence.
- A lack of sufficient education of the employee population on the purpose and role of the ombudsman.
- The skill level of the person in the function to handle all the diverse requests presented.

In March 1982, Maselko presented her proposal for the *Office of Ombudsperson* to Tuomenoksa for review with his staff. The concept was accepted.

The next step was implementation preceded by an extensive education process. Maselko developed some materials and with the assistance of the Graphics Department in the company, created a video slide presentation explaining the purpose of the *Office of Ombudsperson* (the title chosen) and how it would work. (The title of the function varied in companies visited.)

Learning from the failures of others, Tuomenoksa wanted the position to have sufficient influence and decided to have the function report directly to himself, the highest manager in his area of responsibility. A series of meetings were scheduled with the purpose of personally contacting each employee. These presentations were conducted with top managers; then managers and their work groups; and in more open meetings, with many different groups represented. Each person viewed the visual presentation and then heard from Maselko personally. She answered questions and differentiated the *Office of Ombudsperson* function from existing functions. In all, some 25 meetings were held with many one-to-one conversations mixed in. Within two weeks the organization (and even some outside the immediate group) were aware that the *Office of Ombudsperson* was a reality in the Bell Labs organization, which was to become a few months later the Customer Systems area of AT&T-IS.

Overall Description of the Current System

The *Office of Ombudsperson* was established to meet the needs of the organization and the individual needs of all employees at all levels within Customer Systems, from the vice president to the newest entry-level employee. The *Ombudsperson* was available to work with the concerns of all staffs and individuals.

The kinds of issues vary a great deal in scope, from an individual concern to an organizational concern; from one individual to an entire work area or work group. The following is a list of the kinds of concerns or issues covered. Some are more of an individual type, for example:

— Problem with career,
— Retirement,
— Difficulty with supervisor,
— Relocation,
— Promotion inequity,
— Transfer of work area,
— Potential sexual harassment suit,
— New supervisory responsibilities,
— Difficult employee,
— Resignations,
— Identification of proper internal resources to solve problems of Affirmative Action, counseling, and other established functions.

Other kinds of concerns were either organizational or included several individuals. For example:

- Several individuals
  — A group problem with a particular supervisor,
  — Work environment problems,
  — Stress in the work project,
  — Inequities felt by a certain work classification across department lines.
- Organizational issues
  — Questions regarding company policy,
  — Questions regarding salary administration,
  — Training activities,
  — Where else and how to establish other *Ombudsperson* offices both within the AT&T system and outside,
  — Other concerns affecting work indirectly, such as physical fitness, outside training, child care, and community relations,
  — Establishing more effective communication links, such as providing an informal channel to the vice president and management, creating an area newsletter, establishing direct link between the vice president and em-

ployees at all levels through, for example, meetings and breakfasts,
— Assisting in the process of intercompany transfers.

As indicated, an important function of the *Office of Ombudsperson* is to assist individuals in the organization in obtaining proper direction or information. Frequently, resources exist within Customer Systems, but for whatever reason, individuals are unaware of how to access these resources. The *Ombudsperson* role is not to duplicate these resources but to channel the requests to the proper function and area of responsibility. Employees with questions on affirmative action, clarification of sexual harassment, purchasing procedures, and individual counseling are referred to the proper resource.

A key to the effectiveness of the function depends on how the system is communicated to employees. If individuals are to take advantage of the function, they must be aware that it exists. However, other methods of communication also operate to maintain the flow of information. These communication methods include the following:

- A newsletter was created originating from the *Office of Ombudsperson* but written and edited by employees. This newsletter is called *On Line* and is published monthly with frequent communications from the *Ombudsperson*.
- The function received publicity from newspapers at other AT&T locations available to Customer Systems' employees. For example, *Bell Labs News* and *Bell Telephone Magazine*.
- New employee handbooks contain information such as the following example from one handbook: "In Division X, an ombudsperson is available to assist you in resolving problems related to the 'human' side of work. The ombudsperson guarantees confidentiality and anonymity in all contacts and is supportive of the needs of the individual, supervision and the organization. If you are experiencing problems in your work environment, the ombudsperson may be able to help solve the problems or direct you to someone who can."
- The activities of the *Ombudsperson* are reviewed by the vice president and his staff and periodic reviews are conducted with other levels of management.
- The Vice President, Lee S. Tuomenoksa, mentions the *Office of Ombudsperson* in his presentations.

- Other activities such as employment anniversaries, and significant changes are further opportunities to "advertise" and communicate information on the office.

Communication has played a significant role in the quick response the organization has had to the *Office*. People know of its existence and, if they do not make use of the function themselves, they refer others to it. The difficult part of communications has to do with publishing results and specifics since the confidential nature of the work must be protected. Frequently, people are aware of the *Office* but may not be aware of its specific accomplishments.

The location of the *Office* is highly important. Individuals need to have access while their visits remain anonymous and confidential. For this reason the office site selected is accessible yet its location encourages people to contact the *Ombudsperson* without fear of being observed. In Customer Systems the location is near the main entrance.

The Mechanics of the System

While the "system" under which the *Ombudsperson* works is consistent, it is not a formalized or documented system. The outline below captures the flow of the procedure as it is presently used:

The nature of the methods and steps is to establish a procedure that meets both the individual and personal needs as well as those of the organization. Unlike more traditional methods of arbitration which have formal established steps, the procedures of the *Ombudsperson* office are flexible. The *Office* achieves its power and effectiveness from being able to cut short, or at times circumvent, the obstacles of a bureaucratic structure. This is not to advocate anarchy, but to create a method of operation different from the traditional and normal, so that problems are dealt with quickly and effectively. Wherever structured methods of problem solving are in support of effective resolution, these steps are followed. Also, the *Office* in no way sets itself up against appropriate methods of recourse, such as legal, or union contracts, or other established methods. The *Office* is supportive of policy where it exists and works to clarify policy, update policy, and when necessary, question and change policy. This requires that the *Ombudsperson* be seen as following a procedure and not as acting whimsically or capriciously. For this reason, the *Office* makes use of the resources and expertise of the Legal and Personnel Departments.

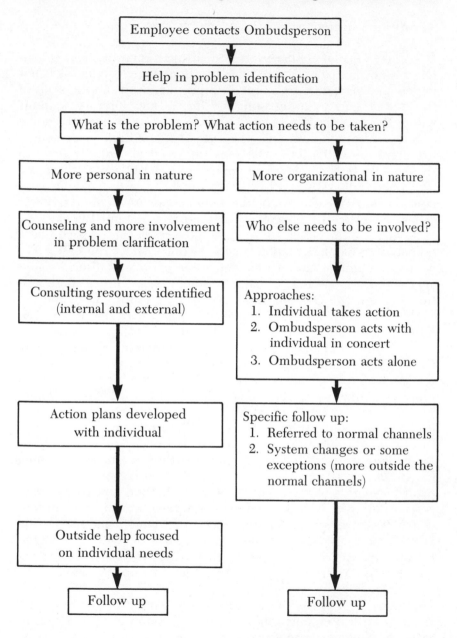

The System in Action

The *Office of Ombudsperson* deals with investigation, concil-iation, and mediation but not adjudication. Its effectiveness is not dependent on formal adjudication procedures, but on the skills of the practitioner in using both the formal and informal systems within the organization. The *Ombudsperson* can frequently solve problems through more effective means of fact-finding, investiga-tion, and mediation which lessens the need for adjudication. In the area of equal employment opportunity (EEO) cases, there is a formal parallel system within AT&T-IS. EEO cases have been ex-cluded from the charter of the *Ombudsperson* deliberately. At times, however, the office plays an important role in EEO matters. In particular, the actions of the *Ombudsperson* can be such that a potentially volatile situation never becomes an "EEO case." On occasion situations have arisen where one party feels discriminated against, or believes that sexual harassment has occurred. Both par-ties seek out the *Ombudsperson*, and in attempting to define the problem more clearly, both parties become aware that it is not an EEO matter but something else. The result is that the case does not go to the EEO function, but rather, energy is invested in solving the real problem that was identified.

An example of this is a case in which several individuals (as a group) felt they were being discriminated against because of age. The problem was later identified as salary compression, a typical problem for today's organizations, and the problem was addressed as a salary administration problem, not as an EEO case. The *Office* has helped in regard to EEO matters in other instances by helping individuals or groups clarify their understanding of what consti-tuted a violation of EEO legislation and what did not. In this way, certain potential EEO cases were withdrawn or never instituted, and the real problems were addressed to the benefit and satisfaction of both the employee and the organization. Likewise, if the *Om-budsperson* clearly discovers an EEO case, the individual is re-ferred to the Affirmative Action Department for appropriate counsel and advice.

Since the *Office of Ombudsperson* is established to deal with all manner of problems otherwise unresponded to by the organi-zation bureaucracy, the types of problems and issues vary greatly. Therefore, a common thread is identifiable only in major issues or concerns such as problems with supervision, performance review process, and career development. In 1984, the *Office of Ombuds-person* was involved with 496 instances of individual or group concerns. In 1985 that number increased to 623. The *Office* goes beyond the statistical reporting of data. There are numerous other instances of contact with people that are not able to be statistically quantified. These are the contacts in the hallways, at other meetings, casual office discussions, the parking lot, the lunchroom, at the local shopping center doing Christmas shopping, or at community affairs. The initiative of Customer Systems in creating the role has a significant impact on individuals and on individuals within their work groups. It is important to give statistical quantifiable results of the *Office*. However, nonmeasured activities also make a contribution in potentially eliminating concerns or at least as a positive living symbol that the organization "really does care about its employees." This value is also exemplified by the fact that those using the services of the *Office* include members from all groups of employees including the vice president and his staff. The following are some examples of the most common types of concerns presented to the *Office* during the last full year of functioning.

Counseling People Who Perceive They Have a Difficult Boss

Individuals and groups sought assistance with situations in which they perceived their boss to be the problem. In most instances the *Ombudsperson* discovered the employees had not articulated their concerns. For the most part, the employees tended to be indirect, assuming that the boss could read between the lines, and know what the problems were. They expected the boss to be able to know what they wanted. The *Ombudsperson* spent time encouraging the employee to be more specific in articulating examples in a way that would open more communication channels, rather than close them. This is never an easy task for employees who view themselves as being in a less powerful position, but it is critical if one is to be productive and not waste energy on noneffective communications. In most of the instances, with the help of the *Ombudsperson*, employees could be clear and set more specific goals with their boss. The results were more satisfied employees who resolved their own problems and operated more productively.

Assisting Managers in Dealing With Personnel Problems

Managers sought advice and assistance from the *Ombudsperson* in ways to deal with difficult employee situations. Some examples of this kind of situation are: peers within a work group having conflict; conflict between peers in different departments; a secretary who constantly cried; and an employee identified as having high potential but who was not being productive. In most cases, managers knew what to do to handle the situation. What they needed was a willing ear to help talk through the situation and to discover strategies and courses of action which would resolve the problem. They wanted to be comfortable and know their action plans would have positive results They also sought alternative ways of handling the situation so they could be assured they thought through alternatives. The *Ombudsperson* was the willing ear and helped to think through alternative solutions.

Working on Getting Ideas Implemented

Individuals felt they had important ideas that they wanted to be heard and implemented. These ideas included effective affirmative action meetings, customer visits, flextime, and ways for a minority group to deal with upper management. In each of these situations, the employees had good ideas and wanted to learn some methods to get them implemented. These individuals and groups sought the *Ombudsperson* as a source of information and help. This involved talking through concepts and ideas, resources required, and appropriate procedures for increasing the probability of implementation. With the help of the *Ombudsperson*, these individuals and groups planned and carried out, *by themselves*, strategies for having their ideas heard. In all the issues identified, with the exception of flextime, the ideas were implemented effectively. In this way, the ideas of all employees have the chance to be heard, which has an impact on their level of satisfaction. This also helps the organization and management, who have the benefit of the thinking of all employees at all levels.

Acting as a Broker for the Services of Others

The *Office* assists individuals in getting to the right source to deal with their issues, problems, or questions. In some instances employees were not sure who was responsible or which department could help. There were such issues as salary information, retirement concerns, transfers, and relocation. The *Ombudsperson* function acts as an information base where people can freely ask where to go for help to solve their problem. The *Office* fills an important void in this area.

Employees Try Every Channel and Nothing Works

The traditional organization has procedures and methods which are not always the best for responding to individual problems and needs. For example, a person attempted unsuccessfully for eight months to correct an error in her paycheck. The *Ombudsperson*, together with the immediate supervisor, solved the problem in three days. Another example was the situation of a technical person who, because of the transition, had no approved method of making a change in a particular specification number from one company to another. There was a problem shifting the specification number from Bell Labs to Customer Systems. By contacting the appropriate departments in each organization, the specifications were transferred, and the employee could continue his work on the project. The problem was solved. The *Office of Ombudsperson* offers problem solving in situations where the usual channels do not exist or prove ineffective.

Voicing Concerns to the Vice President

Individuals and groups have concerns that they feel should be brought to the attention of the vice president. In some instances, they required action, and in others, awareness was enough. One example centered on a van pool problem. Employees were told one thing almost as a matter of policy, and later, management reversed its position. A similar issue centered on problems regarding salary treatment. While no direct changes of policy resulted from information presented to the vice president on these and similar problems, there is a certain level of awareness. Now data are being collected to identify where there might be problems with actual policy, and when the problems are consistent in nature and not just exceptions. The vice president and the *Ombudsperson* are more aware of the need to review and monitor existing policies carefully. There were numerous other issues where no action was required, and just being heard met the needs of the individual raising the concern. In this way, the *Ombudsperson* helped both the employee and the vice president, who is not viewed as distant and unconcerned, but as someone who practices his beliefs in the importance of the individual employee.

Obtaining Information for Special Requests

Individuals seek assistance from the *Office of Ombudsperson* in obtaining special information on how to deal with special problems such as conflict, stress in the work setting, and "employee burnout." The *Office of Ombudsperson* maintains a resource center for this and other relevant information for employees. Employees at all levels make use of this service, and individuals receive help in coping with work-related problems through this additional information source.

Orientation for New Employees

The introduction of new employees into an organization and their quick assimilation has direct impact on their productivity and effectiveness. It is the first of many critical steps in their development and has a direct correlation to their sense of well being, satisfaction, and productivity. For these reasons, the *Office of Ombudsperson* took an active role in initiating, designing, and implementing a "new employee orientation" for both the New Jersey and Denver locations.

Exit Interviews

Another important function of the office is to interview departing employees. This is an opportunity to discuss with an employee reasons for their leaving and any recommendations for improvement for the organization. This information is shared with their management. Information is analyzed on a regular basis to determine trends. In more traditional organizations, these data usually remain within the personnel organization. In Customer Systems, the *Ombudsperson* makes this information available to the highest level of management for appropriate action.

Service Anniversary Acknowledgement for Longer Term Employees

Loyalty and dedication frequently go unnoticed in the minds of individual employees. To help recognize the contributions of longer term employees, the *Ombudsperson* initiated and organized Service Anniversary Breakfasts for people with anniversaries in multiples of 5 years (e.g., 5th, 10th, 15th, and 20th). Upper management is present at these breakfasts and acknowledges the work of the individuals. In times of transition and change, this simple structure responded to individuals who might otherwise feel underappreciated and unrecognized. The impact of these celebrations had a positive impact on those who attended.

Promotion and Welcome Acknowledgment

Success and achievement, when recognized, breed even more success and achievement. Organizations do not always do a good job in publicly recognizing the efforts of individuals. Frequently, this is expected in successful high-tech organizations. The *Ombudsperson* developed a method for achieving wider visibility for individuals, in recognition of those who were newly promoted, newly hired, or transferred to the organization. This public recognition takes place in the form of a display board located in a prominent place within the facility.

Distinguished Technical Staff (DTS) Awards

Special achievement deserves acknowledgement. Several of the employees in the organization were noted for their accomplishments and needed to be recognized in a timely fashion. The *Office of Ombudsperson* initiated a procedure for notifying all employees of a special recognition given to one of their peers. A notice was sent "desk-to-desk" to every employee to inform them of who had received the DTS Award on the very day of the announcement. Plaques were also designed so that recipients will receive public recognition on an ongoing basis. Each year the names of recipients of DTS and Fellowship awards will be added to the list presently displayed.

The above examples are some of the employee issues presently being dealt with through the *Office of Ombudsperson*. Many other ideas have been presented and are still in the germination stage. The one single driving force is a method to address employee concerns as well as methods to enhance the work environment. This enhancement assures employees that they will be heard, recognized, and assisted in every possible way that supports the climate and goals the organization is attempting to reach.

The *Office of Ombudsperson* works in support of the organization and the individual at all levels. Therefore, the attitudes of supervision, line management, middle management, and all the employees have been very positive. The *Office of Ombudsperson* is viewed as a powerful tool in implementing requests and narrowing what in some organizations seems to be a gap between management and the individual. Management is supportive because they see the function as helping them achieve results and not just as a complaint center for alleviating problems.

Effects on Outside Complaints and Litigation

Outside litigation and complaints are not the charter or responsibility of the *Office of Ombudsperson*. These activities remain with the Legal and Affirmative Action departments. At times an individual who has taken outside action may seek the assistance of the *Ombudsperson* for personal reasons, but the issues are kept separate and distinct. It is interesting that while the role of *Ombudsperson* is recent to the private sector as an organizational function, there have been ombudsmen in the public sector for a long time. Several federal government agencies have the function as a method of dealing with employee concerns and some governing bodies have it to assure that the interests of their constituents are met and not blocked by bureaucracy. In Customer Systems the focus of the *Ombudsperson* is almost exclusively inward.

Effects on Employee Relations and Organization Objectives

The effects of the *Office of Ombudsperson* in Customer Systems have been felt for a little over five years. Interview data seem to indicate that the effect on employee morale has been positive. Several individuals who had seriously considered leaving the organization and had been active in job searches stopped this activity and became productive employees. Work groups experiencing difficulties with their supervisor were able to remove the barriers to work effectiveness and personal satisfaction. Inappropriate interpretation of company policy by supervisors who lacked sufficient information have been corrected and what could have been a source of discontent turned into a positive situation. Many individuals whose concerns did not receive an immediate resolution "at least were heard" and their concerns are receiving attention. Some of these concerns are not amenable to simple solutions and require additional investigation. However, the impact on the employees has been extremely positive. The work of the *Ombudsperson* has been to focus on more immediate concerns during the initial start up of the position.

Specific steps are now being planned to investigate the present policies and procedures in place at AT&T-IS. While this is a constant concern for management and other departments, the *Office of Ombudsperson* will seek areas in need of refinement, improvement, or change. This focus will take the *Office of Ombudsperson* into the area of organizational change in addition to responding to individual needs. The function will operate much in the same way as it did with individual concerns. Where appropriate areas of responsibility are identified, the *Ombudsperson* will channel the information to that function. Where no clear area of responsibility is identified, the matter will be raised with the Customer Systems vice president and his staff so appropriate resources can be assigned. In the meanwhile, the function will continue to assist supervisors and individuals in managing equity in policy administration, to eliminate potential problems, and to solve real concerns.

Another indication of the positive response received from employees has been the introduction of a second *Ombudsperson* at the Denver location. The function initially resided in New Jersey with responsibility for Denver as well. The demands for the services of the function became such that it required an on-site person at the Denver facility to respond adequately. Several other areas of AT&T-IS have received letters from employees, on their own initiative, for an *Ombudsperson*. The reputation of the work of the *Ombudsperson* presently in place has created a demand from employees themselves.

The importance of growth and change in increasing the effectiveness of the role must be a constant concern. The reason for some past failures of the function in organizations has been an inability or unwillingness to update and refocus the energy of the function. To guard against this inertia, the *Ombudsperson* in Customer Systems, together with Dr. Mary P. Rowe at MIT and Chris McEachern at Anheuser-Busch, has been active in creating a network of ombudspersons in other organizations. A conference was held for the first time in July 1984 at Falmouth, Massachusetts for representatives from other companies, and 53 representatives from different companies attended. The discussions focused on issues and concerns for effective *Ombudsperson* functions within organizations. This allowed individuals to keep abreast of what others are doing, what is happening in the field, what changes need to be made to improve the function, and to network with each other.

This kind of activity will allow the *Ombudsperson* to identify other changes and improvements as well as what kind of issues are dealt with in other organizations. The success and continued life span of the function will certainly depend on the ability of the *Ombudsperson* to be responsive to change and meet the new demands of the organization.

Chapter 4

Key Factors That Make Internal Fair Procedure Systems Succeed or Fail

The 12 organizational systems that have been presented by managers in Chapter 3 illustrate the considerable diversity of approaches that have been adopted in the search for appropriate and effective dispute prevention or dispute resolution mechanisms. Are there some common principles that can be extracted from these diverse innovations of the past decade? And, do these add up to a basic list of critical elements that can be used as a template by managements considering whether to create a new internal fair procedure system, or expand an existing one?

We believe that a set of core requirements *do* emerge from the experiences of organizations we have studied, and that these can be placed under 15 clearly defined headings.

A Complaint and Appeal System That Fits the Company

Whether done primarily by the Chief Executive Officer (CEO), the human resources department, or a task force drawn from various staff and line functions in the organization, the type and style of program chosen by leading companies reflect the special qualities and environment of the organization. The background and outlook of the employees (e.g., high-tech professionals, entertainment industry figures, and diverse production and clerical workers); the formal or informal atmosphere of operating units; the degree of decentralization or centralization of decisions; the reputation of and employee trust in the personnel department—all of these factors are considered in structuring the program and deciding which responsibilities to assign to various management and employee elements. A good program builds on the basic management style and corporate culture, or is used to help managements that are consciously changing their management style from traditional and authoritarian modes to more participative approaches.

A Positive View of Dispute Resolution Machinery

In some large companies, top management sees employee complaints as a "bad" sign, and the creation of formal dispute resolution systems as only "encouraging" discontent and protest. The companies we studied do not share that view. They see the presence of employee complaints as an inevitable part of managing large work forces for complex business tasks, and they consider it intelligent personnel realtions to create formal mechanisms to solicit, process, and resolve such complaints. *Not* to have such a system, these managements believe, is to leave employee concerns to fester, leading to negative developments such as poor work attitudes, low commitment, absenteeism, possible substance abuse and emotional crises, susceptibility to unionization among unorganized employees, and (in equal employment or occupational safety type situations) unnecessarily high levels of complaints to regulatory agencies and the courts. In short, these managements see a formal dispute resolution system as functionally valuable for sound organizational administration.

Top Management Commitment and Presence

Whether still under the direction of the original founder (as at Control Data), in the third generation (as at IBM in the 1960s), or in firms that never had a "founding family," companies with effective fair procedure systems recognize that a visible committed role by the CEO is imperative. Given the occasional tension between employee fair treatment and hard-driving managers and executives "getting things done," it will always take the prestige of the CEO—or a top executive enjoying the CEO's full confidence—and occasional intervention by that executive, to protect the system from favoritism or the "management-team instinct." Also, only the CEO or other top executive can ensure that the visible and invisible reward system that spurs managers on is geared to recognize allegiance to the fair procedure system, and to punish the occasional abuse of it by managers.

Merit-Oriented Personnel Policies

No fair procedure system can be equitable and just in its decisions if it is called on to administer a subjectively cast, inequitable set of employment and personnel policies. Unless a company acknowledges the new "rationality" standard in the law discussed in Chapter 5 and commits itself to objective standards of excellence, professional performance evaluation, fair promotion policies, strong EEO and affirmative action programs, and similar "merit-based" approaches, it does not have the policy base from which to do justice in daily operations. Such policies have to be seen as right for a company in good economic times or bad, whether expanding or contracting the work force, whether in old-tech or new-tech environment.

A Formal Justice System Without Legalism

In the companies we studied, employees were told that they were valued stakeholders in the total enterprise. They were expected to be wholly committed workers, joining in a common, concerted drive to make the company succeed, and they were also entitled to various positive rights, including equal employment opportunity and fair hearings for grievances. Under this concept of "rights," procedures were *informal* enough to foster use of the system, and to help draw out both the "employee's story" and the psychological feelings that lay behind the sense of grievance. But they were also formal enough to give all participants in the process the sense that *justice*, not "cooling out" or "manipulation," was the commitment of the program. Each company must walk its own line between formalized procedures and a numbing legalism.

Communicating the Program's Availability to Employees

The companies we studied paid serious attention to communicating the availability of their complaint procedures to employees, recognizing that wide publicity and frequent reinforcement of the system's presence are essential to its use, and to influencing the behavior of supervisors and managers who might be tempted to act arbitrarily and unfairly if they felt use of the system by employees would not take place. This communication took place in new employee handbooks and orientation programs, bulletin board announcements, articles in company newspapers, video programs shown throughout the company, and many other publicity techniques. In addition, employees were asked in internal surveys among other things whether they knew about the new program, had used it, and if they had confidence in its fairness. If the results showed low levels of awareness or support, many of these companies stepped up their communication efforts in response.

Providing Expert Resources to Employees

In nonunion companies, the resources of management and the individual employee are not equal. If outside counsel or group representation is not to be brought in to assist an employee invoking the fair procedure system, a committed professional staff unit or individual must be designated to take employee assistance as a moral and practical responsibility. This role must be institutionalized and protected by the organization. (This is especially needed when advice from such an employee counselor seems to help the employee's presentation "too well" against those in management who made the contested decision.) Counselors skilled in dispute resolution techniques must help employees to sort out the facts, identify what they feel their grievance is, specify what relief or action they are seeking, understand the other party's perspective and needs, and formulate a strategy for using the company's fair procedure system effectively.

Installing a "Keeper of the Flame"

In almost every good system that we examined, there is one person who embodies and defends the integrity and pervasiveness of the fair procedure system. This will usually be someone who knows the company intimately from long working experience there, understands the pressures and challenges of operations in that enterprise, knows the informal lines of influence and personality interactions of the senior management group, and has full access to and enjoys the confidence of the CEO. Such a "keeper of the flame" must have the personality to win the respect of employees and managers alike as a person dedicated to *fairness* as an achievable ideal in a real world setting. He or she must also be perceived as someone who will pursue and protect the fundamental requirements of that process no matter who is involved in a complaint.

Protecting Employees Against Reprisals

Employees who challenge the decisions of their supervisors and other managers run the risk of having reprisals taken against them for their actions. Since the employment relationship involves continuous evaluation of the employee for pay, assignment, promotion, and other discretionary decisions, employees are highly vulnerable when they continue to be judged by superiors against whom they have complained. Recognizing this fact, and in the absence of any union to safeguard an employee from such reprisal, the managements we studied explicitly promised employees that reprisals would not be taken against any employee using the system. Many of them had their staff track the progress of employees who had used the complaint system to see whether that promise was being fulfilled. In addition, publicity about antireprisal guarantees and enforcement was widely disseminated among these companies.

Building Support Among Line Managers

The way that line managers and executives relate to fair procedure systems represents an important element in their success or failure. The companies we studied paid special attention to fostering the good will of these managers. They developed management communications and training materials that stressed top management's commitment to this approach, stressed the objectivity that would govern the hearings and appeals in the system, and communicated clearly the expectation that line managers would help to make the system work effectively. As noted earlier, compliance with such policies was not made "optional"; it was built into the reward system of every supervisor and manager.

Accepting the Duty to Change Policies and Remove Poor Managers

A common theme in these programs is a desire to discover and correct possible illegality or inefficiency and to correct such conditions quickly and completely. The remedial action taken must not only be appropriate under the facts of an individual case, but must be in line with company policy without losing the trust of employees. At the same time, where management policies have been revealed in a specific case to be faulty in formulation, or to have outlived their value, or to be creating problems of application, these companies both correct the situation for this employee—and change the policies. They also deal directly with managers whose conduct is shown in a fair procedure hearing to be lacking the sensitivity and fairness that the company expects of good managers. Either additional training is provided or that manager is transferred from a management role to a production, professional, or non-managerial staff position. In clear and extreme cases, managers are terminated.

Publicizing the System's Operations and Outcomes

Since the credibility of a company-managed system cannot be taken for granted, many companies we studied report periodically to their employees about the system's use and results. Such communications generally described how many employees had used the system in a given period, the makeup of the user group, the kinds of issues being raised, and the outcomes of the process—including how many decisions accepted the employee's side, how many the management position, and those that were "mixed" results. Such publicity is also directed at supervisors and managers to make the system's operations visible to them as well.

Honest and Probing Employee Surveys

While some companies either do not conduct specific periodic opinion surveys of their employees or else use surveys that are highly generalized "mood" measurements, most of the companies we studied asked detailed enough questions of all employees to learn how satisfied their employees were with the complaint and appeal system. These survey results were used to spot pockets of discontent by such variables as work location, type of employee, and operating unit, and enabled the personnel experts and senior management to dig deeper into the problem and to take corrective measures. Such surveys were also used to test particular features of the fair procedure system and to help decide how to keep the mechanisms "well tuned."

Employee Representation in the System

Whether it is a "peer review" system or variations that we found at a dozen other companies, building employee representation into the hearing or appeal stage of the system is being seen by many managements as an essential credibility-building technique. In part, this arises from growing employee expectations that such is the fair way for a "management-run" system (without a union present) to protect employee interests. Partly it is a "professional" judgment that employee participation helps achieve better results over the long course, by building employee experiences and attitudes into the decision-making process. Also, employee participation usually makes rulings unfavorable to the complainant more acceptable, and earns more general employee trust in the systems than one entirely presided over by management members.

Recognition That the Fair Procedure System Is "Forever"

Companies that understand why managing in these times requires a good fair procedure system—that management must "do justice well" inside or have it done for them by outside agencies and the courts—are committed to having a fair procedure system permanently. The forms and procedures may change or be modified to reflect new issues and organizational operations. But just as no nation could imagine abolishing its courts, so no effective company managing for excellence today can imagine eliminating its fair procedure system, or allowing it to wither into ineffectiveness. In short, these systems are seen as necessities, not luxuries.

Reasons Why These Factors Will Be Addressed

Are these requirements "realistic" for most companies? Our estimate is that there are probably no more than 50 to 100 organizations that have installed fair procedure systems that meet most or all of the 15 critical requirements just described. Before the glaze of pessimism settles over the eyes of readers, let us cite three reasons why this number is quite likely to expand in the coming decade.

First, the organizations that have installed fair procedure systems profited measurably and visibly from using their systems; by doing so, they have also avoided most of the negative consequences of employee discontent facing peer organizations and employers generally. These systems can be found in leading organizations in various industries, of varying sizes and ages, and with varying styles of management, and we believe they are working well. As this experience is disseminated by books such as this one, many organizations are going to be interested in trying out such systems themselves.

Second, the moment is highly favorable for many other organizations to consider developing such systems. At no time since the rise of the assembly line system in American industry have there been so many changes under way in the content of work, the relationships of supervision, the structures and processes of organizations, and the recognition that new management philosophies and styles are needed to guide businesses and nonprofit organizations through this passage to more effective organizational performance. There would have been little basis for optimism about large scale adoption of fair procedure systems in nonunion firms in the 1950s, or even the 1970s. There is now a considerable basis for believing that such a trend—nurtured by the promise of internal benefits and the minimizing of external exposures—is an idea whose time has come in the late 1980s. This volume has been prepared to help nurture that trend, and to help it become a major force for equity and fairness in the "9-to-5" lives of 80 million Americans.

Third, and by no means last, American employment law is rapidly developing important incentives for nonunion organizations to create and use seriously the kind of internal complaint mechanisms illustrated by our profiles. At the same time, courts are beginning to show signs that they will recognize and give important credit to employers who maintain good internal systems, when employees sue their employers under various common law bases. It is these emerging trends in the law of employment that are discussed in Chapter 5.

Chapter 5

The Legal Stimulus to Develop Fair Procedure Systems

In the opening section of Chapter 5, "The Current Legal Setting of Employment Law," we survey the key judicial doctrines of the 1980s that managers and human resources officials need to understand to adjust to the new legal environment in which their organizational policies and actions will be evaluated by "outsiders."

In "The 'Costs' of Litigating Wrongful Discharge Claims," we describe the considerable costs to private employers that are being assessed when internal procedures do not resolve employee complaints, and these disputes go to external forums. After noting (in "Management Responses to Recent Legal Developments") some of the main responses that employers have adopted to cope with the "employment litigation explosion," we present (in "The Fairness Quotient in Modern Human Resource") what we see as the key elements of "fairness" that courts are insisting upon when they examine dispute resolution efforts within organizations.

"Legal Benefits and Ramifications of Fair Procedure Systems" outlines the legal benefits and organizational values that we believe employer organizations obtain when they respond to the fairness trend and install meaningful internal systems. This chapter concludes, in "Legal Considerations in Establishing Fair Procedure Systems," with some practical guidelines for managers establishing or administering such systems within the current legal environment.

The Current Legal Setting of Employment Law

Resolution of employment disputes in today's evolving workplace is as much determined by legal proceedings and remedies as by the efforts of management.

The patchwork of new remedies for employees created or expanded in the last two decades has effectively rendered all major personnel decisions subject to legal challenge. When is a memorandum critical of an employee's abilities or a discussion of an employee's medical condition defamatory? When is a company's failure to abide by its own personnel policies a breach of contract? When is dismissal for insubordination wrongful discharge? Employers must now concern themselves with these and other questions. Personnel decisions that only recently were promulgated by management fiat are now eminently susceptible to legal challenge.

It was not always this way. Under the long-standing employment-at-will doctrine,[1] management and employees have an unfettered right to terminate the employment relationship without repercussion. The employment-at-will doctrine, however, and its legal underpinnings have come under increasing attack as the 1980s progress. As described by the Illinois Supreme Court,

> Recent analysis has pointed out the shortcomings of the mutuality theory. With the rise of large corporations conducting specialized operations and employing relatively immobile workers who often have no other place to market their skills, recognition that the employer and employee do not stand on equal footing is realistic. [Citation omitted.] In addition, unchecked employer power, like unchecked employee power, has been seen to present a distinct threat to the public policy carefully considered and adopted by society as a whole. As a result, it is now recognized that a proper

---

[1]In 1877, legal scholar H.G. Wood published in the United States a highly influential treatise entitled *The Law of Master & Servant* which announced as the law of the land the legal presumption that the employment relationship is terminable at the will of either party. Wood's statement of the law was well-suited to an age of tremendous economic growth and disruption stemming from rapid industrialization, and one in which laissez-faire policies prevailed. The strength of the American economy depended in part on an abundant, flexible work force. The ability of the parties to an employment agreement to create and terminate the relationship freely was most desirable in this setting. The relationship was no longer familial, but rather impersonal, and functional. Wood's presumption, in addition to being clear and easy to apply, was an indisputable timely social judgment as well.

Wood's legal analysis, however, was seriously flawed. As has been recently been pointed out, "Commentators now agree that Wood invented his own rule." G. Minda, *The Common Law of Employment At-Will in New York: The Paralysis of Nineteenth Century Doctrine*, 36 Syracuse L. Rev. 939, 970 (1985). Nonetheless, Wood's "presumption" soon began to be treated as Wood's "rule" or the employment-at-will doctrine and as such was quickly adopted by the state courts. The employment-at-will doctrine is today in force in every American jurisdiction but Montana.

balance must be maintained among the employer's interest in operating a business efficiently and profitably, the employee's interest
in earning a livelihood, and society's interest in seeing its public
policies carried out.[2]

While the employment-at-will doctrine is still in force, legislative
and judicial exceptions to this rule have made its application uncertain at best. Both the range of employees' remedies and management's stakes have increased dramatically in recent years.
Particularly troubling to management and its attorneys is the difficulty in summarily disposing of these legal challenges by way, for
example, of a pretrial motion, and the potential for large punitive
damage awards with every filing that is tried before a jury. As
discussed in Chapter 1, this uncertainty has fed and indeed is a
prime motivating factor for the search for new dispute resolution
systems in employment.

The most prominent early critic of the employment-at-will
doctrine, Professor Lawrence Blades,[3] foresaw this development.[4]
Blades predicted that unsatisfactory court decisions would prompt
employers

> to resort to arbitration or to create some other machinery for airing
> and adjusting such claims outside the courts. *Thus a lack of confi-
> dence in courts and juries could lead, albeit in a roundabout way,
> to the creation of private means of settlement that might well be the
> most effective and expeditious way of handling such cases.*[5]

Contract Law Developments

Courts in recent years have taken an expansive view of what
constitutes a binding promise, that is, a contract, in the employment context. Many things are said and written in the midst of
establishing and sustaining an employment relationship that may
not be intended to bind the parties. For example, statements of
company policy and goals are often intended merely to be informational. However, courts increasingly are treating as contractual

---

[2]*Palmateer v. International Harvester Co.*, 85 Ill.2d 124, 421 N.E.2d 876, 878 (1981).
[3]*See* L. Blades, *Employment At Will v. Individual Freedom: On Limiting the Abusive
Exercise of Employer Power*, 67 Colum. L. Rev. 1404 (1967).
[4]Professor Blades, having little legal authority to draw on in support of his position,
approached this issue from the perspective of the need of society to protect the rights of
individual employees against "mammoth business corporation[s]" which "now pose a threat
to individual freedom comparable to that which would be posed if governmental power
were unchecked." *Id.* at 1404.
[5]*Id.* at 1431 (emphasis added).

those company statements and policies about job security that management and supervisory personnel communicate to employees whether or not they are intended to be binding.

Today, management needs to know that what it promises in words and actions may be enforceable against it by employees who have a growing legal arsenal at their disposal to raise such claims.

Personnel Handbooks

An employee handbook serves a number of familiar functions: it introduces new employees to the company; it provides management with the opportunity to state its philosophy; it sets forth company rules, regulations, and operating procedures; and it explains employee salaries and benefits. Handbooks are the most often used and convenient technique by which management communicates with its workers.

Communications can create expectations, however, and handbook terms are subject to differing interpretations. Can an employee rely on the terms of the handbook to management's detriment? Courts traditionally have said no—the handbook was merely a company statement of goals and procedures offered for informational purposes only.[6]

What can an employee rely on, if not company policy as put forward by the company in its official documents and through its supervisory personnel? In response to this question, a growing number of courts have concluded that employees may indeed rely on promises of job security contained in company publications like handbooks.[7] The Michigan Supreme Court, in the leading case in this area, offered the following reasoning:

---

[6] *See Johnson v. National Beef Packing Co.*, 220 Kan. 52, 551 P.2d 779 (1976); *Edwards v. Citibank*, 100 Misc. 2d 59, 418 N.Y.S.2d 269, *aff'd*, 74 App. Div.2d 553, 425 N.Y.S.2d 327, *appeal dismissed*, 51 N.Y.2d 875, 433 N.Y.S.2d 1020, 414 N.E.2d 400 (1980); *Shaw v. S.S. Kresge*, 167 Ind. App.1, 328 N.E.2d 775 (1975).

[7] *See Woolley v. Hoffman-LaRoche, Inc.*, 99 N.J. 284, 491 A.2d 1257 (1985); *Toussaint v. Blue Cross & Blue Shield of Mich.*, 408 Mich. 579, 292 N.W.2d 880 (1980); *Pine River State Bank v. Mettille*, 333 N.W.2d 622, 115 LRRM 4493 (Minn. 1983); *Weiner v. McGraw-Hill, Inc.*, 57 N.Y.2d 458, 457 N.Y.S.2d 193, 443 N.E.2d 441, 118 LRRM 2689 (1982); *Southwest Gas Corp. v. Ahmad*, 99 Nev. 594, 668 P.2d 261, 114 LRRM 2633 (1983).

Policy Statements in Personnel Manuals Held to be Contractual: "Policy: It is the policy of the company to treat employees leaving Blue Cross in a fair and consistent manner and to release employees for *just cause only." (Toussaint, id.*, 292 N.W.2d at 903.)

"The company will resort to dismissal for just and sufficient cause only, and only after all practical steps toward rehabilitation or salvage of the employee have been taken and failed. However, if the welfare of the company indicates that dismissal is necessary, then

While an employer need not establish personnel policies or practices, where an employer chooses to establish such policies and practices and makes them known to its employees, the employment relationship is presumably enhanced. The employer secures an orderly, cooperative and loyal work force, and the employee the peace of mind associated with job security and the conviction that he will be treated fairly. No pre-employment negotiations need take place and the parties' minds need not meet on the subject, nor does it matter that the employee knows nothing of the particulars of the employer's policies and practices or that the employer may change them unilaterally. It is enough that the employer chooses, presumably in its own interest, to create an environment in which the employee believes that, whatever the personnel policies and practices, they are established and official at any given time, purport to be fair, and are applied consistently and uniformly to each employee. The employer has then created a situation "instinct with an obligation."[8]

Following this reasoning, employees have challenged, for example, terminations based upon: handbook provisions promising that length of service would be the "governing factor" in determining which of two comparable employees would be laid off in a reduction-in-force;[9] a promise in the management procedures manual that allowed furloughed management to reclaim nonmanagement positions previously held;[10] and the employer's failure to abide by the disciplinary procedures set forth in its personnel handbook.[11]

---

that decision is arrived at and is carried out forthrightly." (Weiner, Id., 457 N.Y.S.2d at 194.)

"Employment in the banking industry is very stable. It does not fluctuate up and down sharply in good times and bad, as do many other types of employment. We have no seasonal layoffs, and we never hire a lot of people when business is booming only to release them when things are not as active."

"The job security offered by the Pine River State Bank is one reason why so many of our employees have five or more years of service." (Pine River State Bank, Id., 333 N.W.2d at 626 n.2.)

"You have been selected for a position because it was felt that you have the qualifications which in time will be of benefit both to you and to the Bank. Unless otherwise specified, you will be employed on a probationary basis for a period of three months. If it develops during that period that you are not pleased with your association or are not suited to the work of the Bank, your employment may be terminated, in mutual fairness, without any other reason." (Wiskotoni v. Michigan Nat'l Bank-West, 716 F.2d 378, 386, 114 LRRM 2596 (6th Cir. 1983)).

[8]Toussaint, supra, note 7, 292 N.W.2d at 892.

[9]Wagner v. Sperry Univac, Div. of Sperry Rand Corp., 458 F. Supp. 505, 519–21, 19 FEP 1567 (E.D. Pa. 1978), aff'd mem., 624 F.2d 1092, 24 FEP 451 (3d Cir. 1980).

[10]Brooks v. Trans World Airlines, 574 F. Supp. 805, 114 LRRM 3136 (D. Colo. 1983).

[11]Pine River State Bank v. Mettille, see supra, note 7. See Flowers v. Area Agency on Aging of S.E. Ark., Inc., 574 F. Supp. 71 (E.D. Ark. 1983), appeal dismissed, 738 F.2d 444 (8th Cir. 1984) (employer that failed to abide by progressive disciplinary procedures outlined in handbook but nonetheless dismissed employee with good cause subject to nominal damages of only $1.00).

Oral Agreements

"Don't worry, Walter, jobs are secure around this place," the supervisor said to the job applicant. "I'll personally review your job performance, and as long as you do the job for us, you won't be let go." Walter took the middle management position and two years later was discharged even though, he argued, he was "doing his job." A jury agreed, and awarded Walter, who was unable to exercise a stock option because of his discharge, a verdict of $300,000. The Michigan Supreme Court upheld the verdict. [12]

Courts have recently ruled that promises made during the hiring process by personnel in positions to bind the company may be enforced against the company. This is particularly true if the promise induces the applicant to take the job. [13] The exchange of the company's promise for the employee's performance may constitute a contract. [14] Management personnel who, in the midst of enthusiastically selling the job to an applicant, make promises beyond what company policies mandate may be selling a job package and employment contract the company may not be able to live with. A job interview, like a labor negotiation, is not the place for company representatives to speak loosely or to misrepresent the company position.

Management discretion, to which courts in the past deferred, no longer supports the abrogation of promises which reach, under today's broader standards, the level of contract.

Implied Contracts

In addition to things written and said, company deeds and long-standing practices may be treated by a court as implied promises enforceable against the company. In effect, an unwritten law of the firm may be established that may serve to limit company prerogatives. [15] Some states have gone further and applied the covenant of good faith and fair dealing, which is implied in every

---

[12]*Ebling v. Masco Corp.*, 408 Mich. 579, 292 N.W.2d 880 (1980).

[13]*See e.g. Grouse v. Group Health Plan*, 306 N.W.2d 114 (Minn. 1981); *Casale v. Dooner Laboratories*, 503 F.2d 303 (4th Cir. 1973); *McNulty v. Bordon, Inc.*, 474 F. Supp. 1111 (E.D. Pa. 1979).

[14]*Southwest Gas Corp.*, *supra*, note 7.

[15]*See e.g. Crosier v. United Parcel Serv.*, 150 Cal. App.3d 1132, 198 Cal. Rptr. 361, 115 LRRM 3585 (1983).

contract, to the employment setting.[16] For example, in several cases, salespeople dismissed for the purpose of denying them large commissions about to come due were able to successfully invoke the covenant and recover their lost commissions (though not their jobs).[17]

In one notable case, Wayne Pugh, a 32-year employee who had worked his way up from dishwasher to vice president in charge of production of a candy manufacturing and retailing company, was discharged without notice following the most successful year in the company's history.[18] When Pugh asked why, he was allegedly told to "look deep within yourself." Pugh believed his discharge was prompted by his refusal to go along with the company's attempt to gain a sweetheart contract from the union. The court concluded that the company's actions through his 32-year employment, as alleged, indicated an implied promise not to treat him arbitrarily. The court pointed to the following factors: "the duration of [Pugh's] employment, the commendations and promotions he received, the apparent lack of any direct criticism of his work, the assurances he was given, and the employer's acknowledged policies."[19]

These cases suggest that many courts today expect management to act in accordance with the employment atmosphere and norms it has established. In short, if promises of fair treatment are part of a management's ethos and practices, this may become the contract-based standard by which courts will measure management's actions so as to give effect to employees' reasonable expectations. (And, as discussed below, where management does *not* promise fair treatment, certain other common law doctrines may nonetheless be applied by courts to protect employees.)

An employee's subjective belief of job security, however, is not enough to bind management on a contract basis. For example,

---

[16]*Cleary v. American Airlines*, 111 Cal. App.3d 443, 168 Cal. Rptr. 722, 115 LRRM 3030 (1980); *Magnan v. Anaconda Indus.*, 193 Conn. 558, 479 A.2d 781, 117 LRRM 2163 (1984); *Fortune v. National Cash Register Co.*, 373 Mass. 96, 364 N.E.2d 1251 (1977); *Dare v. Montana Petroleum Mktg. Co.*, 687 P.2d 1015, 117 LRRM 2442 (Mont. 1984); *Crenshaw v. Bozeman Deaconess Hosp.*, 693 P.2d 487, 118 LRRM 2076 (Mont. 1984) (probationary employees); *Monge v. Beebe Rubber Co.*, 114 N.H. 130, 316 A.2d 549, 115 LRRM 4755 (1974). *Contra Parnar v. Americana Hotels*, 65 Hawaii 370, 652 P.2d 625, 115 LRRM 4817 (1982); *Brockmeyer v. Dun & Bradstreet*, 113 Wis.2d 561, 335 N.W.2d 834, 115 LRRM 4484 (1983); *Murphy v. American Home Prods. Corp.*, 58 N.Y.2d 293, 461 N.Y.S.2d 232, 448 N.E.2d 86, 31 FEP 782 (1983).

[17]*Fortune, supra*, note 16; *Gram v. Liberty Mut. Ins. Co.*, 384 Mass. 659, 429 N.E.2d 21, 115 LRRM 4152 (1981).

[18]*Pugh v. See's Candies*, 116 Cal. App.3d 311, 171 Cal. Rptr. 917, 115 LRRM 4002 (1981).

[19]*Id.*, 171 Cal. Rptr. at 927. The jury rejected Pugh's discrimination and related claims upon remand.

a Michigan court rejected an employee's claim that the following circumstances constituted an implied promise of just cause dismissal: The company was a small, close-knit family operation with low pay and little turnover; the company paid sick leave to its workers even though it had no formal medical benefits policy; its pension plan was available to all employees; and there were periodic claims by a supervisor that the company was ready to "take off." The court found these factors insufficient to constitute an implied promise of job security.[20]

In sum, a promise of job security may be inferred, whether intended or not, from management's words and actions. On the other hand, a promise cannot rest on the purely subjective view of the employee. Where there is a set of circumstances that a reasonable employee could interpret as constituting a contractual promise of job security, these may be treated by a court as enforceable.[21]

Tort Actions Based on Public Policy

In addition to developments in contract law, tort law has expanded to allow for wrongful discharge suits based on violations of public policy. Contract actions, while somewhat troubling to management, allow for only "make-whole" damages. Tort actions, however, provide for punitive as well as compensatory damages. An employee who successfully makes out a public policy exception claim is already entitled to compensatory damages and may be within reach of punitive damages. The increasing threat of these types of cases going to juries provides one of the major incentives to employers to settle out of court, even apart from the merits of the claim.

The term "public policy," however, is difficult to define. Both courts and litigants as we shall see have struggled with defining the bounds of this slippery term.

The court in *Petermann v. Teamsters Local 396*[22] looked to the state criminal code for guidance in defining public policy. The court wrote, "The public policy of this state as reflected in the penal code . . . would be seriously impaired if it were to be held that one could be discharged by reason of his refusal to commit

---

[20]*Schwartz v. Michigan Sugar Co.*, 106 Mich. App. 471, 308 N.W.2d 459 (1981).
[21]*See e.g. Thompson v. St. Regis Paper Co.*, 102 Wash.2d 219, 685 P.2d 1081, 116 LRRM 3142 (1984); *Pugh, supra*, note 18.
[22]174 Cal. App.2d 184, 344 P.2d 25 (1959).

perjury."[23] Perhaps the broadest view of public policy was taken by the Illinois Supreme Court when it upheld, in 1981, the wrongful discharge suit of an employee who reported possible thefts by a co-worker to the police, and then assisted in the ensuing investigation. The court concluded that public policy was implicated by retaliatory discharges that "strike at the heart of a citizen's social rights, duties and responsibilities."[24] The court found that public policy "favored citizen crime fighters" even though there is no obligation on a citizen "to take an active part in the ferreting out and prosecution of crime."[25]

Most courts have taken a more restricted view. Those courts that have recognized a public policy exception have generally required that the discharge violate a clear mandate of public policy as evidenced by existing legislation, regulation, or judicial decision.[26] The New Jersey Supreme Court has gone a step further and acknowledged that public policy may find expression in the ethical codes of the professions.[27] Discharges resulting from service on juries or grand juries are typical of those cases in which courts have recognized exceptions to the at-will doctrine on public policy grounds.[28] In contrast, courts have rejected claims of wrongful discharge on public policy grounds where the employee was fired for going to law school at night;[29] the employee filed a lawsuit against his employer resulting from an accident involving his minor daughter;[30] and the discharge followed the retaining by the employee of counsel in a dispute over wages.[31]

While the term public policy is broad, management, through its counsel, can generally anticipate the scope of activity covered by the public policy exception in a particular case by asking, does the employee's action for which he or she is subject to discipline or dismissal serve to further the specific purposes of enacted legislation or administrative regulation or of recognized constitutional

---

[23]*Id.*, 344 P.2d at 27.

[24]*Palmateer v. International Harvester Co.*, 85 Ill.2d 124, 421 N.E.2d 876 (1981).

[25]*Id.*, 421 N.E.2d at 880.

[26]*Sheets v. Teddy's Frosted Foods*, 179 Conn. 471, 427 A.2d 385, 115 LRRM 4626 (1980); *Pierce v. Ortho Pharmaceutical Corp.*, 84 N.J. 58, 417 A.2d 505, 115 LRRM 3044 (1980); *Harless v. First Nat'l Bank in Fairmont*, 162 W.Va. 116, 246 S.E.2d 270, 115 LRRM 4380 (W.Va. 1978); *Thompson, supra*, note 21.

[27]*Pierce, supra*, note 26.

[28]*Nees v. Hocks*, 272 Or. 210, 536 P.2d 512, 115 LRRM 4571 (1975) (jury); *Wiskotoni v. Michigan Nat'l Bank-West*, 716 F.2d 378, 114 LRRM 2596 (6th Cir. 1983) (grand jury).

[29]*Scroghan v. Kraftko Corp.*, 551 S.W.2d 811 (Ky. 1977).

[30]*DeMarco v. Publix Supermarkets*, 360 So.2d 134 (Fla. App. 1978), *cert. denied*, 367 So.2d 1123 (1979), *aff'd*, 384 So.2d 1253 (Fla. 1980).

[31]*Kavanagh v. KLM Royal Dutch Airlines*, 566 F. Supp. 242 (N.D. Ill. 1983).

principles? If so, public policy may command that no retaliatory act be taken against the employee.

Abusive or Negligent Use of Management's Prerogatives

Tort law has also expanded since 1970 to provide a remedy to employees who are subject to the abusive or negligent use of management power and prerogatives. Management may criticize an employee's work performance, but may not defame the employee in doing so; it may discipline an employee, but must not do so in an outrageous manner that would cause severe emotional distress; management may review an employee's work performance, but may not perform the review in a negligent manner; it may induce an employee to join the company, but not by means of fraud; and while supervisors and staff should be collegial with employees of the opposite sex, they may not harass or impose themselves physically on them.

Most members of management would agree with these general propositions. Many, however, may be disturbed and even shocked by the ways these principles have been applied by courts since 1970. To anticipate potential legal problems, personnel managers should try to put themselves in the positions of courts conducting after-the-fact reviews of personnel decisions. This may help managers to learn an essential rule of survival in the new, heavily regulated workplace—namely, that a personnel decision must be justified not only at the time of its making, but must also be defensible before a court, jury, or administrative body several years hence. Awareness of and adherence to this simple rule may avoid later court review and reversal.

Employer Communications and Defamation

Defamation is the publication of false and derogatory information about an individual. Truth is an absolute defense to a defamation claim.[32]

Employers possess and transmit a great amount of information concerning their workers—some of it factual, some of it subjective. Perhaps the ripest circumstance for a defamation suit is a termination on grounds of misconduct where the employer possesses derogatory information about the employee and needs to transmit

---

[32]*Prosser & Keeton on Torts* (5th ed. (1984)), §116, p. 840.

the fact of the termination (but not necessarily the derogatory information itself) to employees in the company with a need to know.

Certain communications, such as information transmitted to state unemployment compensation officials, are absolutely privileged, even if otherwise defamatory.[33] Most employer communications, however, are only qualifiedly privileged.[34] The privilege can be lost if the publication of the information is made with malice or to too wide an audience.[35] The burden of proving the privilege defense rests with management,[36] as does the financial burden of presenting a privilege defense in court.

Some courts have held that an intracorporate communication can constitute a publication for purposes of defamation law.[37] How does job-related information about an employee get transmitted within the company? The potential for broad intracorporate publication is evident in the following 1980 federal district court decision.[38]

Allegheny Airlines dismissed a ramp agent because the latter informed another employee that he was a target of a company security investigation. The director of ground services drafted the termination letter. The letter worked its way through the company in the following manner. The director of ground services' secretary read the letter, then dictated the letter over the telephone to the secretary for the customer service manager of Allegheny's Boston operation, who transcribed it and showed it to her boss. The customer service manager signed the letter and then returned it to his secretary, who photocopied the letter and sent copies to: the employee, the director of ground services, personnel department, accounts receivable, payroll, tax department, budget department, and the credit union. Copies were later sent to the vice president for customer services and the regional director of ground services. The court noted that other employees knew of the reasons for the

[33]*E.g., Magnan v. Anaconda Indus.*, 193 Conn. 558, 479 A.2d 781, 117 LRRM 2163 (1984) (information given to unemployment insurance board absolutely privileged); *Ezekiel v. Jones Motor Co.*, 374 Mass. 382, 372 N.E.2d 1281, 1284 (1978) (slanderous statement made to management-union grievance board absolutely privileged).

[34]*Arsenault v. Allegheny Airlines*, 485 F. Supp. 1373, 1379–80 (D. Mass.), *aff'd mem.*, 636 F.2d 1199 (1st Cir. 1980), *cert. denied*, 454 U.S. 821 (1981) (termination letter conditionally privileged).

[35]*See e.g., Pirre v. Printing Devs.*, 468 F. Supp. 1028 (S.D.N.Y.), *aff'd*, 614 F.2d 1290 (2d Cir. 1979); *Glynn v. City of Kissimmee*, 383 So.2d 774 (Fla. App. 1980).

[36]*Id.; Banas v. Matthews Int'l Corp.*, 116 LRRM 3110 (Pa. 1984).

[37]*Arsenault, supra*, note 34; *but see Halsell v. Kimberly-Clark Corp.*, 683 F.2d 285, 29 FEP 1185 (8th Cir. 1982), *cert. denied*, 459 U.S. 1205 (1983) (Wisconsin law precludes defamation action based on communication between officers of same corporation).

[38]*Arsenault, supra*, note 34.

employee's dismissal, although they did not have access to the letter. The court concluded, "that there was a publication of the letter when it was distributed among the Allegheny workers and otherwise communicated to persons other than [the employee]."[39] The court held, however, that the publication was qualifiedly privileged and granted summary judgment to the company.

Disclosure of accurate information related to work performance to those with a need to know either inside or outside the corporation generally is held not to be defamatory unless the disclosure is with malicious intent or is overbroad.[40] Unfortunately for management, this determination is typically a jury question not resolvable by pretrial motion.

Courts have held the following communications to be qualifiedly privileged: statements made by the company president to supervisors related to an employee's alleged thefts;[41] a letter sent by the company's general counsel, with copies to certain staff members, to the employee's lawyer who had written requesting certain termination pay for his client disclosing the reasons for termination;[42] allegations of theft made by a company security guard which were repeated in a meeting requested by the employee following his discharge attended by the store and personnel managers;[43] and allegations of theft made by a co-worker at a hearing conducted by a joint management/union grievance board.[44]

Candid, but *truthful*, job references are generally privileged as well.[45] Nonetheless, employers are increasingly limiting disclosure to "dates of service" information as the disclosure of any evaluative information may result, whether or not liability is found, in litigation and its related costs. Even if liability is not found, the cost of the litigation to the employer may be prohibitive.

In one notable instance of a successful employee defamation suit involving the intracorporate transmittal of a supervisor's memo, the court described the employee as a "mechanical and engineering

---

[39]*Id.* at 1379.

[40]*Id. See also Berg v. Consolidated Freightways,* 280 Pa. Super. 495, 421 A.2d 831 (1980); *Banas, supra,* note 36.

[41]*Vlasaty v. Pacific Club,* 4 Hawaii App. 556, 670 P.2d 827 (1983).

[42]*Otteni v. Hitachi Am., Ltd.,* 678 F.2d 146 (11th Cir. 1982).

[43]*Zuniga v. Sears, Roebuck & Co.,* 100 N.M. 414, 671 P.2d 662 (N. Mex. App.), *cert. denied,* 100 N.M. 439, 671 P.2d 1150 (1983).

[44]*Ezekiel, supra,* note 33.

[45]*Alford v. Georgia Pac. Corp.,* 331 So.2d 558 (La. App.), *cert. denied,* 334 So.2d 427 (La. 1976); *Swanson v. Speidel Corp.,* 110 R.I. 335, 293 A.2d 307 (1972); *Duncantell v. Universal Life Ins. Co.,* 446 S.W.2d 934 (Tex. App. 1969). *See* Cal. Labor Code §1053 (West 1983).

genius" who was also "an extraordinarily sensitive man who had to do things in his own way, and was wholly incapable of conforming to any sort of structured discipline."[46] The supervisor's memo, copies of which were sent to supervisors up the line and to the parent company, threatened immediate termination if the employee engaged in further acts of insubordination, continued to challenge management decisions, verbally abused other employees, or failed to complete assignments and to improve the quality and quantity of his work products. The court characterized this document as a "product of thoughtless and clumsy writing." The jury thought it defamatory, and awarded the employee $445,000 in the ensuing libel suit; however, the court ultimately reduced this figure to $45,000.

Intentional Infliction of Emotional Distress

Abusive use of management authority is most often charged in suits alleging intentional infliction of emotional distress. The limits of this potentially boundless tort have been slowly expanding. This cause of action, also identified as the "tort of outrage," requires conduct that is "so outrageous in character, and so extreme in degree, as to go beyond all possible bounds of decency, and to be regarded as atrocious, and utterly intolerable in a civilized community."[47] Emotional distress claims are being appended with increasing frequency to sexual harassment, wrongful discharge, and age discrimination complaints.

Emotional distress claims often present extreme and dramatic factual situations, and such complaints are increasingly surviving summary judgment motions. For example, the widow of a cancer victim whose husband was coerced into not filing for disability benefits by a supervisor who knew of his terminal illness was allowed to sue the company and her husband's supervisors on emotional distress grounds as administratrix of his estate.[48] An employee who was not allowed to leave his work position to go to the toilet, who then evacuated his bowels in his clothing, and who later discovered that his supervisor had told approximately 40 co-workers that he had "crapped in his pants" was allowed to seek damages

---

[46]*Pirre, supra*, note 35, 468 F. Supp. at 1031.
[47]Restatement (Second) of Torts §46, Comment D (1970).
[48]*Harrison v. Loyal Protective Life Ins. Co.*, 379 Mass. 212, 396 N.E.2d 987 (1979).

for emotional distress.[49] In the archetypal emotional distress case, a cashier whose name began with "A" was allowed to sue after she was discharged in accordance with the store manager's decision to fire the cashiers in alphabetical order until someone admitted to stealing from the cash register. Her husband was allowed to sue for loss of her companionship as well.[50]

In addition to instances of outrageous conduct by individual supervisory personnel, courts on occasion have found emotional distress caused by implementation of company policies and practices to be actionable. For example, a telephone installer for Illinois Bell alleged that he was repeatedly asked by his superiors to falsify his work reports which were used to bill customers and to report expenses to the Illinois Commerce Commission. The practice, he claimed, was common among the company foremen and was encouraged by upper management. As a result of his refusal to falsify his work reports, the employee was given less desirable work assignments, denied an equal share of overtime, given unreasonable time estimates for tasks assigned, subjected to excessive scrutiny, and arbitrarily denied leave. In addition, the employee's accurate reports were often rejected and false information was occasionally added to his already completed reports. The employee's claim that this widespread retaliation was part of a company policy and that this policy caused him deep emotional distress requiring hospitalization was held sustainable by an Illinois appellate court.[51]

Merely offensive behavior, however, is not sufficient to support a claim of emotional distress. For example, an employee who was fraudulently induced into remaining with his company, relocating, and forgoing other employment opportunities failed to allege a legally sufficient claim for emotional distress.[52] Similarly, transferring an employee, denying her an annual salary increase, removing her secretary and private office, and giving her a poor performance rating were held not to constitute an emotional distress claim.[53]

As we shall see later in this chapter, some courts have held that the existence and proper use of fair procedure systems such as those described in Chapter 3 serve to rebut claims of reckless or intentionally wrongful actions on the part of management.

---

[49]*Kissinger v. Mannor*, 92 Mich. App. 572, 285 N.W.2d 214 (1979).

[50]*Agis v. Howard Johnson Co.*, 371 Mass. 140, 355 N.E.2d 315 (1976).

[51]*Milton v. Illinois Bell Tel. Co.*, 101 Ill. App.3d 75, 427 N.E.2d 829, 115 LRRM 4428 (1981).

[52]*Cautilli v. GAF Corp.*, 531 F. Supp. 71 (E.D. Pa. 1982).

[53]*Wells v. Thomas*, 569 F. Supp. 426 (E.D. Pa. 1983).

Negligence

Employers undertaking certain personnel management tasks may be required to perform those tasks with reasonable care. The familiar elements of a negligence claim are the existence of a legal duty, its breach, a showing of causation, and damages.[54] As the scope of management's legal duties to its personnel grows, so does its responsibilities to carry out those duties diligently and with reasonable care.

The leading cases in this area are both from Michigan and involve the alleged negligent performance of personnel performance reviews. In *Schipani v. Ford Motor Company*,[55] a Michigan appellate court determined that Ford's system of performance evaluation arose out of the employment contract and was designed to benefit both parties. The court held that Ford may have a duty under these circumstances to conduct evaluations with reasonable care. The court determined that this was a question of fact for the jury to decide.

Another application of this new weapon in employees' legal arsenal appears with the federal district court decision in *Chamberlain v. Bissell, Inc.*[56] In that case, a 23-year employee whose performance deteriorated after he was denied a promotion was found to have a cause of action for negligence as a result of his supervisor's failure to advise him at his last performance evaluation that his discharge was being considered. If Chamberlain had been told, the court reasoned, he would have had an opportunity to reform his behavior. The court noted that the duty of reasonable care was not static, but varied with the circumstances. The court concluded that Chamberlain, as a result of his long-term service, " 'earned' a greater degree of care from his employer . . . ."[57]

If the logic and holdings of these cases were to gain greater acceptance, management might increasingly find itself in court defending its personnel decisions and practices under the legal standard of reasonable care. Because these causes of action are tortious in nature, even though deriving out of a contractual relationship, the resulting damages claims and awards may be large.[58]

---

[54]*See generally, Prosser & Keeton on Torts* §30 (5th ed. 1984) pp. 164–68.
[55]102 Mich. App. 606, 302 N.W.2d 307, 30 FEP 361 (1981).
[56]547 F. Supp. 1067, 30 FEP 347 (W.D. Mich. 1982).
[57]*Id.*, 30 FEP at 359.
[58]*See* pages 241–44, *infra.*

Fraud

Management may be liable for common law fraud if an employee relied on a false statement of material fact made by one in authority who knew such statement to be false. Fraud claims in the employment context typically involve misrepresentations of fact that induce an applicant to take a job, or a new position with the firm, or agree to a different salary or benefit plan.[59] For example, an employee in a company's Boston office was induced to move to Los Angeles by promises of lifetime employment. He moved to Los Angeles and was given a job different from what he was led to expect. When he complained, he was told to either accept the job or leave. When the officer who had promised him lifetime employment was asked if he was "kidding" when he made that offer, he answered yes. The jury awarded the employee $15,000.[60]

Remedies

Why should employers care about these developments in the law? To anticipate and respond to a changing marketplace and legal environment is the essence of good management. Further, simple preventive measures may succeed in avoiding prolonged, costly litigation and large damage awards. In this regard, recent common law developments have precipitated a flurry of lawsuits with heavy damages awards. For example, in one age discrimination/wrongful discharge case, three former executives were awarded $800,000, $600,000, and $500,000, respectively, plus $467,000 in attorneys' fees.[61]

The amount of damages awardable in a particular case depends on whether the action lies in tort or contract. If an employer is found liable under both contract and tort claims, damages under both may be awarded. For example, in one case, a bank was told by an informer (a prostitute) that its branch manager was helping to finance a local numbers operation by cashing checks in the morning and then tearing up the checks at the end of the bank day when the cash was returned. The FBI was unable to prove the

---

[59] *Sea-Land Serv., Inc. v. O'Neal*, 224 Va. 343, 297 S.E.2d 647 (1982); *Shear v. National Rifle Ass'n*, 606 F.2d 1251 (D.C. Cir. 1979); *Casale v. Dooner Laboratories, Inc.*, 503 F.2d 303 (4th Cir. 1973); *Brudnicki v. General Elec. Co.*, 535 F. Supp. 84 (N.D. Ill. 1982).

[60] *Doody v. John Sexton & Co.*, 411 F.2d 1119 (1st Cir. 1969). *See also McAfee v. Rockford Coca-Cola Bottling Co.*, 40 Ill. App.3d 521, 352 N.E.2d 50 (1976).

[61] *Cancellier v. Federated Dep't Stores*, 672 F.2d 1312, 28 FEP 1151 (9th Cir.), *cert. denied*, 459 U.S. 859 (1982).

charge, however, and the investigation was eventually dropped. Soon thereafter, the branch manager was subpoenaed to testify before a grand jury. Before he testified but after he was subpoenaed, he was terminated.

The branch manager sued on two bases: first, that the bank's handbook implied a promise not to discharge him for less than just cause; and second, that his discharge for being subpoenaed to testify before a grand jury violated public policy. The jury found for him on both claims, and awarded him damages as follows: $29,332 back wages, $25,000 loss of professional reputation, $10,000 mental anguish, and $600 moving expenses. All but the award of $10,000 for mental anguish were upheld on appeal to the Court of Appeals for the Sixth Circuit. An award for mental anguish, while recoverable under the tort claim, was disallowed because the branch manager had failed to carry his burden of providing specific and definite evidence of his own mental anguish. The final award was $54,932.[62]

Contract Damages

Damage awards in contract actions are designed to make the injured party "whole," based on the original expectations of the parties.[63] Thus, contract damages in discharge cases consist of back pay and lost benefits, but not an award for such damages as "pain and suffering" or for punitive damages. Back-pay awards may include reasonably anticipated raises and promotions, and generally accrue until the employee has obtained suitable or comparable employment following a diligent search. Front pay (i.e., a series of payments after judgment to continue until the employee is satisfactorily reemployed), although rarely awarded, has been held to be appropriate in a number of age discrimination cases as an alternative to reinstatement, and may in coming years gain greater acceptance in unjust dismissal cases.[64] Income earned from the time of dismissal until the time of the court's award is generally deducted from the ultimate damages award. Lost benefits are similarly awarded with an eye toward making the employee whole.

---

[62]*Wiskotoni v. Michigan Nat'l Bank-West*, 716 F.2d 378, 114 LRRM 2596 (6th Cir. 1983).

[63]*Gulf Consol. Int'l, v. Murphy*, 658 S.W.2d 565 (Tex. 1983). *See Fincke v Phoenix Mut. Life Ins. Co.*, 448 F. Supp. 187 (W.D. Pa. 1978) (punitive damages not available in contract action). *See also* Restatement of Contracts §355 (1981).

[64]*See Whittlesey v. Union Carbide Corp.*, 742 F.2d 724, 35 FEP 1089 (2d Cir. 1984); *Gibson v. Mohawk Rubber Co.*, 695 F.2d 1093, 30 FEP 859 (8th Cir. 1982). *But see Kolb v. Goldring, Inc.*, 694 F.2d 869, n.4, 30 FEP 633 (1st Cir. 1982).

Tort Damages

Tort actions offer the highest damages and broadest scope of potential liability for management. Compensatory damages, including awards for "pain and suffering" and loss to professional reputation, may be awarded in any of the tort actions discussed in prior sections: public policy exception to the at-will rule, defamation, and intentional infliction of emotional distress, fraud, and negligence.[65]

The distinction between tort and contract actions has become blurred in this area. For example, actions based on the implied covenant of good faith and fair dealing have been characterized as tortious by some courts, contractual by others.[66] In one case, the Wisconsin Supreme Court took the novel position that public policy exception cases, even though tort actions, provide for only make-whole remedies, that is, reinstatement, back pay, and lost benefits.[67] The court in that case was bothered by the possibility of exorbitant tort damage awards.

The potential for punitive damages is perhaps the most troubling quality of tort actions to management. The federal circuit court of appeals that upheld the jury award of $1.9 million for three dismissed management employees, discussed above, concluded that "[a] jury may award punitive damages if it finds by a preponderance of the evidence that defendant was guilty of malice, oppression or fraud."[68] In another case, an employee discharged for filing a worker's compensation claim was awarded $25,000 in punitive damages on a back-pay award of only $749.00.[69]

Management's worst fears of juries and juries' awards in wrongful discharge litigation have been borne out in a survey (noted in Chapter 1) conducted by the law firm of Schachter, Kristoff, Ross, Sprague and Curiale of jury verdicts in wrongful discharge cases in California in 1986. The survey revealed that of the 51 jury verdicts in wrongful discharge cases, 78 percent resulted in verdicts

---

[65]*Harless v. First Nat'l Bank in Fairmont*, 169 W.Va. 673, 289 S.E.2d 692, 117 LRRM 2792 (W.Va. 1982) (emotional distress); *Kelsay v. Motorola, Inc.*, 74 Ill.2d 172, 384 N.E.2d 353 (1978) (punitive damages); *Wiskotoni, supra*, note 62 (professional reputation).

[66]*Fortune v. National Cash Register Co.*, 373 Mass. 96, 364 N.E.2d 1251 (1977) (contract); *Gates v. Life of Mont. Ins. Co.*, 205 Mont. 304, 668 P.2d 213 (1983) (tort); *Cleary v. American Airlines*, 111 Cal. App.3d 443, 168 Cal. Rptr. 722, 115 LRRM 3030 (1980) (both tort and contract).

[67]*Brockmeyer v. Dun & Bradstreet*, 113 Wis.2d 561, 335 N.W.2d 834, 115 LRRM 4484 (1983).

[68]*Cancellier, supra*, note 61, 28 FEP at 1156.

[69]*Kelsay, supra*, note 65.

for the plaintiff. The average verdict, including both general and punitive damages, was $424,527. In 16 of those cases resulting in plaintiffs' verdicts, punitive damages were awarded. The average punitive damages award was $494,006. In one case, a furniture department manager was awarded $337,000 in general damages and $2 million in punitive damages. The fear of large damage awards like those often obtained in age discrimination suits may serve as an incentive to management attorneys to settle cases prior to a jury verdict.[70]

In addition to company liability, supervisors who initiate or participate in the employer's wrongful act may be held personally liable for their part in the employee's injury.[71]

Finally, attorney's fees and costs are generally not awardable in either tort or contract wrongful discharge or related common-law actions.

The "Costs" of Litigating Wrongful Discharge Claims

Employers today more than ever must weigh the cost of taking an action against possible legal liability. Damage awards, however, are only a part of the costs of litigating employee lawsuits, in particular, wrongful discharge claims. Among the hidden costs to be considered: (1) employee relations damage, (2) public relations damage, (3) manager's time lost to litigation, (4) plaintiff's discovery, (5) attorney's fees, and (6) company's litigation precedent.

Employee Relations

A lawsuit brought by a co-worker or former co-worker is likely to become an item of discussion at the coffee machine, in the elevator, on the loading dock, or at the Wednesday night poker game. If the employee litigant is still employed, information on the case from the employee's perspective will be freely available to interested co-workers. If he or she is an ex-employee, then friends still on the payroll may serve as an alternative source of information. Whatever the particular facts or equities of the case, the David and Goliath quality to the litigation will give even an unsympathetic employee litigant grounds for co-worker sympathy.

---

[70] *BNA's Employee Relations Weekly*, Vol. 5, No. 9 (Mar. 2, 1987) p. 283.
[71] See *Harless, supra*, note 65.

This is particularly true when a forceful defense is waged against the suit.

Litigation can very quickly become, from an employee relations perspective, a no-win situation for management: if management wins, fancy lawyers and a deep pocket are credited; if it loses, in the eyes of co-workers, justice may be viewed as having prevailed.

From an employee relations point of view, what may be gained in court may be at most a Pyrrhic victory, unless a prompt and strong effort is made to communicate the company's view of the facts and its position on the suit.

Public Relations

IBM, generally known for its effective human resource management, faced a troublesome and well-publicized problem. A supervisor in a California office demanded that a staff sales manager, Virginia Rulon-Miller, stop dating a sales manager with a competing company (an ex-IBM employee) whom she had been dating for four years. When she refused, she was transferred to a position with less responsibility, and then resigned. She sued on wrongful discharge and invasion of privacy grounds, and won a jury award of $300,000. The national press and major television networks covered the story in detail. For IBM's personnel staff, the financial damage caused by the jury award paled in contrast to the injury to IBM's strong reputation as an employer that treats its workers fairly.[72]

A jury verdict is not necessary for severe public relations damage to be inflicted. As most effective plaintiffs' lawyers know, *allegations* of wrongdoing are often treated as newsworthy, despite no *finding* of wrongdoing. Prompt and appropriate responses to workers' allegations of wrongdoing can help alleviate unnecessary injury to a company's valued public image.

Management Time

Litigation is a time-consuming and expensive process, partly as the result of liberal litigation discovery rules. While allowance is often made for the expense of litigation in the company budget, the amount of management time invested in wrongful discharge

---

[72]*Rulon-Miller v. IBM*, 162 Cal. App.3d 241, 208 Cal. Rptr. 524 (1984).

and related litigation is often overlooked. A plaintiff with resources or an ambitious lawyer might involve in the litigation every manager who participated or could have participated in the alleged wrongful act. Time spent in answering interrogatories, responding to attorneys' questions, plotting strategy, or testifying at a deposition or at trial is valuable time spent not managing.

Plaintiff's Discovery

Discovery in wrongful discharge and related cases can be unduly intrusive. For example, in a wrongful discharge suit, plaintiff will want not only his or her own personnel records, but also those of similarly situated employees. He or she may request, and may be entitled to receive, otherwise confidential information regarding management policies and practices. The scope of permissible discovery may in fact be broadened by the defense offered by the company to the plaintiff's claim. For example, assume management defends a wrongful dismissal claim by contending that the employee was released as part of a companywide reduction in force. A persevering plaintiff may seek and be entitled to discover information—companywide—about the reduction in force. Liberal discovery rules in the hands of an astute plaintiffs' lawyer may translate into a high settlement value for an otherwise insubstantial claim.

Attorney's Fees

Liberal discovery, in addition to occupying an inordinate amount of management's time and threatening to disclose otherwise privileged information, also requires a substantial amount of attorney's time for supervision. Defense counsel, with most of the relevant documents in their client's possession, typically require a limited amount of discovery from plaintiff. Much of defense counsel's time is spent in responding to plaintiff's requests and in unraveling the facts surrounding a particular personnel decision. Attorney's time means attorney's fees, and fees may become disproportionate to the amount of potential liability. Decisions to settle are often made not out of the fear of potential liability, but out of the reality of calculable attorney's fees.

Company Precedent

For policy reasons some companies never settle suits they believe to have been wrongfully brought. Others want to be spared the expense of litigation and of paying the judgments entered on these suits by quickly settling these suits. Most address the issue on a case-by-case basis.

The way an employer responds to a wrongful dismissal or related common-law suit (particularly the first) may color all such subsequent disputes. Did the company settle too easily? How were the events communicated to workers, and how did they respond? How bitterly was the contest fought? Who won? Disgruntled employees and future litigants will measure management's litigation stance in deciding on an approach in the same way attorneys read prior decisions written by the judge before whom they appear.

Management Responses to Recent Legal Developments

Developments in EEO and the common law have prompted a variety of management responses. A recent, broad-based survey of personnel executives revealed that three-fourths of the responding firms had taken some action to limit their legal liability in anticipation of wrongful discharge litigation.[73] Personnel managers, concerned with the possibility of judicial review of their practices and policies, are turning increasingly to legal counsel for guidance. Counsel, in turn, have provided suggestions to minimize legal liability. Personnel managers who follow such advice will undoubtedly minimize company liability against employee-instituted litigation. Human resources managers on occasion resist such suggestions when they seem to threaten basic management philosophy and policies—and experience with employees—at their companies.

Whatever approach a particular management adopts, it is essential that it reflect the philosophy and goals of top management. As we saw in Chapter 3, some firms favor an informal set of procedures for employee complaints and a climate of trust in management's openness and fairness that can make such procedures work effectively. Other companies, especially firms with large work forces and operating units, such as Bank of America, may select more formal systems with standardized rules, staff monitoring of the system's results and fairness, and an appeals mechanism that

---

[73]Bureau of National Affairs, Inc., *Employee Discipline & Discharge*, Personnel Policies Forum Survey No. 139 (Washington, D.C.: BNA, 1985).

is both visible and interventionist. Still others like the Massachusetts Institute of Technology and the National Broadcasting Company, with work forces heavily made up of professionals or technical personnel, may opt for a counselor-oriented rather than a hearing-oriented system.

The key point to note is that the makeup of the work force, the organizational structures, management traditions, the expanding or contracting nature of the business, and many similar variables need to be at the forefront of management's thinking when it adopts or revises its internal complaint system in light of new legal exposures and a desire to minimize outside lawsuits. (The company case studies in Chapter 3 amply document the kinds of variations in internal systems that such a reflection of company situation and style produce.)

Legal advice in this area, responding directly to recent court decisions, seeks to avoid the following: creation of expectations of job security in the work force where none are intended, promise of benefits not guaranteed to be provided, and sloppy practices permitting individual supervisors to abuse or misrepresent their authority to the company's detriment. A review of some of the suggestions made by counsel in the significant aspects of personnel management, including hiring, communicating policies, measuring performance, discipline, and termination follows.

Hiring

The hiring process establishes both the terms and the tone of the employment relationship. Problems for management may arise from things said or promises made during that period of good feeling when an applicant becomes an employee. Express and implied promises made by company personnel, when broken, become the elements of a breach of contract action later. The key to effective personnel management at this stage is accurate and forceful communication of the company philosophy and policies and the precise nature and responsibilities of the new employee's job. Counsel's advice to management has focused on the following three areas: the employment application, the employment interview, and the special problems related to fixed-term contracts.

Employment Application

Typical of the type of advice being offered to human resource managers is the insertion of what may be called the standard "at-will/merger" or the "I'm free/you're free and don't let anyone tell you otherwise" clause inserted in employment application forms. Several courts have reviewed the "at-will/merger" clause found in the Sears, Roebuck & Company standard employment application and have rejected wrongful discharge suits brought by employees who signed such applications containing those clauses.[74] The clause reads as follows:

> In consideration of my employment, I agree to conform to the rules and regulations of Sears, Roebuck and Co., and my employment and compensation can be terminated, with or without cause, and with or without notice, at any time, at the option of either the Company or myself. I understand that no store manager or representative of Sears, Roebuck and Co., other than the president or vice-president of the Company, has any authority to enter into any agreement for employment for any specified period of time, or to make any agreement contrary to the foregoing.

The courts reviewing this clause held that it became part of the employment contract when the offer of employment was accepted and it was therefore enforceable against the employee. These decisions are consistent with those court rulings that hold enforceable any promises of just cause dismissal found in personnel handbooks.

Employment Interview

Promises made during the employment interview may be enforceable against the company even if the interviewer was without express authority to make such promises. Express at-will/merger clauses in the employment application or employee handbook, as in the employment application, may be overridden by promises of job security made during (and after) the hiring process. For example, a Ford employee was permitted to introduce evidence of oral promises of employment until the age of 65 despite the presence of an express at-will clause in the employment application.[75]

Counsel have consequently advised that company interviewers be provided with specific directions regarding the conduct of a job interview and what *not* to say. In particular, interviewers are instructed to avoid making representations of job security, promises of "promotions from within," or statements related to job benefits not expressly guaranteed by existing policy.

---

[74]*Batchelor v. Sears, Roebuck & Co.*, 574 F. Supp. 1480, 114 LRRM 3467 (E.D. Mich. 1983); *Novosel v. Sears, Roebuck & Co.*, 495 F. Supp. 344, 117 LRRM 2702 (E.D. Mich. 1980).

[75]*Schipani, supra,* note 55.

Fixed-Term Contracts

Fixed-term contracts traditionally have been terminable only for just cause, even where not expressly agreed to by the parties.[76] The burden of demonstrating just cause is borne by the employer.[77]

Some courts have begun to take a broader view of what constitutes a definite term of employment. For example, the Alaska Supreme Court found that the promise of employment until retirement age constituted a contract for a definite period of time, terminable only for just cause.[78] In addition, dismissal for less than just cause in fixed-term employment contracts is likely to be subjected to the increasingly accepted implied-in-law covenant of good faith and fair dealing.[79] Consequently, counsel are coaching personnel managers, as might be expected, to reserve management's rights under these circumstances.

Three suggestions are generally made. First, include an at-will clause in the fixed-term agreement expressly providing that just cause is not required to terminate the relationship. Such a clause is generally upheld by the courts. Second, short of converting a fixed-term agreement into an at-will relationship, management may insert an arbitration requirement for all disputes on the question of just cause for dismissal that do not raise issues of public policy. Finally, counsel have urged that a liquidated damages clause setting a limit on damages be inserted whether or not at-will and arbitration clauses are also present.

Communicating Policies

Consider this familiar scene. Counsel informs the human resource director that the newly issued employee handbook is a legal time bomb. Any language implying job security will have to be reviewed, and the terms "permanent" and "until retirement" immediately expunged wherever they appear. Ambiguous promises of fairness or equitable treatment are also to be excised. Finally, disclaimers must accompany all promises made in the handbook

---

[76]*Alpern v. Hurwitz*, 644 F.2d 943 (2d Cir. 1981); *Rosecrans v. Intermountain Soap & Chem. Co.*, 100 Idaho 785, 605 P.2d 963 (1980).

[77]*Rosecrans, supra*, note 76, 605 P.2d at 965; *Watts v. St. Mary's Hall, Inc.*, 662 S.W.2d 55 (Tex. App. 1983).

[78]*Eales v. Tanana Valley Medical-Surgical Group*, 663 P.2d 958 (Hawaii 1983).

[79]*See* cases cited in note 16, *supra*.

and all company communications. The Center for Public Resources' 1984 survey discussed in Chapter 1 confirms the frequency of this occurrence. Responding companies reported that they had revised the listed company documents in the following percentages within the prior three years in an effort to clarify the at-will nature of employment with their companies: personnel handbook (43 percent), employment application (36 percent), policy statements (25 percent), and offer letters (20 percent).

Certain human resources managers concerned about enhancing employee morale and commitment may be troubled by this advice, for they know, as does counsel, the importance of meaning what they say to employees. They may choose not to allow the fear of potential legal liability to stand in the way of thoroughly and accurately communicating company policy to company personnel. They recognize that an overly cautious legal approach has its costs. The employee handbook could be eliminated; but so would an effective and efficient communications tool. Disclaimers are enforceable, particularly when signed by the employee,[80] and could be inserted in strategic places in company documents, but may breed employee insecurity and reduce worker commitment. Stock options, which have been viewed by some courts as indicia of job security, could be replaced, but then a powerful recruitment device may be lost. Finally, a "no oral contract clause" that explains to workers that anything said by a manager or by management that contradicts written company policy may not be relied upon, while enhancing top management's position, may undermine the authority of individual low-level supervisors. Thus, legally tenable options may be found by some human resources managers to be unacceptable approaches to the operation of their personnel function.

Other employers may decide that it is in their corporate interest to refine their handbooks to stress management power to terminate and to define what employee conduct can and cannot be raised in internal systems. Ultimately, these are issues that top management must decide, balancing the firm's interests, employee expectations, and sociolegal factors.

The courts may also decide that legal protections surrounding employee communications may survive such efforts at narrowing employee rights. For example, a number of courts have held that

---

[80]*Mau v. Omaha Nat'l Bank*, 207 Neb. 308, 299 N.W.2d 147 (1980); *Ferraro v. Koelsch*, 119 Wis. App.2d 407, 350 N.W.2d 735, 116 LRRM 3092 (1984), *aff'd*, 124 Wis.2d 154, 368 N.W.2d 666, 120 LRRM 2607 (1985). *See also supra*, note 74 and accompanying text.

oral assurances of job security may override signed acknowledgements of at-will employment in an employment application, contract, or personnel handbook.[81] Also, written company policies that contradict a signed acknowledgement of at-will employment may be enforceable against the company.[82] Finally, a substantial change in a written employment term by an employer may be treated as a breach of the employment contract upon review by a court.[83]

Measuring Performance

One of the most difficult arguments company attorneys have had to make to judges and juries in wrongful discharge cases has been that the employee who had received consistently excellent performance evaluations through his long years of employment with the company was legitimately terminated because of suddenly poor performance, particularly when this arose in connection with management actions the employee alleges to have been improper or negligent. Performance evaluations have become plaintiffs' counsel's most important tool in demonstrating that the proffered reason for the dismissal was pretextual.[84]

In response, some company counsel have urged that:

- employee failings be scrupulously documented in employees' personnel files and in subsequent performance evaluations;
- highly favorable performance appraisals be avoided;
- the category "excellent" be eliminated from the possible ratings options;
- performance evaluations more than three years old be destroyed and personnel files periodically purged;
- worker responses to performance appraisals be disallowed; and
- the anecdotal quality of employee reviews be limited in those states that permit employees access to their personnel files.

---

[81]*Schipani, supra,* note 55; *Arie v. Intertherm, Inc.*, 648 S.W.2d 142, 118 LRRM 3436 (Mo. App. 1983). *See Stone v. Mission Bay Mortgage Co.*, 99 Nev. 802, 672 P.2d 629, 116 LRRM 2917 (1983) (oral promises may overcome disclaimer in employment application where no evidence that application constituted employment contract).

[82]*Brooks v. Trans World Airlines*, 574 F. Supp. 805, 114 LRRM 3136 (D. Colo. 1983).

[83]*Sanders v. May Broadcasting Co.*, 214 Neb. 755, 336 N.W.2d 92 (1983).

[84]For a review and the text of a study of court decisions involving employee performance appraisal systems by Feild and Thompson of Auburn University, *see* 1984 Daily Lab. Rep. (BNA) 248:E-1–E-5.

Management concern for the integrity of its performance evaluation system is, of course, warranted. Recent court decisions have held companies accountable for performance criteria that were found to be inherently discriminatory against older employees,[85] discriminatorily or irrationally applied,[86] or overly subjective.[87]

The most dramatic extension of the rights of employees in this area is an unappealed 1982 federal district court decision that held an employer liable for the negligent evaluation of a corporate manager's performance.[88] The court found the company negligent in failing to apprise the manager that dismissal was likely unless his performance promptly improved. The employee was awarded $61,354.02 in actual damages.

This decision suggests that once a performance appraisal system is in place, the evaluations must be diligently and fairly conducted, and results should be shared with the employee.

Discipline and Discharge

No personnel decision is as likely to be reviewed by a court as a decision to discipline or discharge an employee. The Equal Employment Opportunity Commission estimates that 70 percent of all age discrimination lawsuits involve employee terminations.[89] Professor Jack Stieber, a strong advocate of unjust dismissal legislation, has estimated that 1.4 million nonprobationary employees in the private sector are terminated in the average year, and that 140,000 of these employees would gain reinstatement were all private sector employees able to arbitrate their dismissals under a just cause standard.[90] Also, no personnel decision is as likely to be viewed with more hostility by a jury than the unjust disciplining or dismissal of an employee. In response to this fact, many employers now require approval by the personnel department or

[85]*Mistretta v. Sandia Corp.*, 649 F.2d 1383 (10th Cir. 1981).

[86]*Stoller v. Marsh*, 682 F.2d 971, 976–78, 29 FEP 85 (D.C. Cir. 1982), *cert. denied*, 460 U.S. 1037 (1983); *Stephenson v. Simon*, 427 F. Supp. 467, 472–73 (D.D.C. 1976); *Hatton v. Ford Motor Co.*, 508 F. Supp. 620, 626–28, 25 FEP 314 (E.D. Mich. 1981)

[87]*Crawford v. Western Elec. Co., Inc.*, 745 F.2d 1373, 1383–84, 36 FEP 1753 (11th Cir. 1984); *Segar v. Civiletti*, 508 F. Supp. 690, 25 FEP 1452 (D.D.C. 1981) (subjective evaluations having disproportionate impact on blacks, unless justified by business necessity, violate Title VII). *But see Pinckney v. County of Northampton*, 512 F. Supp. 989, 27 FEP 528 (E.D. Pa. 1981) (subjective evaluations of personalities of candidates for management positions may be considered).

[88]*Chamberlain v. Bissell, Inc.*, 547 F. Supp. 1067, 30 FEP 347 (W.D. Mich. 1982).

[89]*EEOC Profile of ADEA Plaintiffs*, 115 LRRM 73 (Jan. 23, 1984).

[90]Stieber & Murray, *Protection Against Unjust Dismissal: The Need for a Federal Statute*, 16 Mich. J.L. Reform 319 (1983).

high-level executive prior to dismissal or severe disciplining of an employee.

Some counsel suggest more ambitious defensive strategies designed to limit liability. The "less-said-the-better" is the thrust of this approach. Formal disciplinary policies are to be avoided, counsel will argue, so that line management is allowed greater flexibility and the ability to fire on the spot when necessary. Written records of the discipline are also discouraged so as to preclude later review. (This contradicts somewhat the desire to develop a full personnel record to support later discipline or dismissal.) If the company favors a policy of progressive discipline, then counsel will probably recommend that it be practiced, but not promised, in order to avoid expressly creating expectations that may rise to the level of contract.

Recommendations of reticence also extend to terminations. Reasons for dismissals, it may be suggested, need not be given employees. Techniques for gaining releases from dismissed workers during the exit process may be discussed. Counsel may also suggest that probation periods be extended, thereby allowing a longer look at new workers and greater flexibility in severing ties if that becomes necessary.

As noted earlier, job security is a principal concern of American employees, both union and nonunion. The increasing willingness of major unions in the 1980s to forgo economic gains in favor of greater job security confirms this fact. Personnel practices that signal a disregard for workers' job security, some personnel management experts argue, may be injurious to employee morale and tend to swim against the tide of legally acceptable practices. For example, some states, like Maine, require that employers provide to workers upon request written reasons for termination of employment.[91] Also, courts, receptive to the notion that proper notice should be required prior to the denial of rights or property, increasingly have required management to abide by a stated policy or practice of progressive discipline preceding termination. Finally, the existence of written policies that establish grounds for discipline often cut in management's favor and make possible proof of the propriety of a discharge to the jury.

In short, discipline and discharge situations will be most carefully scrutinized and required to meet the most stringent tests of propriety and equity.

---

[91]Me. Rev. Stat. Ann tit. 26, §631 (1984).

The Fairness Quotient in Modern Human Resource Management

The movement in the courts, Congress, and among state legislatures toward protecting and enhancing the rights of employees has, in the opinion of some, reached its peak in recent years and is not likely to expand in the near future. They cite the very limited number of legislative enactments in recent years which seek to further the job protection or other rights of workers. In addition, strong stands by such courts as the New York Court of Appeals, the highest court in New York state, against expanding employee rights by judicial fiat lead some to the conclusion that the pendulum of employment prerogatives and rights is swinging back toward management's side. If true, dramatic changes in company policy or practice such as establishing an internal grievance and complaint system, it is argued, are less likely to be needed or implemented.

If the movement in the law of recent decades continues, however, and treatment of unorganized employees is increasingly governed by legislation or judicial decision, as has been suggested by others, then management's need to respond to these developments will be increased. Should these trends continue, and we believe that they will, courts increasingly will demand that management respond to what we have called the "fairness quotient" in employment relations.

The notion of fairness is deeply rooted in the American legal and social systems. America has long been heralded as the land of opportunity and dignity in which a person could receive a fair day's pay for a fair day's work. It became part of our folklore that all that stood between a person and prosperity was hard work. The eminent fairness of such a system was unimpeachable.

From the Bill of Rights to Chief Justice Earl Warren's recurring inquiry of counsel, "but is it fair?" fair treatment has been treated as a value enforceable by law, standing at the very core of the constitutional, political, and social rights of the individual. In the law, due process is often the means by which fairness is measured and meted out.

This fairness quotient in American law and society is being applied increasingly by courts in reviewing the treatment of unorganized employees in the workplace. The disparity between the rights of union and nonunion employees has furthered this development, as has the decline in the percentage of the unionized work force. The demand for broadened legal protection for nonunion employees may also be seen as an outgrowth of the civil rights and civil liberties movements of the 1960s and 1970s.

Recent developments in the courts promise to provide unorganized employees some protections approximating those afforded to union employees under collective bargaining agreements. However, the bounds of this new protection, and of management's potential liability, are not yet known. The absence of established and uniform legal standards to facilitate compliance is perhaps the most troubling aspect of recent developments to management, particularly in light of the potential for punitive damages.

Indicia of Fairness

Despite the uncertainty, certain indicia of court-recognized fairness obligations of management can be discerned. They are: rationality, legality, notice, and appeal.

Rationality

Overly subjective or idiosyncratic policies and practices are increasingly being successfully challenged in court. The intimacy and informality of a less industrial (and litigious) time has passed. The employment relationship is now governed by procedures and rules related and necessary to job performance that must apply to each employee equally and must be uniformly applied. In short, personnel policies and practices today are being asked by the courts to meet the test of rationality.

How has the requirement of rationality been interpreted and applied by the courts? The following types of policies or practices have been found to be irrational, and, on a variety of grounds, illegal: job qualification requirements that are not "job-related" and which disparately impact on a particular group,[92] performance appraisal systems that are overly subjective or discriminatory on their face,[93] disciplining of an employee on the basis of contradictory directions,[94] or for doing an assigned task too well.[95]

---

[92]*Griggs v. Duke Power Co.*, 401 U.S. 424, 3 FEP 175 (1971).

[93]*Mistretta, supra*, note 106.

[94]*Cloutier v. Great Atl. & Pac. Tea Co.*, 121 N.H. 915, 436 A.2d 1140, 115 LRRM 4329 (1981).

[95]*See e.g., Richter v. Ellis Fischel State Cancer Hosp.*, 629 F.2d 563 (8th Cir. 1980), *cert. denied*, 450 U.S. 1040 (1981) (radiation safety officer in hospital suffered retaliation for reporting serious violation to Nuclear Regulatory Commission).

A 1981 New Hampshire Supreme Court decision is typical of these "rationality" cases.[96] David Cloutier had worked for his employer, A&P, since 1939, and in July 1975, was made manager of a new store in Tilton, New Hampshire. Because the store was in an unsafe neighborhood, Cloutier arranged for a police escort for employees depositing store cash in the bank. The police charged $3.00 a trip, or $6.00 for the daily round trip. A&P later terminated the practice "to save costs." Cloutier was solely responsible for deposit of the cash and was instructed to place cash in the store safe on nights and weekends.

One Sunday evening, while Cloutier was off duty, the store was robbed of $30,000 taken from the store safe. Cloutier was suspended after a five-minute meeting with his supervisors, then discharged in summary fashion for his "violation of company bookkeeping procedure." The assistant manager on duty that day was briefly suspended, but then reinstated. The company reasoned that Cloutier, as manager of the store, was responsible at all times for the cash on the premises.

Cloutier sued for wrongful discharge, arguing that the company had acted in bad faith. A jury awarded Cloutier $92,000. The New Hampshire Supreme Court upheld the jury's finding of bad faith on the part of A&P, and the jury's award. The court found several indicia of the store's bad faith.

First, "A&P was willing to terminate a procedure intended to guarantee the safe and regular delivery of deposits to the bank in order to save $3 per trip to the bank. . . . Discharging [Cloutier] because a burglary occurred, when the defendant's loss resulted from actions it condoned, could be found to involve bad faith and retaliation . . . ."[97]

Second, the store was obligated under the Occupational Safety and Health Act (OSHA) to provide a safe workplace to its workers. A&P "breached this duty by requiring [Cloutier] to travel to the bank, unprotected, with substantial sums of money."[98]

Third, "After thirty-six years of employment, the plaintiff was suspended after a five-minute meeting and then discharged in an equally cursory manner. A&P never informed the plaintiff of the allegations against him. The manner in which A&P notified the

---

[96] *See supra*, note 94.
[97] *Id.*, 115 LRRM at 4332.
[98] *Id.*, 115 LRRM at 4333.

plaintiff of his discharge suggests that A&P acted with malice towards the plaintiff."[99]

Finally, the court noted that Cloutier was responsible for the cash in the store at all times, and could not delegate the responsibility. But the law requires what the Lord decreed, a day of rest. The court held that Cloutier could not be "discharged for some action or failure to act during his regularly scheduled day off, when to do otherwise would deprive him of the day off, something which public policy encourages and the law commands."[100]

The rationality requirement is basically a common-sense demand that personnel policies and practices not be inconsistent, absurd, or administered in bad faith.

Legality

An employee may be asked to do much in the name of his or her employment—the unpleasant, the inefficient, and even the silly. But to be asked to violate the law in the course of employment is no longer legally tenable, at least in most states. The broad discretion afforded employers under the at-will doctrine has eroded at least that far. Few would argue, at least publicly, that loyalty to the employer, which remains at the core of a successful employment relationship, requires blind obedience to directions to violate the law or established professional/ethical mandates.

The public policy exception to the terminable-at-will rule embodies this development. For example, dismissals for refusing to commit perjury or to participate in an illegal price-fixing scheme have been held, in the parlance of modern employment law, to be "wrongful discharges" subject to review by judges and juries. A less sympathetic case to present to a jury can hardly be conceived. The inherent unfairness of such personnel decisions pervades courts' analyses and colors juries' decisions. The following 1984 Oregon Supreme Court decision is typical.[101]

Ledbetter, a district manager for Taco Time restaurants, received complaints from some customers that too many blacks worked at one Taco Time restaurant in Portland. Ledbetter spoke to Delaney, the restaurant manager, and suggested that he fire a troublesome black employee, Ms. White. White was dismissed soon

---

[99]*Id.*, 115 LRRM at 4332–33.
[100]*Id.*, 115 LRRM at 4334.
[101]*Delaney v. Taco Time Int'l*, 297 Or. 10, 681 P.2d 114, 116 LRRM 2168 (1984) (en banc).

thereafter, and she filed for unemployment compensation, indicating that she was discharged because of her race.

Ledbetter later asked Delaney to sign a report that gave as the reason for White's termination her unwelcome sexual advances toward Delaney and threat to cause dissension if he refused to accede to her demands. The report, written in the first person by Ledbetter, also alluded to the request made by some customers that more Caucasian help be hired, and continues, "I suggested the addition of one or two white people but in no way did I suggest that [Delaney] terminate anyone because of their color."[102] The report stated that Delaney misinterpreted Ledbetter's suggestion, and fired White. The report concluded that White must be reinstated. Delaney refused to sign the report because it contained untrue statements, and when he refused a reassignment, was fired.

Delaney sued for wrongful discharge: The jury awarded damages for lost wages, emotional distress, and punitive damages. The Oregon Supreme Court upheld the award. In the court's words, Taco Time "required [Delaney] knowingly to commit a potentially tortious act or lose his job."[103] The statements in the report, the court noted, were not only false, but arguably defamatory as well. The court ruled, "[A] member of society has an obligation not to defame others. . . . [Delaney] here was discharged for fulfilling a societal obligation. We hold that [Taco Time] is liable for wrongfully discharging [Delaney] because [Delaney] refused to sign the potentially defamatory statement."[104]

Notice

The two basic components of constitutional due process are (1) notice and (2) an opportunity to be heard. It is not surprising that courts, in reviewing adverse employment decisions, turn to these principles for guidance.

Notice of the company's rules and of the charges made against the worker prior to discipline or discharge is crucial on legal review. The principle of progressive discipline that underlies the union grievance system increasingly is being applied in the nonunion setting.

Notice typically takes the form of communicating company rules and procedures to the employee orally or by written statement, typically a personnel handbook. Policies need not be formally

---

[102]*Id.*, 116 LRRM at 2169.
[103]*Id.*, 116 LRRM at 2171.
[104]*Id.*

expressed; they may be unspoken or implied from circumstance. For example, in one case, United Parcel Service (UPS) was able to withstand legal challenge of its decision to dismiss a manager on the basis of an unwritten rule against management-nonmanagement fraternization. The manager had been living with a non-management UPS worker. In balancing interests, the court found the company's interest in avoiding claims of favoritism and sexual harassment outweighed the manager's privacy interests and claims of unfairness. The employer's case was enhanced because it had warned the manager several times before his discharge about its nonfraternization rule and because it had dismissed a member of management on the same ground a few months earlier.[105]

Similarly, basic to the court decision discussed earlier, recognizing an employee's right to sue for the negligent performance of his performance review, was the failure of the company (Bissell) to give the employee notice of his contemplated termination. The court wrote:

> It is unavailing for Bissell to argue that it had no duty to provide notice, to hold Chamberlain's [the employee's] hand, or to tell him what should have been obvious. Bissell had a duty of reasonable care. By failing to fully inform Chamberlain it increased the risk that he would ultimately be discharged. Bissell's failure is not justified by any counterbalancing benefit or interest. Therefore, Bissell breached its duty of reasonable care.[106]

When proper notice is given, however, management discretion in a court's eyes may be broadened. The fairness of its actions may be perceived as unimpeachable, as exemplified by the following case involving the Federal Express Corporation.[107]

Randall Gee, an experienced pilot, and his First Officer Luana Davis were on a normal cargo run when Gee leaned over to Davis, said "I want to show you something" and rolled the aircraft in a full 360 degree turn. A stunned Davis heard Gee comment, "I always wanted to do that." In addition to being a flagrant violation of Federal Aviation Administration regulations and company flight operations procedures, the acrobatic maneuver could have caused structural damage to the plane, disabled the hydraulic system, and caused the engines to shut down. Davis reported the incident to company officials.

---

[105]*Crosier v. United Parcel Serv.*, 150 Cal. App.3d 1132, 198 Cal. Rptr. 361, 115 LRRM 3585 (1983).
[106]*Chamberlain, supra*, note 88, 30 FEP at 360.
[107]*Gee v. Federal Express Corp.*, 710 F.2d 1181 (6th Cir. 1983).

Federal Express procedures provide for the convening of a Flight Operations Board of Review when crew members are disciplined. The employee is entitled to select three of the five board members. Federal Express officials decided, however, not to convene a review board in this case. Section 1.01 of the *Federal Express Flight Crewmembers' Handbook* provides: "Blatant violation of company or departmental rules may constitute conduct for which an employee may be dismissed without notice or warning." The company flight operations manual expressly stated that aerobatic flight maneuvers were prohibited, and indicated that normal flight operations should not require more than a 30 degree angle of bank. Gee was questioned as soon as the charge was made, and admitted rolling the plane. He was fired that day by the Senior Vice President of Flight Operations, whose decision was immediately endorsed upon review by the company's president and its chief executive officer and chairman of the board. Relying on Section 1.01 of the crew members' handbook, management concluded that a Board of Review was not appropriate where the violation of the rules was blatant.

A federal appeals court, agreeing with the company's interpretation of its rules, upheld the dismissal. The court was impressed with "the prompt and unanimous actions of top Federal Express officials in discharging Gee when they learned of his admitted blatant violation."[108] Gee was on notice of the possible ramifications of his actions, and the company's swift action in accordance with company policy was sustainable upon review.

Appeal

An employee's right to be heard with respect to an adverse personnel decision and the chance to appeal that decision to higher authorities in the company are at the heart of fair treatment in both legal and commonsense terms. Mistakes can be made, and permitting the person most affected by a personnel decision or company policy to argue his or her case provides a valuable opportunity for a second look by management. In addition, the cathartic effect on the employee of expressing the concern cannot be minimized. Finally, in the eyes of a reviewing court or jury, the corporate execution (in the case of a discharge) will seem less the action of a lynch mob and more the imposition of a judicial death sentence

---

[108]*Id.* at 1186.

if the employee has an adequate opportunity to plead his or her case.

Provision for appeal need not be formal or embodied in a structured, multitiered system. The more extensive the procedures, however, the more likely the system will be perceived as procedurally fair. The bureaucratization of the employment relationship, and the need for large, corporate managements to centralize and standardize procedures have furthered this trend toward establishing structured, fair procedure systems for resolution of employee grievances and concerns.

An employee's right to be heard has been to a limited extent legislated into existence. For example, a number of states provide employees, along with the right to review their personnel files, an opportunity to respond to the information contained therein.[109]

In addition to occasionally being legislatively required, providing employees with an opportunity to be heard is viewed by many management experts as good policy. For example, space is often provided on performance appraisal forms for an employee's remarks and signature. One recently issued management guidebook comments:

> The signature merely acknowledges the fact that the appraisal was presented to the employee.
> The space for employee comments is far more important. If the employee registers disagreement with the appraisal, it will provide the employer an opportunity to review its initial determination. Whatever the outcome of this review, the process itself makes fairness more likely and certainly will make it easier to persuade the jury that the employer was acting fairly.
> If the employee does not register objection, it will be difficult for him later to convince a jury that the supervisor's negative appraisal was incorrect.[110]

The fairness quotient in employment relations should not be ignored. Those managements that apply techniques learned in the hard-negotiating collective bargaining setting to the management of nonunion employees are less likely to win the fairness battle, both in the minds of their employees and in the eyes of a court and jury. The greater the failure on management's part to provide

[109]Cal. Labor Code §1198.5 (West Supp. 1985); Conn. Gen. Stat. Ann. §431–128 (West Supp. 1984); Del. Code Ann. Tit. 19 §§719–724 (Supp. 1984); Ill. Ann. Stat. ch. 48 §§2001–2012 (Smith-Hurd Supp. 1984–85); Me. Rev. Stat. Ann. tit. 26 §631 (1984–85 Supp.); Mich. Comp. Laws Ann. §§423.501–512 (West Supp. 1984–85); N.H. Rev. Stat. Ann. §275–56 (I–III) (1983 Supp.); Or. Rev. Stat. §652.750 (1984 Supp.); Pa. Stat. Ann. tit. 43 §1321 (Purdon Supp. 1984–85); Wis. Stat. Ann. §103.13(1–8) (West Supp. 1984–85).
[110]R. Baxter & G. Siniscalco, Manager's Guide to Lawful Terminations, 77–78 (1983).

from within both the reality and appearance of fairness to its workers, the more likely the requirement of fair treatment will be imposed from without.

Fairness and Internal Dispute Resolution

A review of recent legislative and judicial developments in employment law confirms what personnel managers already sense— that the law is increasingly limiting management's discretion and control over its employees.

Loss of discretion, like the loss of youth, requires that the abilities retained be used with deliberation. The internal dispute resolution systems described in Chapter 3 are the most obvious and successful examples of organizational attempts to instill fairness and rationality into the employment relationship. Attempts to resolve disputes promptly and equitably from within satisfy the four recognized indicia of fairness: rationality, legality, notice, and appeal. The internal systems described in this book serve to provide what is at the heart of legal fairness, namely, the values underlying due process. Such attempts are likely to find favor with courts upon review. Professor Blades' prediction, made almost 20 years ago, that developments in the law and "a lack of confidence in courts and juries could lead, albeit in a roundabout way, to the creation of private means of settlement that might well be the most effective and expeditious way of handling such cases"[111] may yet prove true.

The fairness quotient in employment litigation translates into a battle for the heart of the finder-of-fact at trial. In viewing court decisions through the lens of fairness, it is clear that employers who fail to live up to their promises, that fail to acknowledge long years of service, or that act arbitrarily or in an insensitive manner toward their workers are likely to lose the fairness test in employment litigation. In contrast, personnel action that is reasonable under the circumstances, does not circumvent the law, is taken following notice to the employee, and survives an internal appeal is, of course, more likely to be perceived as fair by a judge or jury and sustained. Key to both the appearance and reality of fairness is the existence of a credible internal grievance system.

Is corporate management responding to the new fairness quotient in American employment law? The recent employment litigation explosion has made every responsible manager aware of the hazards of poor personnel management, and an increasing number

---

[111] *Supra*, note 3 at 1431.

of companies are indeed responding by establishing formal internal dispute resolution programs.

Legal Benefits and Ramifications of Fair Procedure Systems

Managers implementing or considering a fair procedure system may ask: What effect will the existence and use of a fair procedure system have on the rights of our employees to seek judicial or administrative review of their claims? Can legal action before the courts or agencies be precluded? Can we require our employees to use our internal system before going outside the company with their disputes? How can we strengthen our internal system to lessen the chances of reversal upon external review? Few definitive answers exist to these important questions. Certain benefits to management, however, as well as problems that it must face can be discerned.

Legal Background: Michigan Example

Legal authority on the subject is sparse but developing. The Michigan state courts have been particularly active in this area. Indeed, in December 1986, the Michigan Supreme Court issued the most thorough and authoritative decision related to the enforceability of the decision rendered by a fair procedure system. A review of this important decision, *Renny v. Port Huron Hospital*,[112] serves as a foundation for the discussion under "Legal Benefits Surveyed" below.

In *Renny*, a registered nurse was terminated for allegedly undermining Port Huron Hospital's new teamwork policy under which, among other things, nurses were asked to perform tasks formerly performed by nurses' aides. The Hospital's employee handbook provided for an optional joint employer-employee grievance board (the Board) as a "fair and effective means to resolve work related complaints and problems." The Board was unilaterally established by the Hospital and employee participation was limited to volunteer service on the Board. Renny grieved her termination and, under the Hospital's procedures, selected the members of the Board to resolve her dispute.

---

[112]427 Mich. 415, 398 N.W.2d 327 (1986). *Cf. Khalifa v. Henry Ford Hosp.*, 156 Mich. App. 485 401 N.W.2d 884 (1986), *appeal denied*, 428 Mich. 900 (1987)(employee bound by decision of procedurally flawed fair procedure system).

The Hospital's procedures severely limited the grieving employee's role before the Board. For example, the grieving employee could not be represented by counsel, review the written complaint against him or her, be present during the testimony of other witnesses, be told the identity of other witnesses, call witnesses or compel their attendance without the Board's consent, cross-examine or rebut witnesses' testimony, be present during the Hospital representative's opening remarks, or make an opening or closing statement. Further, no record or transcript of the hearing was produced and no findings were made by the Board. In Renny's case, the Board upheld her dismissal by a vote of five to one.

Renny sued, alleging that the employee handbook established a "just cause" standard of termination. The Michigan Supreme Court held, under the authority of its prior decision in *Toussaint v. Blue Cross & Blue Shield of Michigan*,[113] that the Hospital's handbook established a just cause requirement for termination.

The court further held that an employer's decision to dismiss an employee for just cause only is "subject to judicial review." The court went on to say that alternative methods of dispute resolution are subject to limited judicial review. Relying on its decision in *Fulghum v. United Parcel Service*,[114] the *Renny* majority concluded that "a decision of a joint employer-employee grievance committee should be granted the same deference as that afforded an independent arbiter."[115] Nonetheless, the court ruled that judicial review is permissible if "a plaintiff alleges that the grievance process lacked elementary fairness."[116]

The court then quoted the following five "essential elements necessary to fair adjudication in administrative and arbitration proceedings" taken from the Restatement (Second) of Judgments:

a) Adequate notice to persons who are to be bound by the adjudication;
b) The right to present evidence and arguments and the fair opportunity to rebut evidence and argument by the opposing argument;
c) A formulation of issues of law and fact in terms of the application of rules with respect to specified parties concerning a specific transaction, situation, or status;
d) A rule specifying the point in the proceeding when a final decision is rendered; and,

---

[113]408 Mich. 579, 292 N.W.2d 880 (1980).
[114]424 Mich. 89, 378 N.W.2d 472 (1985).
[115]*Renny, supra* note 112, 398 N.W.2d at 337.
[116]*Id.* at 338.

e) Other procedural elements as may be necessary to ensure a means to determine the matter in question. These will be determined by the complexity of the matter in question, the urgency with which the matter must be resolved and the opportunity of the parties to obtain evidence and formulate legal contentions.[117]

A grievance procedure unilaterally established by the employer lacking these elements, the court stated, would not ensure "an employee fairness."

In *Renny*, the court pointed to the following specific problems with the Board's procedures:

- Renny was not notified prior to the hearing of the allegations of the complaint;
- Renny was not notified prior to the hearing of the witnesses against her;
- Renny was not given the right to present evidence, including witnesses of her choice and her own work records; and
- Renny was not permitted to be present during the hearing and consequently could not rebut the evidence against her.

The *Renny* majority concluded that the Hospital's fair procedure system lacked "elementary fairness," and, as a consequence, she was entitled "to submit the merits of her claim to the jury to determine if, in fact, she was fired for just cause."[118] Questions for the jury include "whether plaintiff had, in fact, committed the specific misconduct for which she was fired, whether the firing was pretextual, or whether the employer was selectively applying the rules."[119] On the record before it, the Michigan Supreme Court concluded that the jury was entitled to find that Renny's termination was pretextual or that the Hospital's rules were selectively applied against Renny.

Three Justices of the Michigan Supreme Court, in dissent, compared the Hospital's procedures to the arbitration setting and concluded that the decision of the Board could only be vacated upon judicial review if the decision was procured by corruption, fraud, misconduct, bias, or by other undue means. Procedural unfairness, in the dissent's view, was not sufficient to overturn the Board's decision.

In sum, the Michigan Supreme Court in *Renny* was unanimous in holding that the decisions of fair procedure systems: (1) may be

---

[117]*Id.* at 338, *citing* Restatement (Second) of Judgments, §83(2) (1982).
[118]*Id.* at 339.
[119]*Id.*

final and binding; (2) are subject to limited judicial review; and (3) may be vacated upon review only if either (a) lacking elementary procedural fairness (majority view), or (b) procured by fraud, misconduct, or bias (dissent's view).

Legal Benefits Surveyed

The majority in *Renny* declined to give preclusive effect to the decision of the Hospital's fair procedure system under the facts of that case. The legal benefits of internal systems, however, extend beyond the question of preclusion (although this is admittedly a significant concern for many employers). A review of some of these benefits, as well as a discussion of the preclusion issue, follows.

Opportunity for First Review

Empirical studies of employee attitudes have consistently concluded that employees—if presented with the option—prefer to raise work-related disputes inside the company without involving outsiders or the government. An employee dispute presented to an internal system for resolution is perhaps management's last chance to resolve the matter without outside intervention. The issue may be resolvable in a number of ways, including counseling of the employee raising the complaint, or of the employee that is the cause of it, or by resolving the dispute if it is in management's control to do so. On occasion, systemic problems that need attention will be revealed in the complaint of an individual employee. As indicated in the Chicago and North Western Transportation Company's profile in Chapter 3, management at that firm found that "the internal system serves as a type of warning flag that possible, unrecognized, problem areas may exist."

Perhaps the problem uncovered is not resolvable at all due to its nature or the employee's or management's intransigence. Nevertheless, management benefits by being fully apprised of the employee's concerns and the employee is made more fully aware of management's position. Litigation of the claim, should it come about, is made that much easier.

Enhanced Litigation Stance

The existence of an internal system enhances both the appearance and reality of fairness of the company's actions in a later court proceeding. An employee who fails to present his or her claim first to the company system for resolution may be viewed by the judge or jury as rash, insincere, or litigious. In turn, the company may justifiably complain of being denied an opportunity to clean its own house. Finally, the company's litigation position will be significantly strengthened if the employee's claim was thoroughly investigated and fairly reviewed by its fair procedure system. Indeed, the Chicago and North Western Transportation Company was able to report in its profile that two of the three discrimination complaints filed over a six-month period with human rights agencies "were dismissed due primarily to the evidence contained in the internal investigation."

Support for this view may be found in the Supreme Court's 1986 decision in *Meritor Savings Bank v. Vinson,* [120] a case in which the Court for the first time declared sexual harassment to be a form of prohibited sex discrimination. Vinson, a bank supervisor, alleged that her supervisor had sexually harassed her over a period of four years. She admitted having sexual intercourse with her supervisor between 40 and 50 times and testified that she did not report the harassment to management or use the bank's internal complaint procedures out of fear for her job. The Supreme Court held that the "hostile environment" of harassment allegedly created by Vinson's supervisor could, if proven, constitute unlawful sexual discrimination. A majority of the Court declined, however, to hold employers absolutely liable for their supervisors' unlawful sexual harassment in "hostile environment" cases.

The bank argued to the Supreme Court that it should be "insulated" from liability because Vinson had failed to use the bank's internal complaint procedures or notify management of the harassment. The Court rejected the bank's argument that "the mere existence of a grievance procedure and a policy against discrimination, coupled with [Vinson's] failure to invoke that procedure, must insulate [the bank] from liability." [121] The Court noted, however, that these facts, while "not necessarily dispositive" are nonetheless "plainly relevant." The problem in this case, as analyzed by the Court, was that the bank's nondiscrimination policy did not address sexual harassment directly and that the complaint procedure required that Vinson first go to the supervisor who was harassing her to have her complaint addressed. The Court con-

---

[120]447 U.S. 57, 40 FEP 1822 (1986).
[121]*Id.*, 40 FEP at 1829.

cluded that the bank's contention that Vinson's "failure should insulate it from liability might be substantially stronger if its procedures were better calculated to encourage victims of harassment to come forward."[122]

The four concurring Justices, in an opinion by Justice Marshall, took a somewhat different (but related) approach to this issue. Specifically, the concurring Justices took a broader view of circumstances under which management could be held liable for its supervisor's sexual harassment. Justice Marshall's opinion also analyzed in a different manner the extent to which management can protect itself by establishing internal procedures that could redress discrimination in the workplace. Justice Marshall reasoned that the existence of an internal system has an impact not on the question of an employer's *liability* but on the *remedy* available to the employee after a finding of liability and concluded that where an employee who alleges that a

> hostile work environment effected a constructive termination . . . without good reason bypassed an internal complaint procedure she knew to be effective, a court may be reluctant to find constructive termination and thus to award reinstatement or backpay.[123]

The concurring Justices also suggested that an employer whose procedures could have addressed a discrimination complaint filed with the EEOC if the complaint had been filed internally could avoid the imposition of injunctive relief "by employing these procedures after receiving notice of the complaint or during the conciliation period."[124]

The Supreme Court's discussion of this topic should, however, be treated with caution. The majority opinion expressly declined "the parties' invitation to issue a definitive rule on employer liability . . . ."[125] The Court's statements are, in the classic sense, dicta. There can be no doubt, however, that the Court viewed the existence of an effective internal complaint procedure as a positive—and possibly dispositive—factor in defense of sexual harassment (and presumably other discrimination) claims. The bank's litigation stance in *Vinson*, despite some acknowledged flaws in its policies and internal procedures' ability to address sexual harassment claims, was nonetheless enhanced.

---

[122]*Id.*
[123]*Id.* at 1831.
[124]*Id.*
[125]*Id.* at 1829.

A recent Bureau of National Affairs, Inc., study of employer policies and procedures related to sexual harassment revealed that 82 percent of responding companies either had or expected to have in place by the end of 1987 a formal, written policy on sexual harassment.[126] In addition, 84 percent of responding companies requested that their employees follow a particular company procedure in making sexual harassment complaints including: established procedures for EEO/discrimination complaints (31 percent); procedures established for sexual harassment complaints (28 percent); and established procedures for all workplace grievances (31 percent). Personnel executives are most frequently selected to investigate (81 percent) and decide (75 percent) sexual harassment complaints.

Enactment of a model policy, however, is not enough. Courts have emphasized that effective administration of established sexual harassment policies are essential to defense of such claims in court. In *Yates v. Avco Corp.*,[127] the court held that although the company policy to address sexual harassment was "commendable . . . it was vague and ad hoc in its implementation and did not function effectively to eliminate harassment in the Avco . . . plants."[128] In that case, two women complained that they were being sexually harassed by their supervisor. In concluding that the policy was not effectively implemented, the court noted that the women were told not to go to the Equal Employment Opportunity Commission as their complaint would be promptly addressed inside the company (which it was not); they were denied copies of their testimony taken during the investigation; one woman was promised but not provided with an administrative leave to avoid returning to the harasser's supervision and as a consequence was instructed to call in sick, developed a record of excessive absenteeism, and was prevented from explaining her absenteeism by the company's policy of confidentiality. In the court's words,

> Avco's policy of not placing documentation of sexual harassment in personnel files seems to protect only Avco and the harasser, rather than the affected employee. An effective anti-harassment policy does not operate this way.[129]

---

[126]*Sexual Harassment: Employer Policies and Problems*, Personnel Policies Forum Survey No. 144 (Washington, D.C.: BNA, 1987).
[127]819 F.2d 630, 43 FEP 1595 (6th Cir. 1987).
[128]819 F.2d at 635.
[129]*Id.*

Courts prior to *Vinson* had viewed favorably the existence and use of credible internal systems in rejecting employee lawsuits. For example, in *Rogers v. IBM*,[130] IBM dismissed a branch manager whose relationship with a subordinate interfered with his job performance. IBM had received complaints through its *Open Door* policy from other IBM workers regarding this manager's behavior. The termination, the court noted, "followed timely notice and an investigation in which plaintiff participated."[131] The court, in rejecting the manager's claim of wrongful dismissal, concluded that "[t]he procedures followed by IBM, including the 'Open Door Policy' and the investigation, preclude a finding that the dismissal was improper."[132]

Similarly, IBM successfully defended claims of wrongful discharge and intentional infliction of emotional distress in another case in large part through its handling of the plaintiff's *Open Door* complaints.[133] This court, in upholding IBM's actions, spoke of the "manifest reasonableness of defendant's conduct" and commented that IBM "acted fairly and in good faith towards plaintiff." The court concluded that the "procedure followed by IBM in terminating plaintiff's employment, including the three Open Door appeals, precludes a reasonable finding that the dismissal was beyond the bounds of decency."[134]

"Final and Binding": The Preclusive Effect of Internal Decisions

Can the internal resolution of an employment dispute be treated as final and binding so as to preclude a subsequent legal action raising identical issues? The Michigan Supreme Court in *Renny* held that it could, although not under the facts of that case. The answer to this question, although not finally decided for all jurisdictions as evidenced by the Supreme Court decision in *Vinson*, depends on the means by which the dispute was addressed and the legal nature of the issue raised. The few decisions rendered support the following general proposition: The decision reached by a fair procedure system will be given preclusive effect if: (1) the decision-making entity or person and the process itself were both

---

[130]500 F. Supp. 867 (N.D. Pa. 1980).
[131]*Id.* at 869.
[132]*Id.* at 870.
[133]*Lekich v. IBM*, 469 F. Supp. 485 (E.D. Pa 1979).
[134]*Id.* at 488.

fair and impartial; (2) the final decision rendered was based on a full and adequate record; (3) the employee expressly or implicitly consented to the forum's authority; and (4) the legal right claimed was based on the employment contract and not on a statute or on a general legal right or principle embodying public policy. In contrast, decisions rendered by internal systems not providing procedural fairness, the jurisdiction of which was not consented to by the employee, or which address statutory discrimination or public policy claims are less likely to be given preclusive effect by a court or agency. The prospect that an employee may enter into a binding waiver of such claims as part of a claim settlement process, whether in exchange for monetary consideration or the availability of a nonjudicial impartial forum, is addressed by the Center for Public Resources Model Procedures for Employment Dispute Resolution included in the Appendix.

Preclusive Effect Given

An employer that creates certain rights for its employees that are not compelled by law, for example, by establishing a just cause standard for terminations, may generally choose the means by which disputes concerning those rights are resolved. The procedures established must be fair and accord with general principles of due process. For a procedure to be enforceable, an employee must consent to the binding nature of a decision rendered by the system established by management. This can be an express consent, for example, by signing an acknowledgement form, or implied, for example, by remaining in management's employ.

Michigan courts confronted the issue of the preclusive effect of fair procedure systems prior to the Michigan Supreme Court decision in *Renny*. For example, the Michigan Supreme Court, in its landmark decision in *Toussaint v. Blue Cross & Blue Shield of Michigan*,[135] holding that promises made in an employee handbook could be contractual, commented that employers who contractually provide for only just cause dismissals may "avoid the perils of jury assessment by providing for an alternative method of dispute resolution."[136] The court pointed to binding arbitration as an example of such a method.

[135]408 Mich. 579, 292 N.W.2d 880 (1980).
[136]*Id.*, 292 N.W.2d at 897.

The "alternative method," whatever form it may take, must comport with principles of elementary fairness addressed by the *Renny* court in order for a decision rendered to be enforceable. For example, in *Vander Toorn v. City of Grand Rapids*,[137] the decision of an internal personnel board was held not to be final and binding because some of the same individuals who participated in the decision to terminate the plaintiff were sitting on the personnel board designated to resolve his dispute.

Where the procedure is neutral and fair, however, Michigan courts have been willing to give internal decisions preclusive effect. For example, in *Dent v. Oakwood Hospital*,[138] a Michigan circuit court ruled that it lacked jurisdiction over a breach of contract claim where the employer provided a contractually binding grievance procedure ending in binding arbitration. In that case, the employee, a security officer, had been terminated for soliciting business as a private investigator from patients in the emergency room.

Preclusive Effect Denied

The United States Supreme Court has consistently ruled that an employee is not foreclosed from seeking judicial relief because of a prior arbitration decision under a collective bargaining agreement where a statutory remedy exists on a claim. In *Alexander v. Gardner-Denver*,[139] the Supreme Court specifically rejected an appellate court ruling that the employee forfeits his or her judicial remedies by electing to pursue racial discrimination claims through contractually created arbitration processes. The Court, in rendering its decision, nonetheless acknowledged the established federal policy of favoring private resolution of labor disputes. The Supreme Court has expanded its holding in *Alexander*, involving a discrimination claim, to include claims under the federal fair labor standards laws[140] and civil rights laws.[141] In sum, pursuit of a remedy under a fair procedure system is not likely to displace a court of

---

[137] 132 Mich. App. 590, 348 N.W.2d 697 (1984).

[138] Circuit Court, Wayne County, Mich., No. 83-314-505 CK (Feb. 21, 1984).

[139] 415 U.S. 36, 7 FEP 81 (1974).

[140] *Barrentine v. Arkansas-Best Freight Sys.*, 450 U.S. 728 (1981) (Fair Labor Standards Act).

[141] *McDonald v. City of West Branch, Mich.*, 466 U.S. 284, 115 LRRM 3646 (1984) (Civil Rights Act of 1871).

its jurisdiction over federal equal employment, fair labor standards, and civil rights causes of action.

The reasoning that prevails in the *Alexander* line of cases may also apply to internal decisions on issues implicating public policy such as may be raised in other statutory settings implicating strong public policies. For example, a federal district court has held that a claim under the Age Discrimination in Employment Act (ADEA) is not subject to the New York Stock Exchange's standard arbitration procedures.[142] In that case, a stockbroker for Smith, Barney, Harris, Upham & Company sued under the federal age act and state human rights law alleging that his dismissal was motivated by age discrimination. The court ruled that compelling arbitration of the federal age claim would fail to vindicate the rights provided to employees under the ADEA. The court held, however, that the state age claim is subject to arbitration under the stock exchange rules.

Similarly, in *Tuttle v. Bloomfield Hills School District*,[143] a Michigan Appeals court held that a claim under Michigan's Whistleblowers' Protection Act was not required to be initially submitted to the school district's collective bargaining agreement grievance procedures for resolution. Generally, since claims, whether statutory or nonstatutory, based on public policy and tort do not arise out of the employment contract but from public law, courts are less likely to give preclusive effect to the decisions of an employer's contractually created procedures. Parties may agree to limit or waive remedies for rights they create by contract but are on less firm ground in agreeing to waive remedies that public policy may compel.

An argument can be made that an employee can waive his or her right to a judicial forum in statutory rights and public policy cases *after*, rather than before, the dispute has arisen where the waiver is knowing and voluntary.[144] In this situation, the employee is not prevented from exercising an inchoate statutory right or public policy claim but rather knowingly and voluntarily surrenders a legal claim in exchange for some tangible benefit such as an enhanced severance payment. There is no evidence yet, however, that this view will prevail in the courts.

---

[142] *Steck v. Smith Barney*, 43 FEP 1736 (D.N.J. 1987).

[143] 156 Mich. App. 527 (1986), *leave to appeal denied*, 428 Mich. App. 879 (1987). *Cf. Pearce v. E.F. Hutton Group*, No. 86–5281 (D.C. Cir., Sept. 11, 1987).

[144] *See* Mishkind, Barnes, & Vogan, "The Internal Grievance Arbitration Option as an Alternative to the Armorplate/Litigation Approach," paper delivered at American Bar Association Midwinter Meeting, March 8, 1986, Labor and Employment Law Section.

Evidentiary Value of Internal Decisions

Nonetheless, the findings and results of an employer's internal procedures may play some role in a subsequent court or agency proceeding even where preclusive effect is otherwise not provided. The Supreme Court in the *Alexander* decision noted that while a prior arbitration may not preclude a later suit, the arbitration award "may be admitted as evidence and accorded such weight as the court deems appropriate."[145] In a significant footnote, the Court suggested certain relevant factors (in the context of a discrimination case) in determining the evidentiary weight to be given to an internal decision:

> the existence of provisions in the collective-bargaining agreement that conform substantially with Title VII, the degree of procedural fairness in the arbitral forum, adequacy of the record with respect to the issue of discrimination, and the special competence of particular arbitrators. Where an arbitral determination gives full consideration to an employee's Title VII rights, a court may properly accord it great weight. This is especially true where the issue is solely one of fact, specifically addressed by the parties and decided by the arbitrator on the basis of an adequate record.[146]

The Court reiterated, however, that the judicial forum must be fully available to ultimately resolve employment discrimination claims.

Exhaustion of Internal Remedies

Can an employee be required to exhaust internal remedies for discrimination or public policy based actions, whether or not the remedies will be viewed as final and binding, prior to filing a discrimination or public policy related claim? The courts have split on this issue. The Michigan Court of Appeals held in *Tuttle v. Bloomfield Hills School District*,[147] that exhaustion of contractual grievance procedures under a collective bargaining agreement is not required prior to seeking relief under a public policy based statute, in that case, Michigan's whistleblowers' law. Other courts

---

[145]415 U.S. at 60, n.21, 7 FEP at 90.
[146]*Id.*
[147]*See supra*, note 143.

have held that employees can be required to exhaust internal remedies for claims rooted in statute or public policy.[148] An employee who bypasses an expeditious and convenient potential remedy, however, may be viewed as litigious or insincere by a reviewing jury or judge.

Exhaustion of internal remedies may be required, however, of a contract claim if such is provided for in the employment contract. An employer that creates a right under the contract, however, is more likely to attempt to expressly preclude judicial or administative review rather than settle for an exhaustion requirement.

The State of Montana is the first state to enact a wrongful discharge statute protecting against termination of employment: for refusing to violate public policy; which lacks just cause, or; in violation of an express personnel policy of the employer.[149] Employers with "written internal procedures" benefit, under the statute, in that employees are required to "first exhaust those procedures prior to filing an action under" the statute. An employee's failure to do so is a defense to an action under Montana's wrongful discharge statute.[150] This statute and its requirement of exhaustion of internal procedures may very well serve as a model for subsequent enactments.

Rebutting Emotional Distress Claims

In some instances, the mere fact that an internal dispute resolution system exists and is properly utilized prior to disciplining or discharging an employee may be sufficient to rebut certain claims against employers. This is the case with claims of intentional infliction of emotional distress and perhaps others as well. Once again, IBM litigation serves as a model.

In order to establish a claim of intentional infliction of emotional distress, a plaintiff must establish that the defendant's conduct was so outrageous as to be characterized as utterly intolerable in a civilized community.[151] The more measured and rational the company's actions, the less likely it is that a court or jury will find such conduct intentionally or recklessly caused the emotional dis-

---

[148]*Midgett v. Sackett-Chicago, Inc.*, 105 Ill.2d 143, 473 N.E.2d 1280, 117 LRRM 2807 (1984), *cert. denied sub nom. Prestress Eng'g Corp. v. Gonzales*, 472 U.S. 1032, 119 LRRM 2904 (1985); *Wyatt v. Jewel Cos., Inc.*, 108 Ill. App.3d 840, 439 N.E.2d 1053 (1982); *Milton v. Illinois Bell Tel. Co.*, 101 Ill. App.3d 75, 427 N.E.2d 829, 115 LRRM 4428 (1981).
[149]HB241, L. 1987 (effective July 1, 1987), IERM 567:4–7.
[150]*Id.*
[151]Restatement of Torts (Second), §46, Comment d (1965).

tress of another. In *Kelly v. IBM*,[152] an employee was terminated for failing to return to work after having been directed to do so by the company following two years of paid disability leave. IBM's decision was based on the review of her condition by four physicians, including her own and an independent physician hired by IBM. Prior to her dismissal, the plaintiff filed two Open Door claims of disability with IBM's upper management which were denied. The court rejected the claim that IBM acted unreasonably in discounting plaintiff's claim of total disability. The court then stated:

> Moreover, under the procedure followed by defendants, plaintiff was afforded two appeals to higher management from the initial determination that she should return to work. This in itself evidences defendants' fairness and negated plaintiff's claim that defendants acted outrageously.[153]

A similar claim was brought in *Lekich v. IBM*[154] by another IBM employee who was terminated following his admission that he knowingly violated IBM's phone policy regarding personal calls. The court, in denying the employee's emotional distress claim, stated, "We believe that the procedure followed by IBM in terminating plaintiff's employment, including the three Open Door appeals, precludes a reasonable finding that the dismissal was beyond the bounds of decency."[155]

"Opting Out" of Unjust Dismissal Legislation

Enactment of unjust dismissal or job security legislation similar to the 1987 Montana wrongful discharge statute seems likely in the coming years, particularly in such states as California and Michigan where the employment-at-will rule has been engrafted with numerous exceptions and permutations. Indeed, unions such as the AFL-CIO have increasingly endorsed the enactment of such wrongful discharge legislation even though its effect extends beyond their membership. The potential for enactment of such legislation has been, consequently, notably enhanced. It also seems likely that provision will be made in such legislation, which undoubtedly will be modeled after existing unjust dismissal legislation in Western

---

[152] 573 F. Supp. 366 (E.D. Pa. 1983), *aff'd*, 746 F.2d 1467 (3rd Cir. 1984).
[153] *Id.*, 573 F. Supp. at 372.
[154] *See supra*, note 133.
[155] *Id.* at 488.

Europe,[156] for the "opting out" of the legislation by employers whose internal systems match or supersede the statutory requirements for fair resolution of termination disputes.

Models for such opting-out provisions exist. For example, employers in Britain whose fair procedure systems improve on the statutory scheme may obtain permission, upon a proper showing, to contract-out of the system.[157]

A company with its own fair procedure system in place, and when unjust dismissal legislation is enacted, will be in the advantageous position of having experience with adjudicating unjust dismissal claims inside the company and, consequently, will be in a better position to address problems under a new statutory scheme in addition to possibly qualify for an exemption from it.

Legal Considerations in Establishing Fair Procedure Systems

The credibility of a company's internal system is, of course, enhanced if the system's decisions are final and binding on the parties. Management can increase in a number of ways the likelihood that its system's decisions based on the employment contract will be given preclusive effect, that is, preempt legal actions on the same claim. A review of some of these approaches follows. In addition, the question—At what cost preclusion?—that must be weighed in the decision to institute such approaches is considered.

Fair Process as Term of Employment

The requirement that all employment disputes be presented for resolution to the employer's fair procedure system and that the

---

[156]*See* Estreicher, *Unjust Dismissal Laws in Other Countries: Some Cautionary Notes,* 10 Employee Rel. L.J. 286 (Autumn 1984).

[157]Under the British system, private dispute resolution systems embodied in collective agreements that meet certain requirements may be substituted for the statutory provisions. *See Protecting Unorganized Employees Against Unjust Discharge,* ed. by J. Stieber and J. Blackburn, 138 (School of Labor and Industrial Relations, Michigan State University, 1983). These private arrangements must cover all employees, must provide remedies as beneficial as those available under the statute, and must provide the right to arbitrate where an amicable arrangement cannot be reached. Compare the British model to the recommendation of the majority of the California Bar Association Labor and Employment Law Section Ad Hoc Committee on Termination-At-Will and Wrongful Discharge in its report, "To Strike a New Balance," p. 22, that limited statutory unjust dismissal legislation be enacted and that there be an exhaustion requirement for employees with access to internal systems providing substantial due process and deference by arbitration to the decisions under these systems.

decision rendered is final and binding can be made terms of the employment agreement in the same manner as other terms are established, for example, by means of a company policy and procedures manual or other written official documents. Such a term may be enforceable and may serve to preclude a contract action in court not first presented to the internal system for resolution.[158] Proper notice to employees would be required if preclusive effect is to be given. Management may also seek a written acknowledgment from the employee that all disputes will be presented for resolution to the system and that the decision reached is final and binding. On the other hand, management's failure to abide by its own procedures in disciplining or dismissing an employee may confer a breach of contract claim on the employee.[159]

For claims that are not finally resolvable inside the company (e.g., Title VII claims), exhaustion of internal remedies may be made part of the employment contract. An employee, of course, may subsequently present his or her claim to an appropriate court or agency. Failure by the employee to initially present claims inside or exhaust internal remedies, if not sufficient to constitute a breach of contract claim, may nonetheless undercut the employee's credibility in the later proceeding as suggested by Justice Marshall in his concurrence in *Vinson*.[160]

Finally, acknowledgment by both parties of the enforceability in court of the internal decision could be made an express part of the employment agreement.

Choice of Forum and Decision Maker

The two questions that immediately follow the initial decision to establish a fair procedure system are: What will be the structure of the decision making process? and Which person or entity will be designated to make the ultimate decision? Chapter 3 of this book offers a panoply of options in establishing the proper forum and decision maker for dispute resolution. The legal benefits and ramifications of these decisions, however, must be considered.

The forum chosen for the ultimate decision must be credible to both the employees and supervisors who will be its users and

---

[158]*McMillion v. Appalachian Power Co.*, 115 LRRM 4294 (S.D. W.Va. 1982), *aff'd*, 115 LRRM 4295 (4th Cir. 1983).
[159]*Continental Airlines v. Keenan*, 731 P.2d 708 (Colo. 1987); *Jeffers v. Bishop Clarkson Memorial Hosp.*, 222 Neb. 829, 387 N.W.2d 692 (1986).
[160]*Meritor Sav. Bank v. Vinson*, 477 U.S. 57, 40 FEP 1822 (1986).

to outside observers, in particular, federal and state judges, like the members of the *Renny*[161] court, who may be asked to decide what weight is to be given to the decisions that emerge. Management could choose, among other options, outside arbitration as the forum of last resort as has Northrop, a joint employer-employee grievance committee as in *Renny*, or perhaps the office of an executive officer, as discussed in the profiles of Bank of America, Cleveland Clinic Foundation, and Citibank in Chapter 3. A management that wants to maximize the preclusive effect of the system's ultimate decision will choose outside arbitration; one more concerned with keeping its process completely internal will choose top management or a joint employer-employee committee as the final step in the process.

With these or any other alternatives, the fairness more than the neutrality of the process is of central importance. An officer of the company placed in a decision making role can hardly be viewed as a neutral. Similarly, an arbitrator deciding a matter referred by a company (whether or not the company, as does Northrop, pays the arbitrator's entire bill) may be viewed as owing some allegiance to this provider of business. Lack of neutrality, however, is not synonymous with lack of objectivity or fairness. What is key is that the decision maker is structurally in a position to render a just decision based on the facts. For example, Northrop revised its grievance system to allow employees to choose as their representative for the final step arbitration a company employee-relations staff person. As Lawrence Littrell relates in the Northrop profile, "Knowing our Employee Relations people as I do, and based on experiences so far, this gives the grievant a real advocate working in his or her behalf." A decision maker beholden to one of the parties of the dispute or with a stake in the outcome is a structurally unsound decision maker. A decision resolving the dispute under these circumstances is unlikely to be given any weight by a reviewing court or agency.

Procedural Concerns

The process itself can be structured so as to increase the legal effectiveness of the decision.

The employee, in presenting the dispute, should be permitted a full and fair opportunity to present his or her case. The employee

---

[161]*Renny v. Port Huron Hosp.*, 427 Mich. 415, 398 N.W.2d 327 (1986).

must be permitted to present witnesses and should be permitted, particularly at the later stages, to be accompanied or represented by another individual. This representative may be, but is not required to be, a lawyer. As we have seen, Aetna, Michael Reese Hospital, Squibb Life Savers Division, and MIT do not allow an employee's counsel to play an active role in the process. Northrop, in contrast, allows attorney representation. Co-worker representatives are a viable alternative to lawyers. For example, the Cleveland Clinic, Michael Reese Hospital, and Squibb Life Savers Division each make provision for co-worker representation.

The employee should also be allowed to be present during formal fact-finding sessions and should be fully apprised of any claims made against him or her. This holds true whether it is an employee making claims about another employee or supervisor or whether management has made a claim against an employee. Following presentation of the employee's case, the employee may be asked to sign an acknowledgment form attesting that he or she has had a full opportunity to present his or her case or, if not, to provide a summary of the evidence that the employee was not permitted to present or the names of those witnesses that he or she was not permitted to offer.

An "adequate record" should be generated and preserved for judicial or administrative review if the internal decision is to receive any deference on review. An adequate record of the proceedings should include: transcripts, minutes, or summaries of meetings held at which evidence related to the dispute was elicited or arguments made; documents submitted by either party for consideration; copies or summaries of applications, motions, or requests made during the dispute resolution process; and a written decision of the decision maker or decision-making body setting forth factual findings and analysis supporting the ultimate decision.

Only upon an "adequate record" can a court or agency properly review the internal decision to determine whether it will be given preclusive effect or, if not, what weight if any it will be given in the court's or agency's deliberations.

At What Cost Preclusion?

Management can indeed take steps to maximize the possibility that a decision reached by its fair procedure system will later be given preclusive effect by a court or agency. In doing so, however, it should take care not to substitute legal efficacy for (1) suitability of its system to its corporate culture and (2) credibility of the system among its users, namely, the company's managers and employees. A cumbersome and overly formal system, while admired by a court or agency on review, does not encourage use by its prime audience—the employer's staff. Overbureaucratization and legal gridlock is as sure to defeat the effectiveness of the system as is lack of resources or commitment to it on the part of top management.

Expeditious resolution of a dispute is a valuable goal of most internal systems. A system that makes fair *procedure* its principal goal, however, is liable to win the preclusion battle at the great cost of not being used for other, less notable or legal, disputes. As an example, a common issue is whether management should encourage or permit an employee to be represented by legal counsel while pursuing a dispute through the system. The "preclusionists" would say yes—the human resources personnel are more likely to say no. The only "right" answer to this and other issues is an individual one—What is right for the company involved when its corporate culture and the goals of the system are considered?

A model system would include the lawyer's concern for fairness without the legal profession's propensity for burdensome procedures. The most successful internal systems are those that are guided by and instilled with principles of elementary fairness and which have as a desired—but not necessary—goal preclusion of subsequent legal claims.

Appendix

Model Procedures for the Bilateral Resolution of Employment Disputes

In 1987, after several years of gestation, the Employment Disputes Committee of the Center for Public Resources issued two Model Procedures designed to help an employee and an employer in the nonunion setting to resolve a dispute that could not be settled through internal mechanisms but which both parties wished to resolve without resort to the courts. One procedure focuses on mediation, while the other uses private, binding adjudication.

The Chair of the Employment Disputes Committee, Joseph Barbash, described the committee's objectives in the following words:

> To arrive at procedures that would be fair, effective, and acceptable to the parties, the Committee kept in mind a number of concerns, including:
> a. Employer reluctance to empower any outsiders to second-guess their employment decisions.
> b. Employee apprehensions about the fairness of any employer-initiated procedures.
> c. Courts' concerns about the inequality between employers and most employees, in bargaining power and sophistication, in reaching agreements.
> d. Employer concerns about allowing one bite of the apple if a second is possible, and employee concerns about giving up jury awards.

The Committee produced two separate and rather different procedures for the parties to employment disputes to consider. The first outlines arrangements to choose a "skilled neutral" to engage in "private, voluntary, informal and nonbinding" mediation of an employment dispute, including a threat of termination or an actual termination decision.

The second describes the procedure by which a single private "adjudicator" makes a binding decision on a termination dispute submitted to him or her by the two parties, the employee and the employer. It is designed to be "substantially speedier, less costly, and less formal than litigation."

Considerable thought and effort was put in by the CPR Committee—which included counsel for employee plaintiffs as well as for employer defendants—to create procedures that, as Joseph Barbash indicated, would meet fundamental fairness interests for both sides, and also anticipate review by the courts for such fairness criteria.

The report of the CPR Committee explaining its work and presenting the two Model Procedures are reprinted here. These procedures offer new ideas and mechanisms that deserve serious consideration and use, especially since they can be tailored to meet any special needs or criteria that the parties may require.

Alternative Dispute Resolution in Employment Disputes Employment Disputes Committee*

Joseph Barbash, Chairman
Peter H. Kaskell, Staff Director
Elizabeth S. Plapinger, Assistant Staff Director

A. CPR Model Procedure for Mediation of Termination and Other Employment Disputes

The Committee believes that a mediation process conducted by a skilled neutral can be a pragmatic way to resolve many employment disputes. Mediation is private, voluntary, informal and nonbinding.

Mediation is far less adversarial than litigation. An able mediator can defuse animosity and can help the parties come up with a solution rapidly and at modest cost. Other options, including the adjudication procedure described in the following section of this report, may be pursued if the mediation does not result in a solution.

The CPR Model Procedure for Mediation of Termination and Other Employment Disputes is attached as Annex A. (This procedure was developed by a subcommittee consisting of Dr. Mary P. Rowe and Jay W. Waks.) The commentary which follows the procedure sets forth the rationale underlying certain of its provisions.

There is no one correct way to conduct a mediation; however, the CPR model procedure provides the parties and their counsel with a useful working tool, which they are encouraged to modify as appropriate.

CPR Employment Disputes Committee

B. CPR Model Procedure for Employment Termination Dispute Adjudication

The CPR Model Procedure for Employment Termination Dispute Adjudication attached as Annex B (developed by a subcommittee consisting of Professor Samuel Estreicher, chairman, Robert A. Goldstein, Wayne N. Outten, Thompson Powers and Roberta V. Romberg) provides for voluntary submission, *after* the dispute has arisen of unlawful discharge disputes, including discrimination claims, to private, binding adjudication by a single adjudicator selected jointly by the parties. The procedure is designed to be substantially speedier, less costly and less formal than litigation.

The procedure represents a model that the parties are free to modify as they wish. Its key features are:

1. The adjudicator determines whether "the employer discharged the employee for legitimate reasons, taking into account the nature of the employee's position and responsibilities and the employer's stated policies consistent with applicable law."
2. Discovery is limited to that for which each party has "a substantial, demonstrable need" and is to be conducted in the most expeditious and cost-effective manner.
3. Conformity to legal rules of evidence is not required at the hearing.
4. Each party will be represented by counsel, unless the submission agreement otherwise provides.
5. The adjudicator may award back pay. He/she may award reinstatement, *provided that* if the adjudicator considers reinstatement inadvisable, or if the employer opposes reinstatement, the adjudicator instead may award up to two years of front pay.
6. Costs of the proceeding are to be shared equally by both parties, unless they otherwise agree, or unless the adjudicator awards such costs to the employee.
7. The proceeding is confidential.
8. The proceeding will be deemed an arbitration proceeding. The award will be final and binding as to all issues and claims which the parties raised or could have raised and which arose out of the employment relationship or its termination. The award will be subject to vacation or modification only on the grounds specified in the applicable arbitration law, and it will extinguish all other rights of the

parties with respect to the subject matter of the dispute, whether grounded in federal or state statutes, common law, or otherwise.
9. The proceeding is initiated by a "submission agreement" which includes mutual waivers and releases.

The Committee believes that the waiver and release to be executed by the employee are likely to be held effective, even in cases alleging violation of discrimination law, under the "voluntary and knowing waiver" test of *Alexander v. Gardner-Denver*, 415 U.S. 36, 52 n.15 (1974), provided that the employee is fully apprised of the legal impact of the waiver and release, has consulted with counsel, and the employer does not withhold payments to which the employee is otherwise entitled.

An employer may want to offer the adjudication procedure (after disputes have arisen) to particular employees on a case-by-case basis. If experience warrants broader application, the employer might make the procedure available to particular classes of employees, or indeed to all employees not represented by a union.

At the suggestion of committee member John Corbett O'Meara, the Committee also gave consideration to agreements, whereby the employer and employee would agree to resolve *future* termination disputes through private binding adjudication. *See* O'Meara & Massie, *Alternative Dispute Resolution: Some Employment Law Applications*, Oct. Mich. Bar J. 1040 (1985). The concept is that to the extent that an employment contract can mandate the conditions under which an employee may be terminated, it can also mandate the procedure that will be used to test the propriety of the termination. The Committee believes, however, that such an approach raises significant legal and personnel issues which warrant further study, particularly because most wrongful termination contract claims are coupled with statutory and common law tort and discrimination claims.

The willingness of the courts to enforce pre-dispute waivers or releases of litigation rights is unclear. The few authorities suggest that a pre-dispute approach may be effective in foreclosing litigation of contract-based termination claims. *See Toussaint v. Blue Cross & Blue Shield of Michigan*, 408 Mich. 579, 610 (1980); *See also Vander Toon v. City of Grand Rapids*, 132 Mich. App. 590, 598, (1984). In cases alleging violation of statute, other protected activity or common law tort claims, favorable judicial reception is less likely, given decisions requiring a "voluntary and knowing" waiver/release of litigation rights. *See Alexander v. Gardner-Denver*, 415 U.S. at 52 n.15; *see also Runyan v. NCR Corp.* 787 F.2d 1039 (6th Cir.) (en banc), *cert. denied*, 55 U.S.L.W. 3234 (U.S. Oct. 7, 1986) (No. 86-95).

With these and other problems in mind, several approaches suggested by committee members are recited below to begin the discussion (without in any way suggesting that CPR has fully studied or endorses any of these).

1. The employer may make it a condition of initial employment and continued employment that the adjudication procedure will be the sole means of asserting a common law contract claim of improper discharge. Such a policy might be best implemented by requiring each affected employee to enter into an agreement to that effect and by provisions in the employment manual.
2. Company policy might provide that upon termination the employee would be given the option of invoking the adjudication procedure, on condition that the procedure will be binding as to all claims—common law and statutory— and that if the employee declines the procedure but brings suit in court, the employee would waive any rights to continued employment based solely in contract.
3. Company policy might permit the employee upon termination to propose the utilization of the adjudication procedure. If the employee does so, he/she would be required to state whether or not he/she will allege discrimination or other violation of a statute, and if so, whether or not he/she agrees to be bound by the adjudicator's award as to all issues, including discrimination. If the employee will not so agree, the employer may refuse to make the procedure available.

If one of the above approaches were adopted, it would be necessary to provide that if the parties cannot agree on a neutral, a third party such as CPR, the American Arbitration Association or another source, would select the neutral or nominate a roster from which the neutral would be selected.

Regardless of the scope of the private adjudication procedure, it would be advisable in most cases for the parties first to attempt to resolve the dispute through informal means, which may include mediation. If an internal grievance procedure is applicable, that procedure should be invoked. Indeed, the private adjudication might become the final step in such a procedure.

The Committee believes that the CPR Model Procedure for Employment Termination Dispute Adjudication provides an alternative that should be seriously considered by parties to disputes arising out of termination of employment, including situations in which illegal discrimination is alleged.

C. Neutrals

The selection of a capable neutral is critical for the success of the ADR processes described in Sections III A–B. It should be recognized that the skills required of adjudicators and mediators are not identical. The parties are encouraged to select by themselves a neutral in whose impartiality and judgment both parties have confidence.

The CPR Judicial Panel consists of eminent former judges, legal academics and other leaders of the bar who serve as neutrals in ADR proceedings and counsel in structuring such proceedings. CPR frequently recommends neutrals as highly qualified for a particular assignment and is prepared to do so in the employment dispute area. Qualified neutrals also can be proposed by state or local bar associations, law school deans, or other sources identified by the parties.

Amicus Brief in *Runyan v. NCR Corporation*

Richard Runyan served as assistant general counsel of NCR Corporation, specializing in labor law, until NCR terminated his employment at age 59 "for unsatisfactory performance." Runyan and NCR entered into a one year "consulting agreement" which guaranteed a minimum monthly payment. NCR later agreed to increase the minimum payment on the condition that Runyan sign a general release, which he did. After the consulting agreement had expired, Runyan filed suit against NCR in the U.S. District Court for the Southern District of Ohio, alleging that his discharge violated the Age Discrimination in Employment Act of 1967 (ADEA). The District Court granted NCR's motion for summary judgment, holding that the general release Runyan had knowingly signed, for consideration the court found adequate, barred the action. Runyan appealed, arguing that his unsupervised waiver of his statutory rights could not bar his private action under the ADEA. A majority of a panel of the Court of Appeals for the Sixth Circuit held that a release of rights under the ADEA, unsupervised by the Equal Employment Opportunity Commission or by a court, was void as a matter of law. The court thereafter voted, however, to vacate the panel opinion and rehear the case *en banc*.

Our Committee believes voluntary settlements of employment dispute controversies should be encouraged in the interests of both parties, and we recognize that the panel decision, if confirmed, would seriously inhibit such settlements. Following the issuance and vacation of the panel decision, Committee member Samuel Estreicher prepared a brief *amicus curiae* on behalf of CPR in support of affirmation of the District Court order. The full Court of Appeals on April 7, 1986, handed down its decision affirming the order and reversing the panel by a vote of 11–2. 787 F.2d 1039 (6th Cir. 1986). The U.S. Supreme Court thereafter denied Runyan's petition for certiorari. 55 U.S.L.W. 3234 (U.S. Oct. 7, 1986) (No. 86-95).

The CPR Employment Disputes Committee
March 1987

Center for Public Resources
680 Fifth Avenue, 9th Floor
New York, New York 10019
(212) 541-9830

Annex A
CPR Model Procedure for Mediation of Termination and Other Employment Disputes

This model represents an approach for mediation of a discharge or other important employment dispute between an employer and an employee who is not covered by a collectively bargained grievance procedure. Mediation is a most informal and flexible procedure. There is no one right way for the mediation process to function. PARTIES ARE URGED TO ADAPT THE MODEL TO THEIR OWN CIRCUMSTANCES AND NEEDS AND TO READ THE ATTACHED COMMENTARY.

I: Proposing the Mediation Process

Either the employer or the employee involved in an employment dispute arising out of the employer's decision to discharge the employee or another cause directly affecting that employee may unilaterally propose a mediation process by contacting the other party, orally or in writing, and suggesting the use of a neutral mediator to mediate efforts to resolve the dispute. At this and other steps in the mediation process, each party may be represented by another person of whose identity the other party shall be informed promptly.

II: Selecting the Mediator

Once the parties or their representatives have agreed in principle to a mediation process, or at least seriously to consider mediation, they will discuss the desired qualifications of the mediator, and who possesses such qualifications. The mediator must be selected by agreement of both parties and their respective representatives, if any, from suggestions made by either party or a list of mediators or ombudsmen made available to both parties.

Each party shall promptly disclose to the other party any circumstances known to that party or that party's representative which would cause reasonable doubt regarding the impartiality of an individual under consideration or appointed as a mediator. That individual shall promptly disclose any such circumstances to the parties. If any such circumstances have been disclosed, before or after the individual's appointment, the individual shall not serve, unless both parties and that individual agree in writing.

The amount and terms of the mediator's compensation will be agreed upon among the parties and that individual before the appointment. Such compensation, and any other costs of the process, will be shared equally by the parties, unless they otherwise agree in writing.

The parties may agree in writing to appoint as mediator an executive of the employer if the executive is not involved in the employment dispute and the executive is prepared to serve without additional compensation.

III: Ground Rules of the Mediation Process

Once a mediator has been selected and has agreed to serve, the representatives of the parties will meet jointly with the mediator to discuss the following ground rules and any different or additional ground rules the mediator or a party wishes to propose as to the manner in which the process is to be conducted:

(1) The process is voluntary and non-binding.

(2) Each party may withdraw at any time prior to execution of a written settlement agreement by written notice to the mediator and the other party.

(3) The mediator shall be neutral and impartial.

(4) The mediator controls the procedural aspects of the mediation. The parties and their representatives will cooperate fully with the mediator.

    (a) There will be no direct communication between the parties or between their representatives without the assent of the mediator.

    (b) The mediator is free to meet and communicate separately with each party.

    (c) The mediator will decide when to hold separate meetings with the parties and when to hold joint meetings. The mediator will fix the time and place of each such session and the agenda, in consultation with the parties.

(5) The mediator may withdraw at any time by written notice to the parties (i) for overriding personal reasons, (ii) if the mediator believes that either party is not acting in good faith, or (iii) if the mediator concludes that further mediation efforts would not be useful.

(6) The representative of a party may, but need not, be an attorney. Each party shall be solely and exclusively responsible for any fee for services and disbursements charged by that party's own representative.

(7) At least one person—the party or the party's representative—will be authorized to negotiate a settlement of the dispute, and that authorization will be communicated to the mediator in a writing signed by the respective party.

(8) The mediation process will be conducted expeditiously. Each party and representative will make every effort to be available for meetings.

(9) The mediator will not transmit information given by any party or that party's representative to another party, the other party's representative or any third party, unless

authorized to do so by the party transmitting the information.

(10) The entire mediation process is confidential, except that, to the extent permitted below, the parties need not retain in confidence the fact that the process has taken place.

   (a) The parties and the mediator will not disclose information regarding the process, including any settlement, to any person not a party to the mediation process; provided, however, that any settlement may be disclosed by either party in any governmental investigation, arbitration, action or proceeding relating to the subject matter of the mediation.

   (b) Any written or oral statement, admission or settlement proposal made during the course of the mediation process, other than that in the form of an executed settlement, shall be inadmissible as evidence in any governmental investigation or administrative, arbitration or judicial proceeding involving the parties, their representatives or any person not a party to the mediation process.

   (c) The mediation process shall be treated as a Compromise and Offer to Compromise pursuant to the Federal Rules of Evidence in any investigation or administrative, arbitration or judicial proceeding under any state or federal law.

(11) The parties will refrain from pursuing administrative and/or judicial remedies during the mediation process, insofar as they can do so without prejudicing their legal rights. If an administrative action and/or litigation is pending between the parties regarding the subject matter of the mediation, the parties will inform the court or agency of the mediation process and the name of the mediator, and the parties will consent to and request a stay of such proceeding. Discovery in any such proceeding will be suspended while the mediation is ongoing.

(12) The mediator will be disqualified as a witness, consultant or expert in any pending or future investigation, action or proceeding relating to the subject matter of the mediation (including any investigation, action or proceeding which involves persons not party to this mediation). The mediator and any documents and information in his or her possession will not be subpoenaed in any such in-

vestigation, action or proceeding, and both parties will oppose any effort to have the mediator and documents subpoenaed.

(13) If the dispute goes to arbitration, the mediator shall not serve as an arbitrator, unless the parties and the mediator otherwise agree in writing.

(14) The mediator shall not be liable for any act or omission in connection with his or her role as mediator.

(15) The mediator, if a lawyer, may freely express his or her views to the parties on the legal issues of the dispute.

(16) The mediator may obtain assistance and independent expert advice with the agreement and at the expense of the parties.

(17) At the inception of the mediation process, each party and representative will agree in writing to all provisions of this Model Procedure, as modified by mutual written agreement of the parties. A model Submission Agreement is attached hereto as Appendix A.

IV: Submission to the Mediator

Once the mediation process has commenced, each party will submit to the mediator such information, including statements by the employee, the employee's supervisors and others, as each party deems necessary to familiarize the mediator with the dispute. Submissions may be made in writing and orally.

The mediator may request any party at any stage of the proceeding to submit clarification and additional information, including the employee's personnel files and other relevant documents. The mediator also may request the opportunity to inverview the employee's supervisor or other employees of the employer having relevant information.

The mediator may raise legal questions and arguments in order to evaluate the likely outcome of the dispute if it were to be litigated in court or before an arbitrator or an administrative agency. The parties and their representatives will make reasonable efforts to submit promptly an explanation of the respective party's position on such legal questions and arguments.

The mediator may request each party, at separate or joint meetings or at a combination of both, to present its case informally to the mediator.

The mediator shall keep confidential any written materials or information submitted to him or her. The parties and their representatives are not entitled to receive or review any such materials or information submitted to the mediator by the other party or representative, without the concurrence of the latter. At the conclusion of the mediation process, the mediator will return all written materials and information to the party who had provided them to the mediator.

V: Negotiation of Settlement Terms

The mediator may promote settlement in any manner the mediator believes appropriate. Once the mediator is familiar with the case, the mediator will hold discussions with the parties or their representatives or both. The mediator will decide when to meet or confer separately with each party and when to hold joint meetings.

The parties are expected to initiate proposals for settlement unless the mediator elects to be the first to propose the terms of settlement. Each party should provide a rationale for any settlement terms it proposes. If the parties fail to develop mutually acceptable settlement terms, before terminating the procedure the mediator may submit to the parties a final settlement proposal which the mediator considers fair and equitable to all parties. The parties will carefully consider the mediator's proposal and, at the request of the mediator, will discuss the proposal with the mediator. If either party does not accept the final proposal, that party shall advise the mediator of the specific reasons why the proposal is unacceptable.

Efforts to reach a settlement will continue until (a) a written settlement is reached, or (b) the mediator concludes and informs the parties that further efforts would not be useful, or (c) one of the parties or the mediator withdraws from the process by written notice.

VI: Settlement

If a settlement is reached, the mediator or a representative of the employer will draft a written settlement document incorporating all settlement terms, including mutual general releases from all liability which may relate to the subject matter of the employment dispute and to the mediation process. This draft will be circulated among the parties, amended as necessary, and formally executed. The settlement shall not be considered to be an employment agreement between parties unless the settlement expressly provides that it is an agreement of employment.

If administrative action or litigation is pending, the settlement will provide and the parties will arrange for dismissal of the case promptly upon execution of the settlement agreement. The settlement will be conditioned upon that dismissal.

Neither party to a settlement will bring or maintain any action or proceeding, including any charge, complaint, action or proceeding to enforce a contractual, common law or statutory right, which may be inconsistent with the terms, purpose and spirit of the settlement even if otherwise permitted by law. The settlement will constitute a waiver of any such right and a complete defense to any such charge, complaint, action or proceeding.

A model Waiver and Mutual Release of Claims is attached hereto as Appendix B.

Appendix A
Submission Agreement Pursuant to CPR Model Procedure for Mediation of Termination and Other Employment Disputes

AGREEMENT made _____, 19__ between _____ of _____
represented by _____
("Employee"); and _____
of _____
represented by _____
("Employer").

Employee was employed by Employer from _____, 19__, until _____, 19__, when Employee's employment was terminated by Employer [or, when Employee's employment was adversely affected by Employer]. Employee alleges that his/her employment was terminated [or adversely affected] for other than legitimate reasons and in violation of _____.

Employee seeks _____
_____.

Employer denies Employee's aforesaid claim.

Employee and Employer both wish to dispose expeditiously of their differences without resorting to litigation in court or before an administrative agency. The parties hereby agree to private and confidential mediation of their dispute pursuant to the CPR Model Procedure for Mediation of Termination and Other Employment Disputes ("the procedure"), a copy of which is attached hereto. The parties hereby adopt and agree to all provisions of the procedure, except as modified by this Submission Agreement.

The procedure shall be conducted before _____, who shall serve as Mediator, who has agreed to serve, and whose compensation has been agreed to between the parties and the Mediator. Neither party knows of any circumstances which would cause reasonable doubt regarding the impartiality of the person named as Mediator.

Both parties and their representatives have read the procedure. The Employee hereby affirms that he/she is entering into this Submission Agreement and the procedure voluntarily, knowingly, and after full consultation with a representative or counsel of his/her own choosing.

Signed by: _____
  Employee

Signed by: _____
  Representative of or Counsel for Employee

Signed by: _____
  Employer

Signed by: _____
  Representative of or Counsel for Employer

Appendix B
Waiver and Release of Claims and Liability in Connection With a Settlement Reached Pursuant to CPR Model Procedure for Mediation of Termination and Other Employment Disputes

Employee hereby affirms that he/she entered into the Submission Agreement pursuant to the CPR Model Procedure for

Mediation of Termination and Other Employment Disputes (the "CPR Mediation Procedure") and participated in the mediation procedure voluntarily, knowingly, and after full consultation with a representative or counsel of his/her own choosing. Employee affirms that he/she understands and agrees that the Settlement Agreement incorporates all settlement terms agreed to by the parties and will be final and binding. Employee hereby waives any and all rights that he/she may now have arising out of his/her employment [or its termination], whether grounded in contract or in federal or state statute, common law, or otherwise, with the exception of vested pension rights and rights, if any, pursuant to the aforesaid Settlement Agreement.

Employee further releases Employer and all of its officers, directors, employees, agents, successors and assigns, from any and all claims, demands, causes of action and liabilities of any kind whatever, whether known or unknown, arising out of Employee's employment [or the termination thereof], up to and including this date.

This waiver and release is binding on Employee and his/her heirs or assigns and may not be changed orally.

The Employer and Employee understand and agree that neither of them may bring or maintain any action or proceeding which may be inconsistent with the terms, purpose and spirit of the Settlement Agreement even if otherwise permitted by law. The Settlement Agreement will constitute a waiver of any such right and a complete defense in any such action or proceeding.

Signed by: _____
Employee

Signed by: _____
Representative of or Counsel for Employee

Signed by: _____
Employer

Signed by: _____
Representative of or Counsel for Employer

Dated: _____

(Provide for notarization of signatures, using applicable forms)

Commentary on CPR Model Procedure
for Mediation of Termination and
Other Employment Disputes

Introduction

In increasing numbers, terminated employees are seeking redress through the courts and administrative agencies. Lawsuits of this nature typically result in high lawyers' fees and other expenses for both parties, and often several years elapse before a case comes to trial. The employee hopes for a substantial damage judgment at the end of the litigation road, but many such cases are decided in favor of the employer.

Many companies have adopted internal complaint systems which enable non-union employees to voice their concerns and grievances. While these procedures differ, many are not well suited for the complaints of employees whose employment has been terminated, or who have received notice of termination.

The alternative dispute resolution movement has gained momentum, as more and more parties to a controversy eschew the burdens of litigation and recognize that the eventual win–lose decision of a court is not necessarily the best solution. Collaborative approaches, such as mediation and the mini-trial, are aimed at bringing about a settlement fashioned by the parties themselves. Time and again, parties using these processes do in fact settle; but if they do not, they still are free to go to litigation, or to arbitration.

CPR and its Employment Disputes Committee, chaired by Joseph Barbash of Debevoise & Plimpton and comprised of leading experts in the field, believe that a mediation process conducted by a skilled mediator is a pragmatic, effective way to resolve, preferably at an early stage, important employment disputes.

Mediation has been used widely to settle disputes between organized labor and management. Its use in disputes between employers and non-union employees is increasing.

A member of our Employment Disputes Committee who has served as a mediator in a substantial number of such cases reports being called on particularly in cases involving unusual or sensitive fact situations; for instance, an engineer who could steal ideas or otherwise cause trouble, a case of possible sexual harassment, a politically active employee, an incompetent family member in a closely held firm. Our member advises that the motives of the parties typically include:

- a mutual recognition that the dispute is best regarded as a problem to be resolved, that a legal showdown should be avoided;
- a desire to protect privacy and personal reputation or corporate image;
- the employer's wish not to set a precedent.

In some cases an impartial manager, perhaps an "ombudsman," serves as mediator; in others an external mediator is used. A number of firms have been organized to provide mediation services, and individual practitioners are available.

I. Proposing Mediation*

Employers and employees contemplating mediation should consider that mediation is private, voluntary, informal, and nonbinding, unless, of course, a settlement is reached. A mediation typically is concluded expeditiously, at modest cost. The process is far less adversarial than litigation or arbitration; perhaps permitting the relationship to be preserved. Since other options are not foreclosed if mediation should fail, entering into a mediation process is essentially without risk. Indeed, either party may withdraw at any time.

Generally, it is preferable for the disputants to agree to a mediation process early in the history of the dispute and before resorting to litigation; however, the pendency of litigation does not preclude mediation. Indeed, some courts have adopted non-binding court-annexed processes which resemble mediation, for certain types of cases.

The mediator's fee and other expenses of a mediation are normally shared equally. However, the employer may offer to pay the entire cost, or more than an equal share of the cost.

The human dimension of conflict is most significant. Emotions easily become barriers to a solution in the best interests of both parties. The employee typically feels a need to state his or her case, to be heard, and a sense that he or she is being treated fairly.

---

*Headings I–V refer to sections of the model.

A critical event in the mediation process is the first step—getting agreement to use it. A skillful mediator will defuse hostility. In the mediation process, psychology works for settlement. The parties are challenged to find a solution. The momentum of mediation leads toward settlement. Settlement equals success.

II. Selecting the Mediator

The selection of a capable mediator is vital. The mediator is not vested with the legal authority of a judge or arbitrator. He or she is not given a script but must rely on his or her own resources. The mediator must:

- be absolutely impartial and fair and so perceived;
- inspire trust and motivate people to confide in him or her;
- be able to size up people, understand their motivation and relate easily to them;
- set a tone of civility and consideration in his or her dealings with others;
- be a good listener;
- be capable of understanding the law and facts of a dispute, including surrounding circumstances;
- know when to intervene, and when to stay out of the way;
- be articulate and persuasive;
- be patient, persistent, indefatigable, and "upbeat" in the face of difficulties.

The mediator should have a personal stature that commands respect. Occasionally, a dash of humor helps.

The mediator can come from various disciplines. He or she might be a former judge, an executive, an experienced attorney, a professor at a law school or business school, an ombudsperson. Prior experience in personnel matters would be desirable, but expertise in employee relations is not required. Normally, the mediator will not be an employee of the employer; however, with the agreement of both parties, an executive of the employer also could mediate the dispute.

III. Ground Rules of Proceeding

A mediated negotiation has substantive, procedural and human dimensions. The mediator should control procedure and have influence on the substantive and human dimensions. He or she may encourage the parties to take the lead with regard to the substance of the dispute, if necessary taking a more active role as the process unfolds, proposing settlement terms and urging their acceptance.

The mediator, to be effective, must keep fully informed of all developments and must be able to control dialogue between the parties. He or she may conclude at a given stage that it is preferable to keep the parties apart. It is important, therefore, that the parties and their representatives do not communicate with each other directly without the mediator's concurrence while the process is ongoing.

At separate meetings a party can share information with the mediator which it is not then willing to share with the other party. Such a meeting also provides an opportunity for the mediator and the party to consider the party's underlying interests and to informally explore settlement options. Joint meetings can provide an opportunity for cooperative exploration of possible solutions among the parties and the mediator.

During the mediator's first meeting with the parties, he or she may well wish to have them confirm that they have a genuine desire to settle their dispute.

V. Negotiation of Settlement Terms

The mediator can help the parties crystallize their own interests and concerns and understand each other's. He or she can defuse adversarial stances and develop a cooperative, problem solving approach. It is common for parties to various types of disputes to start out with extremely divergent and quite unrealistic views as to the value of the claim. A mediator can be particularly useful by deflating unrealistic expectations and circumscribing the ballpark for realistic negotiations.

The mediator's role can run the gamut from that of a faciliator who arranges meetings between the negotiators in a setting conducive to cooperation, to that of an activist who will early on announce settlement terms and will urge the parties to accept such terms. The roles mediators play can include

— urging both parties to agree to talk
— helping parties understand the mediation process
— carrying messages between parties
— helping parties agree upon an agenda

— setting an agenda
— providing a suitable environment for negotiation
— maintaining order
— helping participants understand the problem(s)
— defusing unrealistic expectations
— helping the participants develop their own proposals
— helping the participants negotiate
— suggesting solutions
— persuading participants to accept a particular settlement

What a mediator should do will depend on the issues in dispute, the kind of parties involved, and their relationship with each other and the mediator. It will also depend on the mediator's experience, judgment, and intuition.

If the mediation process should fail, litigation is likely to follow. The mediator, if a lawyer, might give the parties an educated, objective appraisal of the strengths and weaknesses of their positions and the likely outcome of a trial. The mediator also can help each party make a realistic estimate of the tangible and intangible costs of litigation.

VI. Use of Model

This model or any variation of it may be used on an *ad hoc* basis or incorporated into a personnel manual for application in enumerated types of disputes.

When an employer and an executive enter into an employment agreement, the parties may wish to provide that they will attempt to resolve any disputes which may arise out of the employment relationship by use of this mediation procedure before resorting to litigation.

Annex B
CPR Model Procedure
for Employment Termination
Dispute Adjudication

This model procedure calls for a speedy, binding, private adjudication by a jointly selected adjudicator of a claim of improper discharge against an employer by an employee who has been or is about to be terminated from employment. It should be read in conjunction with the Commentary on CPR Model Procedure for Employment Termination Dispute Adjudication.

1. Initiation of Proceeding

The purpose of the CPR Model Procedure for Employment Termination Dispute Adjudication is to provide a voluntary option for adjudicating disputes between employers and employees who have been or who are about to be discharged. This proceeding is initiated when the parties enter into a Submission Agreement (the "Submission Agreement") and accompanying Waiver and Mutual Release of Claims, substantially in the form attached hereto as Appendix A. This proceeding contemplates, and the Submission Agreement reflects, that the affected employee will have the benefit of his/her own counsel, both in considering whether to participate in the proceeding and in the conduct thereof. This proceeding can be initiated at any point from the time an employee has been notified that a final decision to terminate has been made until 180 days following the effective date of the termination.

2. The Adjudicator

2.1. *Single Adjudicator.* The proceeding shall be conducted before a single Adjudicator (the "Adjudicator"), who shall be neutral and impartial. The Adjudicator shall be selected by agreement between the parties and shall be designated in the Submission Agreement. Should the parties be unable to agree on the selection of the Adjudicator, the proceeding shall terminate and any agreements made in contemplation of the proceeding, including any waivers, shall be void.

2.2. *Compensation.* The Adjudicator's compensation rate shall be established at the time of his/her appointment.

2.3. *Communication with Adjudicator.* Except as otherwise provided in this agreement, no party or anyone acting on its behalf shall have any private or ex-parte communication with the Adjudicator on any matter related in any way to this proceeding.

3. Standard for The Adjudicator

3.1. *Scope of the Submission.* Unless the parties otherwise agree in the Submission Agreement, the issue to be decided by the Adjudicator is whether the employer discharged the employee for legitimate reasons, taking into account the nature of the employee's position and responsibilities and the employer's stated policies consistent with applicable law.*

3.2. *Remedial Authority of the Adjudicator.* Unless the parties otherwise agree in the Submission Agreement, if the Adjudicator finds for the employee (under the standard set forth in Para. 3.1 above), he/she may grant backpay (and fringe benefits) less interim earnings. The Adjudicator may also award reinstatement, with or without backpay. If the Adjudicator determines, however, that reinstatement is warranted but inadvisable under the circumstances, or the employer is opposed for any reason to reinstatement, the Adjudicator may award up to two years of frontpay in lieu of reinstatement, in addition to any severance pay to which the employee is entitled. Depending on the circumstances, the Adjudicator may also award costs of the proceeding, including reasonable attorney's fees, to the employee. (See Para. 10.2 below.)

4. Discovery

4.1. *Discovery.* Discovery shall be limited to that for which each party has a substantial, demonstrable need, and shall be conducted in the most expeditious and cost-effective manner possible. The parties' attorneys and the Adjudicator shall meet not more than fifteen days from the date of the Submission Agreement, at a place and time fixed by the Adjudicator, to agree on a discovery plan. The Adjudicator shall resolve any differences, and his/her decisions with respect to the scope, manner and timing of discovery shall be final and binding, except that the employee shall be entitled to a true copy of his/her personnel file and each party shall be entitled to take at least one deposition. All discovery shall be completed within forty-five days of the aforesaid meeting date, unless the parties otherwise agree.

---

*See Commentary on CPR Model Procedure for Employment Termination Dispute Adjudication, Para. 3.1, *infra*.

5. Pre-Hearing Statements and Submission of Exhibits

5.1. Not less than ten days before the hearing, each party shall deliver to the other, and to the Adjudicator, a concise statement, setting forth its factual and legal position on the issues of the case, as well as all documents and other exhibits on which the party intends to rely at the hearing.

6. The Hearing

6.1. *Place and Date.* The hearing shall commence not more than seventy-five days after the date of the Submission Agreement, on a date and at a place to be fixed by the Adjudicator upon consultation with the parties.

6.2. *Duration.* The hearing shall be limited to __ days unless extended pursuant to Para. 10.3 below.

6.3. *Notice.* The Adjudicator shall cause written notice of the place and time of the hearing to be served in person or by mail on each party not less than fifteen days before commencement thereof. Appearance at the hearing shall constitute waiver of such notice.

6.4. *Adjudicator Presides.* The Adjudicator shall preside at the hearing.

6.5. *Evidence.* The Adjudicator shall afford each party full and equal opportunity to present any material or relevant proofs and to cross-examine witnesses. The Adjudicator shall be the judge of the materiality and relevancy of the evidence offered. Conformity to legal rules of evidence shall not be necessary, except that the applicable statutes, rules and decisional law with respect to attorney-client privilege and work product shall apply.

6.6. *Order of Presentation.* The employer will ordinarily present its case first, subject to the Adjudicator's discretion.

6.7. *Transcript.* The hearing will not be transcribed, unless the parties otherwise agree.

6.8. *Adjournments.* The Adjudicator may postpone or adjourn the hearing for good cause, and shall do so upon the request of both parties.

6.9. *Oaths.* The Adjudicator shall sign or otherwise take an oath of office. He/she shall require all witnesses to testify under oath and shall administer such oaths, to the extent authorized by law.

6.10. *Preliminary Hearing.* The Adjudicator may call one or more preliminary hearings to narrow or better define the issues to be adjudicated, to determine procedure, or for other purposes.

6.11. *Representation by Counsel.* The parties shall be represented by counsel at all phases of this proceeding, including at hearings, unless they make provision to the contrary in the Submission Agreement.

6.12. *Attendance at Hearings.* The Adjudicator, upon the request of any party, may in appropriate circumstances require the exclusion of any person not a party or its legal representative from the hearing, and of any witness when not testifying.

6.13. *Subpoenas.* For the hearing, the Adjudicator may subpoena witnesses or documents upon his/her own initiative or upon the request of a party, to the extent permitted by law. Consistent with the scope of discovery allowed under Para. 4.1, counsel for the parties may issue subpoenas to the extent permitted by law.

6.14. *Absence of Party.* The hearing may proceed, at the discretion of the Adjudicator, if any party, after due notice, fails to be present.

6.15. *Submission of Briefs.* Unless the parties otherwise agree, each party shall submit a brief within thirty days of the close of the hearing.

7. The Award

7.1. *Basis of Award.* The Adjudicator will base his/her decision and award on the facts and authorities presented. The award shall be in writing and signed by the Adjudicator. The award shall contain an opinion including a discussion of the bases of the award but, unless both parties so request, the Adjudicator need not prepare findings of fact and conclusions of law.

7.2. *Effect of Award.* The award shall be final and binding as to all issues and claims which the parties raised or could have raised and which arose out of the employment relationship or its termination. The award shall extinguish all other rights of the parties with respect to the subject matter of the dispute, whether grounded in federal or state statutes, common law, or otherwise. The award shall not serve as precedent or authority in any subsequent proceeding, other than as provided in Para. 7.4. (See also Para. 9.1.)

7.3. *Delivery of Award.* The award shall be mailed or delivered to each party's attorney no later than thirty days from the close of the hearing, and if briefs are submitted, no later than thirty days from the date of submission of such briefs.

7.4. *Confirmation of Award.* If the losing party should fail to comply with the award, the prevailing party may apply to any court having jurisdiction for an order confirming the award in accordance with the applicable arbitration law.

8. Court Proceedings

8.1. *Commencement or Dismissal of Litigation.* The Submission Agreement is accompanied by a written waiver of all other rights and remedies that might otherwise have been available to the employee arising out of the employment relationship or its termination. After executing the Submission Agreement and accompanying Waiver/Release of Claims, neither party shall commence in any manner any litigation or administrative proceeding with respect to the subject matter of the proceeding (except as provided in Paras. 7.4, and 10.1). If any litigation or administrative proceeding is pending at the time of the Submission Agreement, the parties, promptly after execution of the Submission Agreement and accompanying Waiver/Release of Claims, will file a stipulation dismissing the pending action with prejudice.

9. Confidentiality

9.1. The substance of these proceedings, including the content and result of the award, shall be kept confidential by all parties, their witnesses and other participants, and by the Adjudicator. The *fact* that such a proceeding exists or that an award has been rendered, need not be kept confidential.

10. Miscellaneous

10.1. *Applicability of Arbitration Statute.* The proceeding shall be deemed an arbitration proceeding subject to the arbitration law applicable in the state in which the hearing is to be held. If this procedure is in conflict with any mandatory requirement of such statute, the statute shall govern. The Adjudicator shall have all powers granted to arbitrators under the applicable statute. The award may be vacated or modified only on the grounds specified in such statute.

10.2. *Costs.* Each party shall bear its own costs of the proceeding, including costs of witnesses, and the compensation of the Adjudicator and any other costs of the proceeding shall be shared equally by the parties, unless the parties otherwise agree in the Submission Agreement or the Adjudicator (pursuant to Para. 3.2 above) otherwise provides in his/her award.

10.3. *Time Extension.* The parties may extend any period of time by mutual agreement. The Adjudicator may extend any period of time for good cause, except for the deadline for issuance of the award.

10.4. *Actions Against Adjudicator.* The parties agree not to make any claim against the Adjudicator based on any act or omission in his/her role as Adjudicator in the proceeding.

10.5. *Settlement Negotiations.* The Adjudicator, at his/her discretion, may urge the parties at any time to engage in settlement negotiations. If at any time settlement is reached by the parties, it may be incorporated in an award issued by the Adjudicator, and all provisions of this proceeding, including waiver, enforcement and confidentiality shall apply.

Appendix A
Submission Agreement Pursuant to
CPR Model Procedure for
Employment Termination Dispute Adjudication

AGREEMENT made _____, 19__ between _____
of _____
represented by _____
("Employee"); and _____

of _____
("Employer").

Employee was employed by Employer from _____, 19__,
until _____, 19__, when Employee's employment was terminated by Employer.

Employee alleges that his/her employment was terminated for other
than legitimate reasons and in violation of _____
_____.

Employee seeks _____
_____.

    Employer denies Employee's aforesaid claim.
    Employee and Employer both wish to dispose expeditiously
of their differences without resorting to the courts. The parties
hereby agree to a final and binding private adjudication of their
dispute under the CPR Model Procedure for Employment Termination Dispute Adjudication ("the procedure"), a copy of which
is attached hereto. The parties hereby adopt the procedure, as
modified by this agreement.
    The procedure shall be conducted before _____,
who shall serve as Adjudicator, who has agreed to serve, and whose
compensation has been agreed to between the parties and the
Adjudicator. Neither party knows of any circumstances which would
cause reasonable doubt regarding the impartiality of the person
named as Adjudicator.

Signed by _____
                 Employee

Signed by _____
                 Counsel for Employee

Signed by _____
                 Representative of Employer

(Provide for notarization of signatures, using applicable forms.)

Waiver and Mutual Release of Claims
Pursuant to CPR Model Procedure for
Employment Termination Dispute Adjudication

    Employee hereby affirms that he/she is entering into this Sub-
mission Agreement and this proceeding voluntarily, knowingly,

and after full consultation with counsel of his/her own choosing. Employee further affirms that he/she understands and agrees that the award of the Adjudicator in the proceeding referred to above will be final and binding, and hereby waives any and all rights that he/she may have now or in the future arising out of his/her employment or its termination, whether grounded in federal or state statute, common law, or otherwise, with the exception of vested pension rights and rights, if any, pursuant to the aforesaid award.

Employee further releases Employer and all of its officers, directors, employees, agents, successors and assigns, and Employer releases Employee, from any and all claims, demands, causes of action and liabilities of any kind whatever, whether known or unknown, arising out of Employee's employment or the termination thereof, up to and including this date. This waiver is binding on Employee and his/her heirs or assigns.

Signed by _____
          Employee

Signed by _____
          Counsel for Employee

Signed by _____
          Representative of Employer

(Provide for notarization of signatures, using applicable forms.)

Commentary on CPR Model Procedure for Employment Termination Dispute Adjudication*

Purposes

The purpose of the CPR Model Procedure for Employment Termination Dispute Adjudication is to provide a voluntary option for adjudicating disputes between employers and employees who have been or who are about to be discharged. The Model Procedure envisions an out-of-court proceeding before an impartial adjudicator jointly chosen by the parties who would have the authority to determine whether the employer discharged the employee for legitimate reasons and, if not, to award backpay and reinstatement

---

*Drafted by Samuel Estreicher, with the advice and assistance of Robert A. Goldstein, Wayne N. Outten, Thompson Powers, and Roberta V. Romberg.

(or frontpay in lieu of reinstatement). In exchange for the employer's agreement to make available such a proceeding and to abide by the adjudicator's award, the employee would execute as part of the submission agreement a waiver and release of all claims arising out of the employment relationship or its termination, whether grounded in federal or state statutes or common law or otherwise. Although CPR is not in a position to give legal advice, it believes that such a waiver/release will be held effective under the "voluntary and knowing waiver" test of *Alexander v. Gardner-Denver*, 415 U.S. 36, 52 n.15 (1974), and *Runyan v. National Cash Register Corp.*, 787 F.2d 1039 (6th Cir.) (en banc), *cert. denied*, 55 U.S.L.W. 3234 (U.S. Oct. 7, 1986), provided that the employee is fully apprised of its legal impact, has consulted with counsel, and the employer does not withhold payments to which the employee is otherwise entitled.

The CPR Model Procedure contains several provisions which may not be strictly necessary to secure a legal effective waiver/release. These are nevertheless included in order to present an alternative to litigation that is likely to be attractive to some employees and their counsel. The Model Procedure offers what might be termed the "default" position: unless the parties provide otherwise in their submission agreement, the Model Procedure will govern the adjudication. In this manner, CPR hopes to convey its model of appropriate procedures for this type of proceeding, while permitting the parties complete flexibility to draft procedures more to their liking.

The CPR Model Procedure may not be appropriate for all situations, and certainly particular employers and/or employees may simply choose to pursue their legal remedies before administrative agencies and in court. It nevertheless outlines an alternative that should be seriously considered by all.

Model Procedure

1. Initiation of the Proceeding

CPR believes that there are advantages to making the Model Procedure available not only after the discharge has become effective, but also after the discharge decision has been made but while the employee remains on the payroll under whatever exit arrangement has been agreed to. Conceivably, if the hearing can be held promptly, an award in favor of the employee would work minimum disruption to the employer and the prospects for successful reinstatement would thereby be enhanced.

We see no legal bar to making the option available only for particular categories of employees or particular claims. Making the option available entirely on an ad hoc basis should create no problem in most jurisdictions, although conceivably in California and perhaps a few other states, the refusal to make available the adjudication option might be viewed as an element of the unfairness of the discharge. To minimize this problem, the employer may wish to keep its ordinary personnel procedures for handling a termination entirely separate from the adjudication option, which would then be viewed exclusively as a dispute resolution mechanism for a termination decision that already has been reached.

2. The Adjudicator

2.1. *Single Adjudicator.* CPR favors a single adjudicator on grounds of practicability. In any event, the adjudicator should be jointly chosen by the parties before entering into the submission agreement.*

2.2. *Compensation.* The submission agreement should provide for the adjudicator's compensation. As provided in Para. 10.2, CPR recommends that the costs of the arbitration should be jointly shared by the parties. We recognize that some employers may wish to pay for the entire costs as a way of encouraging employee utilization; if so, the consent of the employee and his/her counsel should be obtained, and this fact should be set forth in the submission agreement.

2.3. *Communication with Adjudicator.* This is self-explanatory.

3. Standard for the Adjudicator

3.1. *Scope of the Submission.* Absent agreement to the contrary in the submission agreement, the issue for the adjudicator is whether the employer discharged the employee for legitimate rea-

---

*Employment disputes are likely to raise different issues than the usual labor or union contract arbitration, and thus the parties need not necessarily select a labor arbitrator as the neutral.

sons, taking full account of the nature of the employee's position and responsibilities and the employer's lawful stated policies. We have deliberately avoided language of "just cause," because we believe that the standards for scrutinizing terminations as developed in labor arbitrations may not be appropriate to non-unionized settings or to high-level employees with discretionary responsibilities.

The parties may provide in the submission agreement for a different scope of authority for the adjudicator than the proposed "legitimate reasons" formulation, such as an "existing rights" standard which would confine the adjudicator to the particular causes of action available to the employee under federal or state law. A "legitimate reasons" standard is more likely to encourage employees to utilize the Model Procedure and would, moreover, focus the proceeding on what is often the real reason for the employee's grievance and eventual resort to the courts—the perception that the discharge was not motivated by legitimate business considerations. The "legitimate reasons" standard is also more likely to ensure judicial acceptance of the release/waiver envisioned by the Model Procedure.

3.2. *Remedial Authority of the Adjudicator.* Again absent agreement to the contrary, the adjudicator would be empowered to award backpay (and fringe benefits) and reinstatement. Reinstatement may not be appropriate, however, in all circumstances. If either the adjudicator or the employer for any reason deems reinstatement inadvisable under the circumstances, the adjudicator may award up to two years' frontpay in lieu of reinstatement. We believe that the two-year period approximates what most courts will award in Title VII litigation. If, however, the adjudicator awards reinstatement, without objection from the employer, and the employee declines to return to his/her former job, this should operate to terminate any further frontpay obligation. *See Ford Motor Co. v. EEOC*, 458 U.S. 219 (1982).

In order to encourage utilization by employees, the adjudicator is authorized to award to the employee the costs of the proceeding, specifically defined to include reasonable attorney's fees, absent provision to the contrary in the submission agreement.

4. Discovery

4.1. *Discovery.* CPR does not recommend incorporation of the Federal Rules of Civil Procedure, for one purpose of the Model

Procedure is to provide an expedited, less formal, less costly proceeding than would obtain in court. Nevertheless, some pre-hearing discovery is essential to a fair proceeding, and the adjudicator would be empowered to resolve differences over the scope, manner and timing of discovery. At a minimum, however, the employee should receive a true copy of his/her personnel record and both parties should be permitted at least one deposition. Further discovery should be based on a proffer of need and relevance satisfactory to the adjudicator. We recommend the time limits that should generally be followed.

5. Pre-Hearing Statements and Submission of Exhibits

5.1. Both the prospects for pre-hearing settlement and, failing that, the proceeding itself, would benefit from complete disclosure of all arguments and evidence in advance of the hearing.

6. The Hearing

6.1. *Place and Date.* Because prompt resolution is particularly important to the employee, and has implications for the prospect of successful reinstatement, if ordered, the Model Procedure provides that the hearing will begin not later than 75 days after the execution of the settlement agreement.

6.2 through 6.6. These provisions are self-explanatory.

6.7. *Transcript.* In order to minimize costs to both parties, and because most disputes are not likely to be complicated, the Model Procedure provides that the hearing will not be transcribed, unless the parties otherwise agree.

6.8 through 6.10. These provisions are self-explanatory.

6.11. *Representation by Counsel.* Because representation by counsel is likely to be critical to judicial acceptance of the fairness of the adjudication, and insistence on such representation may itself operate to screen out meritless claims, the Model Procedure precludes pro se representation or use of non-lawyer representatives. Provision to the contrary should be set forth in the submission agreement. We understand that insistence on representation by counsel may discourage utilization by employees; we have endeavored to minimize this effect by authorizing the adjudicator to award reasonable attorney's fees (absent agreement to the contrary in the submission agreement).

6.12. *Attendance at Hearings.* Subject to the discretion of the adjudicator, and consistent with the confidentiality provisions set forth in Para. 9.1, representatives of the parties (in addition to counsel) may attend the hearing.

6.13. *Subpoenas.* The adjudicator or legal representatives for the parties may issue subpoenae to the extent authorized by law and consistent with the scope of discovery allowed under Para. 4.1.

6.14 through 6.15. These provisions are self-explanatory.

7. The Award

7.1. *Basis of the Award.* An opinion should accompany any award; this is essential to acceptability of the result and will bolster judicial receptivity to the entire proceeding.

7.2. *Effect of the Award.* The award rendered by the adjudicator would be final and binding, subject to impeachment only on the narrow grounds for vacating an arbitration award set forth in the applicable arbitration law. Moreover, the award would act as a complete adjudication of any and all issues that were raised or could have been raised arising out of the employment relationship, and should extinguish any and all claims whether grounded in federal or state statutes, common law or otherwise. Of course, the parties have complete freedom to frame a narrower submission and narrower waiver/release, reserving certain claims for litigation in the courts. The award represents only a resolution of the particular dispute between the parties and will not serve as precedent or authority in any subsequent proceeding, save as provided in Para. 7.4.

7.3 through 7.4. These provisions are self-explanatory.

8. Court Proceedings

8.1. *Commencement or Dismissal of Litigation.* Again, the purpose of the envisioned proceeding is to provide a complete "bill of peace," precluding all pending or subsequent resort to the courts (save for purposes of confirmation or on the narrow grounds of vacating an arbitration award).

9. Confidentiality

9.1. Confidentiality is essential to the success of the envisioned proceeding. Employers may legitimately be concerned that the decision to make available this option in a particular case not be viewed as a "right" available to all employees under all circumstances. Similarly, employees may have chosen this alternative to avoid the publicity that would attend litigation in the courts. We have included a proviso to permit employers, should they so desire, to communicate the availability of the adjudication option.

10. Miscellaneous

10.1 through 10.5. As stated above, in Para. 10.2, we recommend that absent provision to the contrary in the submission agreement, and except as awarded by adjudicator in his/her opinion and award, the parties should jointly share the costs of the proceeding, including the adjudicator's fee. We believe that some may consider the impartiality of the adjudicator tarnished if the employer were to fund entirely the adjudicator's fee, and that many highly-compensated employees would not find responsibility for 50% of the fee a prohibitive barrier. We understand, however, that this is not always true, and certainly employers should be receptive to paying the entire fee, but only after securing the agreement of the employee and his/her counsel. The other provisions are self-explanatory.

Submission Agreement

As mentioned above, the parties retain complete freedom to modify any feature of the CPR Model Procedure in the submission agreement; such variations should be explicitly set forth therein. In addition, the submission agreement should name the adjudicator chosen by the parties, and should set forth by separate attachment the terms of the waiver/release to be executed by the employee. The entire document, including the waiver/release, should be signed both by the parties and their legal counsel.

Waiver and Mutual Release of Claims

We recommend that the parties and their counsel execute, as a separate instrument, a waiver and mutual release of all claims arising out of the prior employment relationship between the parties. There is a slight asymmetry between the release and the scope of the submission to the adjudicator, for claims arising out of the manner of, rather than reasons for, the discharge, *e.g.*, defamation, false imprisonment, intentional infliction of emotional distress claims, may be waived yet not clearly submitted to the adjudicator. The parties may provide for a broader submission coextensive with the waiver in their agreement.

Index

About the Authors

Alan F. Westin is Professor of Public Law and Government at Columbia University, where he has taught since 1959. A lawyer (Harvard, 1951, Member of the District of Columbia Bar) and political scientist (Ph.D., Harvard, 1965), Westin has authored or edited 25 books, including *The Anatomy of a Constitutional Law Case* (1958); *Freedom Now: The Civil Rights Struggle in America* (1964); *Privacy and Freedom* (1967); *Individual Rights in the Corporation* (1980), with Stephan Salisbury; *Whistle-Blowing: Loyalty and Dissent in the Corporation* (1981); *The Changing Workplace* (1985), with Baker, Schweder, and Lehman; and *Managerial Dilemmas* (1988), with John D. Aram.

Professor Westin's articles on employee rights and labor issues have appeared in the *New York Times*, *Wall Street Journal*, *Business Week*, *Fortune*, *Personnel Administrator*, *Across the Board*, and other periodicals, as well as in leading law reviews and social science journals.

Since 1978, he has conducted on-site field studies of new employee-rights programs at more than 200 corporations and government agencies. He has been a consultant on these issues for IBM, Security Pacific National Bank, General Mills Restaurants, Federal Express, the Social Security Administration, and many other employers. He has helped design innovative programs on employee privacy, equal employment opportunity policies, and internal dispute-resolution systems in nonunion employment.

Alfred G. Feliu is an employment law attorney associated with the national law firm Paul, Hastings, Janofsky & Walker, in its New York City office. He represents management in all facets of employment and labor law, including federal and state litigation, human rights proceedings, labor arbitrations, and National Labor Relations Board proceedings and counsels clients on issues related to discharge and discipline, employment discrimination, breach of contract, defamation, civil rights violations, unfair labor practices, union campaigns, privacy, and immigration law, among others. His articles have appeared in such journals as the *Employee Relations Law Journal, Columbia Human Rights Law Review, The American Journal of Nursing,* and *Technology and Society,* and he most recently co-authored the chapter entitled "Privacy In the Employment Relationship" in the *Privacy Law and Practice* treatise edited by George B. Trubow. Feliu is a graduate of Columbia Law School and a former law clerk to a federal magistrate.

DATE DUE